SCHOOLS, PARENTS AND GOVERNORS

EDUCATIONAL MANAGEMENT SERIES
Edited by Cyril Poster

Schools, Parents and Governors

A New Approach to Accountability

JOAN SALLIS

First published 1988 by Routledge
11 New Fetter Lane, London EC4P 4EE
Reprinted 1990

Printed and bound in Great Britain by
Biddles Ltd, Guildford and King's Lynn

British Library Cataloguing in Publication Data

Sallis, Joan
    Schools parents and governors : a new
    approach to accountability. —
    (educational management series).
    1. Great Britain. Schools. Accountability
    I. Title
    379.1'54
    ISBN 0-415-00930-8

CONTENTS

Foreword

CONTENTS

FOREWORD

I have known Joan Sallis for a number of years and always had a profound respect for her deep commitment to the advocacy of an effective role for parents within our education system. When she accepted my invitation to contribute to this series a book on the theme of Schools, Parents and Governors I was delighted. Disarmingly she had described herself repeatedly as 'just an ordinary parent'. In fact she has a knowledge, as every reader of this book will readily detect, of the education system here and overseas which many a scholar would envy. Yet, however deep her reading and research, its presentation is always in a language easy on the eye and ear; and her personal involvement makes each page glow with life.

I have to say that this is not the book that we originally planned. As the events within the political arena unfolded during 1986 and 1987, early ideas of the contents of the book were modified and, particularly, extended. Indeed, there were times when we have jointly wondered whether we might not appeal for a moratorium in national educational developments - in particular in legislation - for just long enough for the author to write FINIS on the last page and not 'to be continued'. However, I think it can be said without contradiction that this book contains the most up-to-date commentary on the recent Education Acts and the impending - at the time of writing - Great Education Reform Bill that can be found in print.

This is a book about accountability. It is also a vigorous plea for shared responsibility: within schools, with parents, among all the partners in the education service. It is unlikely that her readers will agree with all that she says; but there will be surely none who will dismiss her arguments out of hand, and many who will think twice even though they may still end up in disagreement. The book is permeated with her direct experience of parental involvement in schools and education over many years. It will, I know, be widely read and often quoted. I am proud to have it appear in this education management series.

Cyril Poster

Chapter One

BEYOND THE SCHOOL GATES

'A school is not an end in itself', said the Taylor Committee confidently (1) as it began its work in 1975. Not on the face of it, a controversial statement. Yet the mood which it identified was surely to dominate the quarter century which followed. 1975 was indeed a watershed. It ended the years of expansion in public education. It marked the beginning of a period when schools could no longer count on public indulgence. The clamour for greater accountability was insistent, if not always coherent.

In retrospect the previous quarter century, from about 1950, will seem the golden age of teachers' independence. The worst ravages of war were being repaired, and although it was to be some time before there were roofs over all heads, and enough teachers trained to fill those heads, limbs were already beginning to stretch, ideas were everywhere fermenting, classroom walls exploded with colour and life, and some children were saying they loved school. The 1944 Act was still new and shiny, with its vision of an education as broad as it was long, of a steady advance towards a service meeting new aspirations and removing old inequalities, offering appropriate opportunities throughout life. There was an ample supply of babies to enjoy those opportunities, by present standards a strong public will to find the money, and certainly no shortage of ideas or freedom to develop them.

Perhaps chances were missed in those years to share with parents and the public all the excitement of what was going on, for the time would come when public understanding of the changes which had taken place would have afforded a great deal of protection for those ideals. But we were not to know. When the voices from outside the gates began to be critical, when the children and the money began to dwindle, when all at once words like 'relevance' and 'accountability' began to disturb the happy buzz of classrooms, teachers' workshops and curriculum committees, we could really have done with a few ordinary people who knew what it was all about.

1

BEYOND THE SCHOOL GATES

Many of those classrooms and teachers' centres were holding exhibitions in 1970 to mark the centenary of free universal schooling. Like sepia pictures bursting into colour, they shouted with progress. No sombre notes intruded, no hint of rigours to come, no awareness that if you wanted it in colour it cost more, that if you wanted one for everybody it would cost an awful lot, and that in future you were going to have to justify it. Yet the first of the falling birthrate babies were already in reception classes.

THE LONG DEBATE

In retrospect it was more long than great. The speech made by Prime Minister James Callaghan at Ruskin College in October 1976 was, although there had been many warnings, a bombshell. Consensus about the objectives and effectiveness of the school curriculum had begun to break down. Industrialists had been rumbling for some years. The 'Black Paper' group was beginning to attack school standards. The Organisation for Economic Cooperation and Development had criticised the Department of Education and Science for its weak policies earlier in 1976, and the DES itself had begun a series of internal enquiries which was leaked before the Ruskin speech as the 'Yellow Book', which argued that young people were underprepared for employment. Callaghan expressed concern that education was not meeting the needs of industry and commerce, a theme amplified in the Green Paper (2) which summarised the so-called Great Debate which followed. This debate was a series of regional meetings of educationists, employers and parents, the actual conclusions not very memorable, but the tone very much so. The theme did not go away, and in fact inaugurated a long period of increasing centralisation of curriculum initiatives and a strongly vocational thrust in curriculum and examinations. It fed the growth of the Manpower Services Commission's involvement in education and the introduction of new 16+ examinations and the Certificate of Pre-Vocational Education. At the same time primary education became the subject of much more rigorous general inquiry by Her Majesty's Inspector.

In parallel with this growth of concern about school and work came more general rumblings about the standards of work and discipline in schools, and a feeling that teachers enjoyed too much independence in pursuing their trendy theories and experimenting with other people's children. These feelings were stirred up by the publication of a book by Neville Bennett about 'Teaching Styles and Pupil Progress' (3) which introduced some doubt about informal teaching methods, and above all by the crisis in the William Tyndale School in Islington in 1975-6 (4), where all the agencies of public intervention proved incapable of averting a total

2

collapse of parental confidence.

Finally, in May 1975, the then Secretary of State for Education, Reg Prentice, in conjunction with the Secretary of State for Wales, set up a Committee to look into the composition and functions of school governing bodies and their relationships with Local Education Authorities, teachers, parents and the wider community. This Committee, under the chairmanship of Tom (now Lord) Taylor of Blackburn, reported in September 1977. That report, 'A New Partnership for our Schools' (1), itself provoked a lengthy debate and led to radical legislation in 1980 and 1986. Both the report and the legislation are discussed in detail elsewhere in this book, so I will merely say at this point that it proposed a governing body for every school, representing the public interest in that school, with fair representation of LEA, staff, parents and community, to share as partners in promoting the success of that school in all its life and work, and its good relationships with parents and the wider community.

THE ATTITUDES OF TEACHERS

This is not, of course, the place to discuss the attitudes of teachers to all aspects of the school's relationships with parents, governors and the public. The feelings of teachers, their problems, their actual and potential contribution to the development of whole school partnerships will form an integral part of more detailed examination of such partnerships in practice. Here I want merely to look in a very general way at the reactions of teachers to the increasing pressures on them to involve lay people in the work of schools in the last twenty years or so.

Teachers work very hard. In primary schools it is much harder to teach effectively by modern child-centred methods than in the old days of straight rows and multiplication tables and because-I-say. In secondary schools it is much harder to teach under one roof an assortment of young adults, of widely varying ability and motivation, than it was to teach a limited and well-understood curriculum to children up to 14, and a different but equally circumscribed curriculum to volunteers after 14. Most of these teachers believe in what they are doing, but it is demanding. It takes more skill to teach in a society where, rightly or wrongly, respect has to be earned and not demanded, and authority comes from the kind of human being you are, not the position you hold. The curriculum of both primary and secondary schools has vastly expanded, and new initiatives constantly make more demands on teachers. They are not just educators. Increasingly in our troubled world they have to be social worker, doctor and nurse, priest, even mother and father, for many children suffer things which children should not suffer, and it is not

3

surprising that so many children behave in a disturbed way. It is a miracle that they do not behave much more badly. Teachers feel that parents do not fully understand these things, even that they are expected to do things parents cannot do, like say 'no!'. They may also feel that too many children come to school when they are not well, when they have had no breakfast or insufficient sleep, and that in all social classes many children lack enough adult time and interest, nursery rhymes, games and encouragement.

Teachers also feel that they are more at the mercy of enthusiastic amateurs than anyone except perhaps the paper-hanger, and that every know-all on the bus has something to say about what it has taken them years to learn. It is not therefore easy to get them switched on to the idea of that organised interference we call participation! Indeed they feel that the pressure for more accountability is the last straw, and puts them in a position we should not dream of expecting from the plumber or the doctor. They accept the need to satisfy their employers, their seniors and their professional consciences. Can anyone ask more?

Many teachers also think their critics are very ill-informed about what schools do, and have very old-fashioned expectations. They resent the constant sniping of the press, and they feel generally beleaguered. Since retrenchment began in the mid-Seventies, they often work with inadequate resources and in a depressing environment. Their salaries have failed miserably to keep up with other graduate professions, and above all they feel that state education itself is undervalued.

SEEKING COMMON GROUND

In 1982, out of the blue, the Australian Department of Education invited me to be their guest, look at their schools and their arrangements for involving parents and tell them what I thought. It was very unusual, indeed I think unknown, for them to invite someone who was not an educationist, and I really wondered whether I had anything profound enough to say to all those Ministers, high officials, professors and teachers at all levels who were rather unnervingly wheeled in to listen to me. In order to prepare myself for this ordeal, I tried to think what the problems were which those responsible for providing a good public education service had in common everywhere. Alas for the profundity, the more I thought about the subject, the simpler it seemed to become, so I stopped before things got too serious and wrote down the issues as I saw them. I tried them on lots of people to see if they looked the same upside down. Not only was I assured they were the same, but I now think they are not too bad a check list for both parents and teachers.

How can we create and sustain enough public commitment to an adequately resourced system?

How can we reconcile acceptable minimum standards in all schools with the demand for local variety and freedom, the need to foster creativity and the desire of parents for choice?

How can we reconcile choice for parents with equal opportunity for children, given that the desire for choice arises from, feeds on and perpetuates inequality?

How can we demand accountability from teachers, when all research shows that home support is essential to a child's success, and teachers can not demand home support?

Valuing parental support for the child, and parental involvement in the school as we do, how can we ensure that they do not actually increase inequality, given that it is so hard to involve many?

How can we persuade the less confident parents to get involved?

How can we compensate schools where, despite all our efforts, home input remains low?

How can we lead away from narrow and selfish pre-occupations the confident minority who find it easy to get involved, and instead enlist their commitment for whole schools, whole neighbourhoods and even whole nations?

How, in short, can we foster a sense of common purpose among the strong and the articulate, those who alone in the short run can fight for a good education system?

I am sure you will have spotted how the last question leads back to the first, and how indeed they all interlock. They constitute my agenda for this book, since they leave out none of the problems I have discussed with teachers somewhere every week of every term in the past ten years. They have all agreed with the analysis, all been eager to discuss the programme and all been encouraged to find even one optimist who thinks that together we can win.

There is an obstinate belief that somewhere there must be a magic formula which can solve all the problems of schools. Hence the astonishing trade in ideological gadgetry which goes on year in, year out, whose catalogues I dip into in Chapter Two. This is not surprising. Education is so basic to the quality of life, can bestow so much power, status and happiness, and involves human beings so touchingly defenceless, that we are bound to look for Cinderella's coach, Aladdin's lamp, the philosopher's stone. It is not surprising either that it attracts more than its share of doorstep salesmen and pedlars of dreams. Disillusionment is rapid: at midnight the coach vanishes and last night's dishes are still waiting. Aladdin's lamp is a poor old thing, about 40 watts, and in the morning his mother is doing other people's washing as usual. Of course we would like all the children to go to the ball, all visit the caves, and we would like to offer them something a bit more lasting than dreams. Most teachers know there is no magic, only very hard work.

Recently even hard work sometimes does not seem enough. Because there is not enough public understanding there is not enough pressure for a good service, one which meets the varying needs of children, including those to whom life has given less; for choice which is real, not another name for privilege; for partnership with all parents, even sad ones.

THE CASE FOR PARTNERSHIP

It was my final obligation as a member of the Taylor Committee to go around the country explaining to audiences of headteachers and teachers what the Report had said, and why. They listened to me because they sensed my sympathies, but on the whole the reception for the ideas themselves was hostile. For all the reasons given in the preceding pages, they were unwilling to accept further burdens, as they saw them, or yield to threats to their professional territory.

One of the frustrating things was that there was then, in the late Seventies, scarcely a shadow of the hard times to come in their minds. For me it was like one of those nightmares in which you are in a foreign country, trying to warn of danger, but cannot make yourself understood. It was not because I was wise that I saw the dangers, but only because I wandered as a privileged stranger through town and county hall, picking up the messages only dogs can hear. Everybody in education seemed drunk with the heady scent of expansion, like Keats' bees in the poem, thinking 'warm days will never cease'. Yet expenditure on education, after twenty years of unparalleled growth, had begun to level off in 1975, and declined sharply after 1979. I wanted to say that arguments about territory were luxuries we could not afford, that we did need our partnership now if we were to keep resources in education as child numbers fell. The falling rolls had already then begun to affect the secondary schools. It seemed naive to think schools and teachers would even hold their own, without a fight. In that fight state education needed all its friends.

There were other things too. The clamour for more central prescription was not going away, and I saw properly constituted school governing boards just as the first President of the Board of Education had seen them when he introduced the 1902 Education Bill: an essential defence of the independence and variety of our schools against the excesses of bureaucracy.

As for the poor press schools received, I pointed out that the argument was scarcely about whether the public had any right to comment on schools. Right or not, it would continue, and most of it would be ill-informed and destructive. The only way to get a better image for state education was to build up in the local community a body of people who would not believe the rubbish they read.

Most of all, I wanted teachers to see the dangers of a two-tier system developing within state education as a result of cuts, falling rolls, and the inevitability that parental choice would be an object of a public policy designed to make a virtue of parsimony. I do not think I fully understood then quite how bad this was going to get. Now it is a platitude that there are not two kinds of schools, state and private, but three, private, parent-assisted, and deficient. If you live in the right place, have transport, know how to choose, can write a good appeal, and above all dip into your pocket for extras, you can get a very good bargain. No such luck for the poor children and teachers trapped in the twilight schools, robbed of their skilled parent campaigners, who have been bought off, with the differences in the education you can get in Linden Close and Gasworks Road yawningly wide. All this makes it ever easier to economise on state education as a whole. The strong will be segregated, and will protect themselves. The weak will become more isolated, and the soup can be watered down for them.

The greatest frustration comes from the knowledge that savage cuts were made in education in the Eighties with scarcely any public protest. If parents had begun to understand the significance of what was happening, particularly to the breadth of the primary school curriculum, they would have been stopping the traffic in protest. The fact that they do not understand must in part be the responsibility of the educators, who in the good days failed to communicate their policies. 'If something has to go,' parents will say, (terrible horse-trading politicians' words, nothing to do with children's needs), 'better the music than the maths.' They still think there is an essential and a less essential curriculum. Nobody reminds them what HMI said in their Survey of Primary Education in 1978 (5) about how the basics were not better taught when heavily concentrated on, but more effectively communicated in the framework of a broad curriculum. Therefore they did not understand how cuts robbed children, or even more important, how they did not rob children equally. For cuts fall always on the most vulnerable areas of the curriculum, and on those families least able to bear them. In the lucky homes, the music lessons will still take place even when the school cannot provide, the interesting outings will happen, the books will be bought, even the remedial teaching will be purchased when children have learning problems and the school cannot help. Those children who depend entirely on school for that experience and that help may lose forever their view beyond the mean streets, but their parents do not complain, because they never had that view themselves.

I do not at all blame teachers for being sceptical about what participation can achieve. Some of them have had very bad experience of it. This is especially so in the operation of school governing bodies, where we have been lumbered so long with a system at best comic and irrelevant, at worst corrupt and harmful. It is only because I have now had a good experience that I am keen to share it.

When, as a parent of three children due to enter an infant school in rapid succession more than twenty years ago, I encountered in the playground a real white line and a notice which stated 'No Parents Beyond This Point', I did nothing about it. Parents I spoke with in Australia, unlike those I meet in England, all wanted to know just one thing, which is what I did about that white line while my children were in the school. I concluded that they were still bothered about physical access, how you got in to look for the left Wellington, never mind interfere in the curriculum. They were very disappointed with my reply. You see I never had believed that participation was a good thing in itself. I believed a very wise doctor who once told me that his job was to produce live babies, not to give me a beautiful experience. The same goes for schools. If greater understanding of what they are trying to do makes them able to do a better job for children, then it's worth working for. Schools are not there to provide fulfilment for those adults who lack it, and I do not blame those teachers who, having seen more than enough such people, wish they would go and have their beautiful experience somewhere else.

I only became worried when I realised how little public pressure there was for state education in the place where I had come to live. Looking innocently around, I thought the schools would be as much an object of civic pride as the fine public buildings and parks. Nobody had told me about private affluence and public squalor, and my own formative years were spent somewhere where it was the other way round. Today I know that there are many beautiful towns everywhere in which it is very clear that the people in the big houses with the blossoming trees do not ask for better schools because they do not personally use them. I have never recovered from that shock. I joined the local Campaign for the Advancement of State Education, which was trying to get more parents concerned about the fact that education here was a soup kitchen service, and I began to think more deeply about that white line.

How sad, I thought, in a place where education has no powerful friends, to discourage even the unpowerful ones who together might have been able to make a noise. Even then I did not start making a nuisance of myself in that school, as I do not think you get anywhere by nagging about bad practice. The only way to advance is to find a little bit of good practice, however small, and praise that, encourage it and advertise it.

I still think education has few powerful friends, but unfortunately the scene has become much more sombre, and I now think it has also quite a few powerful enemies. It is becoming too well known that educating the whole child, which the primary schools had been trying to do before someone caught them at it, and educating all the children, which secondary schools are attempting, are very expensive undertakings, but they are also potentially subversive, because they are making people aware of needs which society may not be able to meet.

Back in Richmond-upon-Thames, we began a process which took 15 years trying to get state education upgraded in local consciousness and priorities. Part of that process was working at partnerships of all kinds, simple constructive stuff, better induction programmes in infant schools, more consultation about children's progress, parent help in schools, holiday play centres. But we also saw the system of governing schools, corrupt though it had become, as capable of reform into a very powerful agency of change. We had a Taylorised system before the Taylor Committee was thought of, and that, along with other things we did, transformed the status and the quality of state education locally beyond our wildest expectations. For confirmation, let any Doubting Thomas ask any headteacher or teacher who has worked in the borough for all or most of the period concerned.

The words with which I began this chapter, 'A school is not an end in itself', have now been set in concrete. Whether or not one agrees with giving the public more involvement in schools is not the point. Those teachers who hate it all must know that it will not go away, for it has widespread popular backing and is supported strongly by all political parties. The demand for teacher accountability takes many destructive and cruel forms, as Chapter Two demonstrates, and it also leads to the adoption of other models of expectation which do not in practice take the relationship between parents and their schools forward in any constructive direction, as I try to show in Chapter Three. Since this is not a whodunit, I can reveal the end of the story, which is that I think true accountability can only exist in an acceptance of shared responsibility for success at the level of the child, the school and the service. In dismissing or accepting with grave qualifications the other ways in which accountability is sought, I am counting on my ability to argue for something better.

The point in saying so cruelly that the public claim to share in school policies is not going to go away is that head-teachers and teachers have enormous influence in turning threats into promises. The way in which schools use the now inevitable new structures can be more important than the structures themselves, and the rewards are beyond calculation. In this book I intend to write extensively about what teachers see as the problems of parental involvement, suggesting some helpful approaches, looking at how schools can influence the climate of commitment in which governing bodies approach their work, spreading some good practices and discussing the many ways in which relationships based on the needs of children can be fostered. I shall also provide a full guide to current law affecting school accountability, and suggest how attitudes of LEAs, as well as schools, need to change if the new partnership with the public is to work well for children.

But first we have to take that walk through the market place.

NOTES

1. The Taylor Committee, A New Partnership for our Schools, (HMSO, September 1977).
2. DES, Education in Schools, a Consultative Document, Cmnd 6869, (HMSO, 1977).
3. Neville Bennett, Teaching Styles and Pupil Progress, (Lancaster University, 1976).
4. Robin Auld, QC, William Tyndale Junior and Infants School Public Enquiry; a report to the Inner London Education Authority, (ILEA, July 1976).
5. DES, Primary Education in England: A survey by HM Inspectors of Schools, (HMSO, 1978).

Chapter Two

THE POWER OF THE MARKET PLACE

We have seen that the need for schools to be more accountable to those who use them is a dominant theme of the Seventies and Eighties. Overwhelmingly during these years the
most common model of accountability debated is taken from the
market place. If schooling is seen as a commodity, so it is
claimed, it must respond more accurately and more rapidly to
the tastes of parents, just as the suppliers of other goods
and services must respond to consumer wishes if they are to
survive.

The appropriateness of this analogy will be scrutinised
later in this chapter, but meanwhile the consumerist view of
education has occupied the headlines for so long, and is
superficially so beguiling, that it must be taken seriously
even by those of us who find it unconvincing or distasteful.
It is advocated with great sincerity by many academics, with
passionate conviction by generations of right wing politicians,
and the popular newspapers love its rallying cry. As for
parents, it so often seems to them to provide an easy remedy
for the anxieties and frustrations which many of them
undoubtedly suffer from time to time.

The market place philosophy is promoted by two distinct
groups. The larger and more vocal one believes that this
monopoly service has increasingly been run without regard
for parents' aspirations and with insufficient rigour; that it
panders to the whims and the self-interest of teachers, whom
it protects excessively; that it indulges the waywardness of
children; that it follows the vagaries of fashion; that it
provides target practice for the half-baked egalitarian theories dear to the hearts of political extremists. A much
smaller and certainly less noisy group of critics see the
service as over-preoccupied with economies of scale, with
authority and with orthodoxy, and unresponsive to the needs
of children in all their rich and tender variety. This group
does not, like the first, crave a return to the standards of
some imagined golden age, but rather a move towards a
system providing more variety and more flexible and open

11

ways of working. But although its aims are so different, this group is equally concerned with direct responsiveness to consumer pressures.

Many teachers cringe at every word of this familiar analysis. Can you be surprised, they will ask, when people have such ill-informed notions about schools, that so many of us try to protect our professional territory, wishing only to be left alone to do on behalf of children the job we have been trained for? Especially, they say, we must be free to exercise responsibility for the disadvantaged, whose poverty of experience we could never make good through schooling if we took note of the narrow aspirations of the back-to-traditional-values brigade, or the self-indulgent whimsy of the small-schoolers, free-schoolers and de-schoolers. This is all understandable, but it is dangerous. The market place philosophy is so robust that only massive public pressure can save the values it threatens to destroy, so that the task of winning popular support for those values is urgent. If we fail, the shouts of the market stallholders will drown the voices of all the unrepresented children, and those children's needs will be trampled underfoot like the squashed remains of fruit hosed from the market square at the end of the day. The clever shoppers surge homeward with their bargains, which perhaps do not look so good when they come out of the bag, but it will be too late.

THE SIGNIFICANCE OF CHOICE

We must first look very carefully at the consumerist point of view, accepting that many influential people and hundreds of thousands of ordinary ones see in it the very essence of school accountability. Firstly, it has nothing to do with participation. I don't want to run the shop, is the cry, I merely want the freedom to shop elsewhere if I don't like what they sell or the way they serve it. The customer knows best, and the way to raise standards and drive out shoddy goods is to favour good schools with our custom and withhold it from the others, for thus, the theory is, good schools will flourish and bad ones wither. Only thus, say the prophets of the market place, can the general standard be raised. We shall make our point, they say, against the bureaucrats, with their vested interest in pretending that all schools are the same, against the trendies and the levellers, against the protectors of incompetence. We'll show them what they can do with their learn-as-you-like regime, their sand and water, their integrated day, their new maths, their peace studies, their pastoral curriculum. Oh yes, and their projects!

The simple faith of consumerism is that, in some weird reversal of Gresham's Law, good schools will drive out bad, and that this can be achieved by exposing them all to market forces. The weapon, in this fight against the flab, is choice, a word with a magic sound, if an elusive meaning.

It would be a foolish politician, administrator, but especially parent campaigner, who tried to argue that because the pursuit of choice had some fraudulent motives and some destructive consequences it should have no place in the relationship between parents and their schools. For me, indeed, it would be like a turkey voting for Christmas. For it is a monopoly service, and it would be dangerous to bestow upon it the unfettered power derived from a captive market. Moreover, it cannot be denied that schools benefit from the positive feelings of parents and children who have chosen them.

The problem is, as briefly indicated in Chapter One, how to reconcile the rights of some parents with the needs of all children, how to provide the maximum choice compatible with the interests of the majority, and how to maintain for that majority a stable and reasonably cost-effective service. The 1980 Education Act (1) which is examined in detail below is a fairly moderate attempt to achieve just that, but between a statutory assertion that you must at least let people have what is there, and the extremes of consumerism propounded by, for instance, the Institute of Economic Affairs (2), is a range of options leading to the complete privatisation of schooling. The feature they all have in common is that they make the quality of education available to a child dependent on the ability of parents to choose, to support and ultimately to pay. They vary only in degree. One could add that it is not only by manipulating the operation of choice systems that privilege can be bestowed on children whose parents can provide more support. There are many who would argue that in the Eighties we have seen a sort of voucher system in operation without any pieces of paper changing hands, simply by reducing public expenditure on a scale which has in effect shifted more of the burden of school spending on to parents' shoulders, thus favouring those children and those schools whose parents can supplement the basics. It was estimated by the National Confederation of Parent Teacher Associations from a survey made in 1985 (3) that 84% of secondary schools had asked parents to buy essentials, and that on average 30% of primary school capitation was provided by parent effort. If the principle of voucher schemes is that it is possible to 'top up' the child's basic entitlement, it has been in operation for some time.

WHY PARENTS CARE SO MUCH ABOUT CHOICE

Were parents to be found chaining themselves to the railings, or throwing themselves under the Chief Education Officer's car, it would quite likely be about choice. Choice plays an

important part in our feelings about everything, but there
are two reasons why it assumes an almost obsessional quality
in education. Firstly parents still feel, despite the improved
home-school relationships of recent years, that they do not
really have much say once the gates close. So it becomes
vitally important to choose the right school gates in the first
place. If parents had more influence, they could well settle
for less choice. Any hope that the school they got might
through their association with it become more like the one
they would have chosen, might make more parents willing to
throw in their lot with the nearest school. All sorts of
improvements could follow from such voluntary abdication of
choice. In later chapters on the nuts and bolts of partnership
I shall discuss some of these.

Parents also harbour a shrewd suspicion that, whatever
'they' say, we are still a long way from equal opportunity in
schooling, and among the many respectable ways of sharing
out what is available, choice is a front runner. If all parents
could choose among equal, if different alternatives, with equal
mobility, equal confidence, equal access to information and
equal skill in using it, choice would indeed be a reality for
all parents and all children; but it would also become totally
uninteresting, and no parents would chain themselves to the
railings about it. I believe there are ways in which we can
come somewhat nearer this ideal, but only if we can increase
parents' awareness of some of the pitfalls of consumerism, and
entice them in adequate numbers from the spell of the market
place. Let us look now at the ways which have been tried, or
talked about, for increasing choice.

THE EDUCATION ACT 1980 (1)

This legislation was presented as a fulfilment of the Conservative election pledge to extend parents' rights. In fact,
however, a Bill in many respects similar fell with the outgoing
Labour government, and any administration at that time would
have been faced with the need to adjust the process of
admission to school to take account of falling school rolls. The
Labour Bill was stronger on mechanisms to 'manage' contraction, with its attempts to make planned admission limits water-
tight to parental pressure, but both parties had recognised
the inevitability of allowing parents to benefit to some degree
from slack in the system.

The 1944 Act had enunciated in Section 76 the 'general
principle' that children should be educated in accordance with
the wishes of their parents, subject, however, to compatibility with the provision of efficient instruction and training
and the avoidance of unreasonable public expenditure. But
the only right of appeal for parents against decisions which
conflicted with this principle was under Section 68, a general

right of appeal against 'unreasonable behaviour' by LEAs or school governors. In practice, these provisions gave little joy to dissatisfied parents, since a judgment in the case of Cumings v. Birkenhead in 1971 ruled that the 'general principle' of Section 68 was just that, and not, to quote the judgment, 'the sole or overriding consideration'. Furthermore, in the famous House of Lords ruling in the Tameside case, Section 68 was held to give the Secretary of State the right to substitute his judgment for that of the LEA only if the unreasonable behaviour complained of was such that 'no reasonable authority would engage in it'. If parents took the extreme step of withholding a child from the school, however, and thus brought upon themselves an order under the school attendance provisions of the 1944 Act, they could ask the Secretary of State for a ruling. It was then for the Secretary of State to determine under Section 37 of that Act the school to be named in the attendance order. This had caused problems, since under Section 37 the Secretary of State could only find in favour of the LEA if the chosen school in the individual case was unsuitable or involved unreasonable expense, conditions less restrictive than those applying in choice of school appeals generally. The 1980 legislators sought to remove this anomaly, reduce the number of appeals to the DES and at the same time give parents clearer rights.

Under Section 6 of the 1980 Act parents have a right to express a preference for a school. LEAs and governors must honour this preference unless it would 'prejudice the provision of efficient education or the efficient use of resources, be incompatible with the arrangements for admission made between the LEA and the governors of a voluntary aided school, or unless in a selective school the child has not met the requirements as to ability and aptitude'. Thus there are still qualifications which deny absolute freedom of choice and which protect the power which aided schools have over admissions, and selection where it still exists. Disappointed parents may appeal to a local appeals committee (Section 7) on which the LEA or governors may have a majority of one, but may not provide the chairperson. The parent concerned must appeal in writing and be informed in writing of the decisions and the reasons. There is still recourse to the Secretary of State under Section 68 of the 1944 Act, but no separate recourse in school attendance proceedings. The decision of the appeals committee is binding on the LEA, and determines the school to be named in the attendance order. Parents may opt for a school in the area of another LEA, and under Section 31 of the Act the home LEA may not refuse to pay recoupment if the child secures a place. LEAs and governors must publish their criteria (Section 8) and must include the numbers to be admitted to each school. Furthermore, to assist parents in choosing, schools are obliged by regulations made under the Act (4) to publish information about their curriculum, organisation, discipline and examination results.

In the early days of the Act there was a great deal of scepticism about its alleged extension of parental rights. It was often pointed out that no law can give you what is not there, and that in the terms in which LEAs' duties to meet parental wishes were qualified, it was not very different from the previous legislation, which most parents had judged mere window-dressing. In practice, the 1980 Act had had rather more impact, though how much of a part falling rolls have played we cannot be sure. In the first year of its operation, 1982, there were some 9,000 appeals, of which about one third were successful. In 1983 there were 10,000, and some 3,500 were successful. In 1985, 9,100 appeals were heard, and 3,997 of those parents were granted their choice of school (5).

Before 1980 many LEAs tried to give parents as much choice as the practicalities permitted, and some had appeals procedures. It could be said that the legislation brought all up to the level of the best in these respects, as well as in the degree to which parents were informed and the procedures were open. One must remember that in some LEAs rigid catchment areas were applied, parents were not even informed that they were allowed to choose an alternative and the whole system was run for bureaucratic convenience or in an extreme adherence to the neighbourhood ideal. In others the allocation methods were mysterious and the object of suspicion. Whatever reservations one has about the effects of market forces on the fairness of the system, one cannot justify these extremes.

A very important decision in the courts was made in 1984 in the case of a South Glamorgan appellant, in which the point at issue was the meaning of 'efficient use of resources' in Section 6. Previously LEAs looked like getting away with interpreting the law as giving them the right to consider the need to avoid uneconomic use of space in schools other than the chosen one. The South Glamorgan judgment (6) indicated that to refuse admission to a chosen school it is necessary to prove that the admission of that one child is likely to produce inefficiency or disproportionate expense. This judgment may have had something to do with the much higher percentage (44%) of successful appeals in 1985.

One undeniably effective section of the Act is Section 31, which allows the choice procedures to operate across LEA boundaries. Previously squabbles about payment were common, and many LEAs would not accept out-county pupils because the home LEA would not pay. In my LEA, the outer London borough of Richmond, something like a quarter of the eleven year olds entering our schools in 1986 were from neighbouring LEAs, notably Kingston which was very slow to respond to public pressures for an end to selection. Thus one LEA was assisted to keep its schools and its teachers' jobs while parents in neighbouring areas were making clear their feelings about what was on offer locally. I am not sure how far this makes any contribution to better schools for all: the parents who make positive choices are generally also the ones with the capacity to exert positive influence for change.

No statistics, indeed, can tell us how far the legislation might have achieved its avowed intent of making schools more responsive to parents. In a study of the operation of parental choice carried out by the National Foundation for Educational Research from July 1983 to June 1985 the following very pertinent comment is made:

> Whilst it might be difficult to determine admissions solely or even partly on educational grounds, it is difficult to see how schools might benefit from the expression of the parents' views if they are never made aware of them... In numerous LEAs no information about why parents preferred some schools over others reached either the education officers or any of the schools themselves. (6)

Nor can we ever quantify the negative effects of extending parental choice, the impoverishment of those schools less able to attract custom. Such impoverishment arises from the absence of parents able to press for improvements; from the loss of parents able to supplement what is offered; from the loss of staff as numbers decline; the consequent curriculum erosion; and the vicious downward spiral starting again with further decline in numbers. I only know that in almost all of the LEA areas where I speak to headteachers on in-service courses – and I would estimate that there have been in round terms 200 such occasions in 50 LEA areas in the years 1982 to 1987 – I am told of this tendency for these self-selective processes to damage some schools for no good educational reason. It could to some extent have happened of course as a result of falling rolls, with no help from the law.

IDEAS FOR EXTENDING CHOICE

Many advocates of a free market in education are not satisfied with the limited extension of choice and therefore, in their view, accountability, provided by the 1980 Act. This, in the summer of 1986, was the theme of a publication by a group calling themselves 'Save Our Schools' advocating the direct government funding of schools on a per capita basis, said to have found favour with senior Ministers. In such a system the income of schools would derive solely from the pupils they attracted in a free market. Writing about the idea in The Times on 13 August 1986, Stuart Sexton, for many years the powerful adviser behind the scenes on the present government's education policy, wrote:

17

> We have moved a long way to restoring the rightful, central place to parents and children, but so far we have refused to accept the logic of that in management of schools. In any other enterprise it is the clients, the customers, whose demands and needs have to be met by the suppliers if they are to stay in business. (7)

Note how the parallel between education and purely commercial services is taken for granted. Note too the subtle identification of this extreme form of consumerism with mainstream parent involvement. How many readers of that letter would have guessed that exactly a year later we should be considering plans for new legislation based upon its ideas?

The theorists, who include academic-sounding organisations like the Institute of Economic Affairs, the Centre for Policy Studies and the Hillgate group have moved us by easy stages from free choice within a still basically public system to an extreme in which we forget 1870 and all that, and make education a parental responsibility. At the near end we have 'open enrolment', tried on a limited scale by Kent in the early Eighties, and giving parents by administrative decree a free choice of existing state schools, expanded if necessary, and at the far end a virtual dismantling of LEAs with direct funding of all schools which can establish viability. In between are all the variants of the voucher idea, the essence of which is to turn a child's basic entitlement to education into a piece of paper, to be exchanged at the parents' chosen school. Some versions confine vouchers to state schools, while others would allow the use of vouchers in part-payment for private schools. This would in effect give parents their share of rates and taxes to spend as they wish.

There are many expositions of these ideas (8). So far no working model exists. Experiments in the USA, at Alum Rock, received some attention years ago but they have petered out, while in Kent a feasibility study (9) in the late Seventies and the Kent open enrolment scheme referred to above produced disappointing verdicts and have not been pursued further. But the philosophy behind all these schemes is extraordinarily robust, and alternative routes to better schools seem too much like hard work to have any glamour. It would be very dangerous to underrate the market's allure.

THE WEAKNESSES OF CONSUMERISM

The market place philosophy rests on superficially reasonable comparisons between education and other goods and services. Firstly one must question whether education is a transaction at all, in the sense of a bargain struck between buyer and seller at a particular time and in a particular place. As compulsory reading to equip me to serve as a member of the

Taylor Committee, I had to delve into the history of public sector education and indeed of public involvement in the schools which existed long before there was universal schooling. Surely, one would think, when education was a minority activity, it would be seen as a private arrangement like the purchase of a horse, concerning only buyer and seller? Yet in all the educational writings of former centuries, I was struck by the sense that education was even then an activity of such a character as to concern also those who had no hope of receiving it. This was the origin of the idea of the governing body, so we shall return to it.

Surely we are all consumers of education? In reading books, seeing plays, looking at pictures, buying goods and services, benefitting or suffering from our country's economic health, walking down a dark street at night, we are compulsory participants in this 'transaction' just as surely as the parent who is obliged by law to see that the child is educated. If this is accepted, the parents, important as they are, cannot be the only ones involved in the choice of what is offered to children.

One step on, and we accept education as a public purpose. This provides the answer to those who claim an individual right to spend their share of education rates and taxes as they like. They cannot claim exemption from the cost of refuse collection because they are garden pyromaniacs, or libraries because they cannot read. Why else are the childless required to support schooling?

On a much simpler level, it is the parent who chooses, the child whose life is forever affected by the choice and children do not make that most important choice of all, the choice of the parents who do the choosing on their behalf. Teachers will always argue passionately that children's needs and parents' rights do not always add up, and that teachers may be the sole means whereby children will rise above the aspirations of their homes.

At this point the market place philosopher will only protest that we are talking about life's incurable inequalities, and will point out that children's chances depend in hundreds of ways on the accident of birth. Why deny parents who care passionately about education the right to spend their own money on it, the right to get the best deal they can, especially as their pressures will produce better schools and all will benefit? You do not after all try to stop them giving their children better food, a pleasanter environment, a bedtime story, even though good choices in these matters benefit only their own.

This is the sense in which choice of schools really is different from all other consumer choices. As you walk on your new stair carpet, knowing that it will not fade or develop bald patches, that it will give your family of five ten years' wear or 108,900 treads, because you have read your consumer magazines and done your sums, and got good value for your money, you can feel good without hurting anyone. There is still plenty left on the roll, and if people choose five years' wear at two thirds of the price, it may be the right decision for them. But every act of choice in education changes the school which is chosen, and the one which is not chosen, so that you are not just securing something good for your child, but also making it harder for those who are working to provide something better for the others.

This is all very philosophical, and suggests a moral stamina beyond the reach of most of us. It is only intended to cast doubt upon the simplistic assumptions of the consumerists, who would have us believe that better schools for all, and a service more accountable and responsive, can be so easily won. Choice pursued in isolation from other goals could indeed produce lower general standards and a less responsive service overall, since it could concentrate the parental pressures on a smaller number of schools. This does not mean that efforts to increase choice are misguided, but that the task of enlisting more effective parent and public support for better schools is a far more complex one than is dreamed of in the market place.

A voucher system is only a genuine extension of choice if (a) it provides in whole or in part the income of the school (which both removes public control and gives the parent more clout), and/or (b) it allows for an element of 'topping up', either by being usable at private schools or by giving parents the option even in state schools of buying extras over and above the voucher value.

The supermarket appeal of these proposals is obvious. They give parents the illusion of power, and they will particularly attract three groups of parents. First is the group naturally inclined to private education, either using it already and welcoming the subsidy - 'Why should we pay twice?' - or craving the chance and not quite able to afford the whole cost. Any money spent on this group would clearly represent a net loss to the funds available for state education. Then there is the rapidly growing number, at a time when the living standards of those lucky enough to have jobs are improving, who find state education a reasonably good bargain even if they do have to pay for a lot of extras or even essentials themselves, and who would therefore welcome improved access to the kind of school where this is the norm. Again there is great scope for saving public funds, since once you have placed a cash value on a child's entitlement, there is nothing to say that that level must in real terms be maintained, so you have an ideal opportunity to make what it will buy ever more basic, and shift the cost of the rest of the curriculum on to the parents, a process, as we have said, now already well under way. This offers a poor outlook for the third group who would be attracted by vouchers,

since this consists mainly of those without educational
sophistication who feel intimidated or patronised by schools,
whose aspirations have never advanced much beyond a very
old-fashioned basic education for their children, who vaguely
sense that their children in a number of ways lose out as
things are, and who would grasp the piece of paper which
offered a bit of Dutch courage to ask for what they want. It
is only fair to add that many on the educational right claim to
be especially concerned about this group, arguing that
working class children have suffered most from the
broadening perspectives of the curriculum, and deserve a
better grounding in basics. I have commented on this folly,
as I see it, elsewhere (10). It is interesting that the third
Conservative government elected in 1987 claimed support for
its educational policies from the discontents of certain
'ordinary' parents with traditional views, mainly in areas
under extreme left-wing control.

If it seems unkind to see in voucher schemes yet another
device for reducing expenditure on education, one need only
look at the practical consequences for these three quite
substantial groups in the long term. Once the options
included the private sector, one could expect a proliferation
of crummy establishments trading down to a price at or near
the voucher value, and in some areas state schools might be
forced to compete for the same market. I was told repeatedly
in the course of my contacts with parents and educationists
as I travelled across Australia in 1982 that this had been the
effect in many areas of the Fraser government's policy of
subsidising private schools, which in Australia include all
denominational schools, on a per capita basis. Indeed I was
told that districts could be found where it was actually
cheaper to pay fees at a private school thus subsidised, and
offering a very basic curriculum and unstimulating environment, than to send your child to a good government school
offering the kind of rich educational experience an 'enlight-
ened' parent would seek, since in the government school you
would be buying books, art materials, and the like, contributing to unofficial school funds, and doing your bit in
parental fund-raising. Privilege can take many strange forms!
Yet in Australia there was widespread support among unsoph-
isticated parents for what they saw as a system offering
choice and freedom, and readers will have observed what
difficulties the Hawke government encountered in trying to
implement its promises to change it. Many parents were
clearly making sacrifices to buy their children what we should
consider a very inferior deal, and grateful for the chance. I
say this to emphasise yet again that one must not under-
estimate the strength of the consumerist lobby. It also affords
a sombre warning, for, during the debate leading up to the
Education Reform Bill of 1987, many indications were given
that the 'radical Right' considered this only an instalment of

far more wide-ranging measures which would allow independent schools to 'opt in' as well as LEA schools to 'opt out'.

Because I believe that these extreme forms of consumerism in education would tragically damage the interests of the most needy and defenceless in our schools, I consider it urgent to encourage parents to look at them realistically and ask searching practical questions. Firstly, is it right to assume that schools can respond as effectively to parents' wishes as the providers of more tangible wares? Surely the ethos of a successful school is something built up over years, a blend of tradition, leadership, teamwork and parent support. Can such a school expand rapidly and remain as successful? May not its size have been one of the most appealing things about it? If you add temporary classrooms to accommodate the previously disappointed pupils, without increasing the facilities for science, the arts, recreation, is it not just a cup of water in the soup? Meanwhile what of the schools not so favoured by the wayward public, and the children in them, who have only one chance? They will be on the vicious downward spiral already described. Is it good to encourage schools to put so much effort into packaging and marketing? Falling rolls have already pushed us some way along that path. Most important of all, when schools have reached the limit of expansion, who decides how places are allocated? Are we choosing them, or are they choosing us? What shall we have gained from making education a sort of shanty town, littered with yesterday's false prospectuses? Not influence, since schools will rightly say that we pay our money and take our choice, and they do not really want to know what we think as well. True sharing with parents could be set back years, since a market economy is unlikely to produce more secure and confident teachers.

If accountability is to be real, it must be for everybody, just as choice, if real, has to be for everybody. What voucher schemes and the like would undoubtedly do successfully is concentrate limited resources on those who 'appreciate them most', which could be freely translated as 'need them least'. This is not really news, since throughout the Eighties it has been an orderly, if not actually deliberate process aided by cuts, abetted by falling rolls, and inadequately combated by a too slowly developing awareness of the scope for genuine public involvement in schooling. If we want to end for ever the dominance of market place vocabulary and ethics in education, we must recruit an army to say loudly and often that individual achievement means nothing in a world made up of other people's children, whose rights we ignore at our peril.

NOTES

1. DES, Education Act 1980, (HMSO, 1980).
2. Institute of Economic Affairs, Choice in Education by H.R. Dennison (Hobart Paperbacks No 19) and The Riddle of the Voucher by Arthur Seldon, (Hobart Paperbacks No 21 1986). Also a series of articles by various authors under the title Politics of the Education Voucher, in Economic Affairs, (Vol 6, No 4, April/May 1986).
3. NCPTA, The State of Schools in England and Wales, (NCPTA, 43, Stonebridge Rd., Northfleet, Gravesend, Kent, October 1985).
4. DES, Education (School Information) Regulations 1981, (SI 1981, No 630, HMSO).
5. Source DES Schools Branch, August 1986.
6. Andy Stillman and Karen Maychell, Choosing Schools: Parents, LEAs, and the 1980 Education Act, p. 183 (NFER -Nelson, 1986).
7. Stuart Sexton, Schools: and still the parents wait, p. 12, (The Times, 13 August 1986).
8. In addition to works under (2) above, see especially D. Sugarman How parental choice could enhance school power, (Education, two articles, 17 and 27 April 1979); M. and R. Friedman, Free to Choose, (New York, Avon Nonfic 1981); Anthony Flew, Power to the People, (Centre for Policy Studies 1983) and Power to Parents: Reversing Educational Decline, (Sharwood Press, November 1987); the Centre for Policy Studies, Whose Schools? (December 1986); and the Hillgate Group, Reform of British Education, (Hillgate Group, September 1987). Also of interest is an article by Roger Scruton in The Times of Wednesday 10 June 1987 entitled Power to the Real Parents. The author is editor of the Salisbury Review.
9. Kent County Council, Education Vouchers in Kent, (Kent County Council, Maidstone 1978).
10. See especially Chapter One, pp. 7-8.

Chapter Three

PARENTS: CLIENTS OR PARTNERS?

Teachers reading these words will be relieved that we have
left the market place behind us. They will have needed no
convincing that their precious commodity cannot be sold over
the counter like groceries. They know that the most vulnerable in our schools will suffer grievously if we try to make
their life chances even more dependent on their parents'
skills as consumers. On the other hand, there can be few
who still cherish the hope that some day they will wake as
from a terrible dream to find that the one who has the book
is the only one allowed to tell us what is in it. Few still
believe that they will ever again enjoy the unquestioned
power they think we accord to the doctor, the lawyer, the
bank manager or the architect. But many feel very sore that
no other professionals work under the same pressures to
consult and to justify. You do, they say, let experts design
your homes, dissolve your marriages, whip out your vital
organs, without a word of protest, and you are sometimes
even grateful.

Accountability of the more orthodox kind is more often
demanded than defined. At least those who see schooling as a
transaction know precisely the sense in which the schools will
be made to answer for their failure to please the customer.
But when you visualise it as a community enterprise, lightly
regulated by national law, entrusted to locally elected councils
who employ officers to organise it, produced at school level
by teachers but subject to last minute design modifications by
governors and all sorts of pressures from agencies outside
the school, then inspected by representatives of both local
and national government, you could be forgiven for wondering
how anyone can be held to account if it goes wrong. If the
teachers feel bewildered about where responsibility lies, how
much more bewildering must it be for parents.

Yet if we accept that the educator's total freedom will
never return, and we reject the market place approach, we
must accept the obligation to find some alternative. In the

24

present climate any heads in the sand will emerge to find that false gods hold sway.

WHAT DOES ACCOUNTABILITY MEAN?

We can choose among a range of definitions. I have heard many teachers say that they are accountable only to children. I know that they mean well, and that the remark indicates their solemn feeling of responsibility, their care and seriousness, their desire to put children first and to protect them against their many enemies; but as a response to the widespread belief that they should justify their actions to those who need to know, it is meaningless. It does their cause a disservice.

At the other extreme we have those who dismiss any definition of accountability which does not have the possibility of sanctions. Thus Maurice Kogan told the British Educational Administration Society (1) that accountability was 'the duty to render account of work performed to a body that has authority to modify that performance by the use of sanction and reward'. That is precise and rigorous thinking, but it is very difficult to apply it to the untidy way in which responsibility is at present shared in our education service. The teacher trying to respond to all the agencies which together impinge on the task is like a chameleon on a tartan.

Between these extremes accountability is seen as a requirement to have one's work tested, debated and judged within some more or less formal structure. Success may not be rewarded or failure punished, but there is an obligation to give reasons for action, to review outcomes and to submit to judgement on the performance, in all the circumstances, of the task which one accepts is one's own.

WHAT ARE PARENTS CONCERNED ABOUT?

Parents might be momentarily impressed by the claim of being answerable only to children. They want their teachers to be caring people. But they also want them to be listening people, and they sometimes have a shrewd suspicion that listening to the unvoiced concerns of children is an excuse for not listening to the clearly voiced concerns of elected members, the press, governors and parents. These may or may not coincide with the interests of children, but it is still unwise to treat them with studied indifference.

Probably most parents would be reassured to know that formal structures existed within schools for monitoring teachers. One of the things which makes them panic about a bad teacher is that they fear no one else even knows about the situation, let alone does anything about it. If they should

dare to voice concern to the head, they often get an understandably defensive response, so they panic even more. If,
when their children joined the school, and at intervals after
that, they could be given an explanation of what mechanisms
existed to appraise teachers and help any who were having
difficulties, it would greatly increase both their confidence
and their forbearance. This is rarely mentioned in the debate
about appraisal, but is surely a major additional benefit.

But sanctions? In extremis the irate victims of a situation in which someone has allegedly made a hash of teaching
children see only one sanction as appropriate, namely the
prompt denial of the opportunity to teach any more children.
Such prompt removal from the scene is, they know, only
possible in the direst emergency. Much more commonly there
is no emergency, the rights and wrongs are far from clear,
powerful forces leap into action to defend the teacher - and
on the whole it would be more worrying if they did not - and
the whole process is hazardous and very slow. Nor are sanctions of a punitive kind appropriate in the vast majority of
cases, where most commonly we are talking about brief depar-
tures from rigour or vigilance, ill-judged surrender to
momentary anger, or poor communication, which have caused
tensions. Such lapses are inevitable in dealing with children,
but so often pride turns a small matter into a big one. Explanations and remedies then take a great deal of time, and
children may well suffer in the process.

It is surely only the rare parent who becomes
obsessional about 'making them pay' for real or imagined
failure, and even when it happens it is usually because the
matter has dragged on too long and there are no defusing
mechanisms. All that most parents want is a system in which
they routinely get simple explanations of school policies and
methods, a chance to question and even doubt without making
a meal of it, some assurance that if a problem develops they
will be promptly told and encouraged to help, and that they
themselves can similarly approach the school if they have
worries. I doubt whether many are interested in making
schools do penance for failure. Since children have only one
chance, parents are surely more concerned with an opportunity to share in the avoidance of failure.

ANOTHER WAY

There is no escaping the need for more precision, which we
hope the 1986 Act will bring, on where the last-resort
responsibility on every issue rests, whether it is the inclusion of a subject in the curriculum, the choice of a reading
scheme, the safety of laboratory equipment, the suspension of
a pupil or the collapse of confidence in a whole school.
Surely, however, given the concern of parents with so much

more than the last resort, and the complexity of influences operating on schools, accountability must also mean the acceptance of a commitment to build, day by day, for all concerned, structures within which explaining, questioning, listening, become routine. Such structures would not be immutable, but would develop and grow in an organic way. They would indeed afford great protection for teachers in disagreements with seniors or excessive political interference with their work, since their judgement would have the consent of others and their policies will have been the subject of debate. Their professional authority will be strengthened by the very process of seeking that consent and promoting that debate.

If we are to explore this new dimension of accountability, we shall have to look honestly at attitudes and roles, and especially clarify our thoughts on whether parents can properly be considered 'clients' at all. But we must also look at the frequent complaint by teachers that we expect to be able to question their actions in a way other professionals would not allow.

COMPARISONS WITH OTHER PROFESSIONS

In a survey of voluntary help with reading in schools undertaken in 1985 by Stierer (2) a hostile teacher is quoted as saying: 'I should also refuse surgery from a hospital porter.' This seems an extraordinary statement in the context of such an innocent and well-established form of intervention as parents hearing reading, and I am sure most teachers would repudiate it. Nevertheless there is hardly a week in which I do not hear a similar thought expressed.

Few other professional relationships involve anything so precious to the 'client'. The Victorian lace shawl sent to the dry cleaners may be priceless, but nothing competes with the future. Anyway the dry cleaners frequently seek permission to try more drastic treatment if the stains will not yield to the normal process - many teachers might envy them the opportunity! In no other professional/client relationship are we in effect compulsory consumers. Even the pursuit of health is not obligatory - the freedom to die remains. The doctor seeks consent too for the more risky enterprises. And while few of us would express a view on the merits of a vertical rather than a horizontal incision, if you woke up missing your appendix instead of your gall bladder you might well go back and say you did not feel much better.

This is good knockabout stuff, but there are more serious and relevant points to tease out of such comparisons. You would not question the architect's choice of materials, or the plumber's judgement on the best route to the water tank. But the architect would know it was a conservatory, not a laundry room you wanted. The plumber would tell you if your bedroom floorboards had to be up over the weekend. The solicitor clothes our intentions in some pretty specialised language, but it is for us to tell him the grounds for the divorce or the beneficiaries of the will. In all these relationships there is discussion about the objectives and the methods and a chance to comment on the outcome. Traditionally there has not been much of that sort of discussion about schooling, and such consensus as maybe once there was has been fragmented.

If we consider consent to be an important element in a harmonious relationship between professional and client, we soon have to come to terms with the client's need for information, since without knowledge of what the objective is, what methods are to be used and what outcome can be expected, consent has little meaning. As we shall see, the information available to parents has in many ways increased in recent years, though it may still be judged less than adequate by some. Before we look at parents' information needs in relation to schools, however, we ought to consider how far they are properly informed and involved in the education policies of the LEA, since schools have to operate within this framework.

THE ACCOUNTABILITY OF THE LEA

The democracy of the ballot box provides us with some influence, as citizens, on the general education policies to be carried out in an area. Since 1974 that area has for many of us been a bigger one. If most parents were satisfied that the ballot box gave them a significant and sufficiently detailed influence, it would be easy to see the teacher's simple line of accountability through line management to employer to citizen and parent. There have, it is true, in recent years been some useful improvements in the way local authorities generally relate to their electorate. Since the Maud Commission pronounced itself very dissatisfied with that relationship in 1969 (3), referring to the indifference and contempt with which the citizen regarded local government, and concerning itself particularly with issues of 'accessibility and responsiveness', we have successfully won access to council committees and subcommittees, the right (under the Local Government Act 1980) to a statement showing how the rates are spent, and access (under the Local Authorities (Access to Information) Act 1985) to documents leading up to local authority decisions.

Parents have manifestly not been satisfied that such broad-brush accountability has much bearing on the way their local schools function. Education is rarely a vital election issue at all, and even on the rare occasion when it is, the questions relate to very general matters such as whether there is selection for secondary education. No one votes on whether children are to be allowed water with their lunch, whether they can opt for geography and physics, whether they have homework diaries, whether they can go into the library during wet playtimes, whether parents are consulted about showing a film on child molestation. This dissatisfaction with the degree of direct influence they can exercise in such matters explains parents' interest in having effective Parent Teacher-Assocations and representation on governing bodies. They clearly feel that they need some focus of concern within the school, some structure within which policies can be explained and discussed, and consent and support sought. This has become more, not less, important in recent years, partly because a harsher economic climate makes a child's success or failure at school an even more vital matter, partly because the process itself becomes ever more complex, and partly because even as accountability within local government has been somewhat improved, there has been increased central government intervention in the education service, and more power given to agencies outside education, such as the Manpower Services Commission. This reduces the value of LEA accountability, and by putting more territory outside parental influence has strengthened the case for more say at school level.

It is only right to record that LEAs now have to provide a good deal more information about the choice of schools available to parents, and both LEAs and governors have to publish their admissions criteria. This requirement of the 1980 Act has without doubt opened up a process which was in some areas mysterious and even the object of suspicion. Since 1983, HMI reports on schools have been published and are available free. Some parents think it anomalous that reports by LEA inspectors/advisers are not similarly open. In judging this issue it is important to remember that although local inspectors outnumber HMI by four to one, inspection is a very limited part of their role. Their time is mainly spent giving friendly support to teachers, which means weighing openness against goodwill. Nevertheless, in September 1986, the Parliamentary Select Committee on Education, Science and the Arts, in its Report on Achievement in Primary Schools, recommended (Paragraph 10.12) that reports of local advisers on schools should, subject to certain safeguards, be published.

We look below at the information individual schools provide for parents; but, before leaving the relationship of LEAs with the public, we should say something about local reorganisation proposals. Both the 1944 and 1980 Acts required LEAs to give public notice of their intention to close schools, establish new schools or change the character of schools, and the Secretary of State has a role in endorsing such plans. Since 1980 he need only be involved in disputed proposals or those involving voluntary schools. Since most changes in the pattern of local provision will require at least technical closures, it does mean considerable public involvement. LEAs have to consult parents and governors of affected schools before publishing notices. Already at least two LEAs, Brent and Gateshead, have been prevented from carrying out reorganisation plans because they were found on appeal to have had inadequate consultation with parents.

INFORMATION FOR PARENTS

Apart from the rights given to parents in the 1980 Act itself to information affecting their choice of schools and to consultation about proposed changes in local schools, parents were given important new rights to information from individual schools by regulations (4) made in 1981 under Section 8 of the Act. Individual schools are required to publish specified details about their staff, organisation, curriculum, rules and sanctions, and, in the case of secondary schools, examination results.

I would be the first to complain that these requirements have a strongly consumerist flavour, and are related more or less directly to the support of choice, rather than to the concept of parents in partnership with schools. For instance, schools are not required to tell parents what arrangements they make to involve them in the school, inform them of their children's progress, enlist their help. They are not required to tell them whether there is a parents' association or give them the names of their parent representatives on the governing body - just the chairman. This seems extraordinary when the information rights form part of the same legal package that gives parents for the first time statutory representation on governing boards. The strong implication is that parents need to know more about schools in order to compare them, not so that they may through their understanding play a more supportive role in their own. It is precisely this element of comparison of schools which made many people so fearful of the requirement to publish examination results.

The motivation underlying this whole process of opening up to public scrutiny what the schools offer and how they perform is undoubtedly that of the market place. Yet I cannot accept that it has been a bad development, so far as it goes, or that we should try to reverse it. What we must try to do instead is to move forward to better and more complete information services, join up the dots, flesh out the bones. No one in a public service should be allowed to withhold information about its performance from those who have a legitimate interest, and the fact that the information, because it is incomplete, may be used to make misleading judgements is not a reason for denying people the means to make those judgements, but rather an urgent reason to assist them to make better and more rounded judgements. It is essentially the same issue as I raised on Page 7 about the bad press schools get. There is no means of suppressing criticism based on misinformation. One can only build up knowledge and experience to counteract it. To do violence to Gresham's Law once more, I do believe that good information drives out bad.

On the specific question of examination results, I happen to live in the area of the first LEA to publish, three years before the law required it. The decision to publish was taken when the first cohort reached the fifth year of our comprehensives. I was just as nervous of the outcome as the many teachers who were later to oppose the government's plan to require publication. I had an intense commitment to the system for which I had helped to fight, and hostages in it. I knew that confidence was still fragile and there were many mischief-makers only too ready to exploit any problems. That first cohort was not balanced: parents' timidity had led many who could afford the fees to opt out until things settled, and at the time the LEA had still been buying places for the top 5 per cent in the private sector, a practice we succeeded in persuading them to end, but not for two years. I knew that our schools, like everyone else's, had intakes of varying quality, had been reorganised in varying circumstances and had headteachers who had responded with different degrees of skill to the challenges of change, and there were many of us who feared that such differences as there were would be harmfully widened.

We have been amazed how well it has gone. We are lucky to have fairly mixed catchment areas for all our schools, to have a good number of parents both concerned and sensible, to have a very large local Association for the Advancement of State Education, to have had since 1974 governors widely representative of parents, teachers and community, and an LEA concerned to explain and caution, and willing to use the results to tackle problems they bring to light. This last is crucial. Why publish information if no one draws any conclusions other than those which harden existing inequalities?

In fact there have been quite wide variations among schools, and even now after eight years it is possible to have schools with no more than the national average of pupils with four or more O levels and others with 50 per cent or more. Yet now all eight schools are well supported, and all parents have for several years had their first choice, which itself indicates that no widespread desertion of the neighbourhood school has taken place. There is no evidence that parents are choosing on the basis of examination results alone. The secret is that we have a very high level of parent and governor involvement in the schools, which fosters awareness of all the factors making for a successful school. There is also ground for confidence that constructive comments will be listened to and acted upon, and that the LEA will deal promptly with any problems the results reveal.

Against this background, the press have taken remarkably little interest in the examination results. One reporter said that you needed an A level in maths to understand them! If there were large numbers of parents who had not got places at their chosen comprehensives there might have been some mileage in highlighting the differences in performance, but when all are suited those differences are not very newsworthy. It is good that the regulations provide for the schools themselves to publish their results, for though it is still possible for league tables to be constructed, they are not spoon-fed to the public, and the silent point is made that the information concerns the school, its governors, and its parents and prospective parents. It is also wise that it is the proportion of the age group succeeding which has to be shown, not the proportion of those entered, since it both discourages and fails to give false glory to those schools which restrict opportunity.

One of the most encouraging experiences I have had as a governor is to see governors brushing quickly aside any consideration of where we come in the charts, and focussing sharply on what we can learn for our own school in our own circumstances. 'Weren't we wise to put in some extra strength there!' 'We should perhaps have used that spare scale point in the modern languages faculty after all.' 'Why so many Grade 1 CSEs in biology? Were we perhaps a bit conservative with the O level entries?' Above all, while we have at different times been both top of the league and not top, what has given us most pleasure is that over three years in our own school, with as far as we know no change in the intake, we have actually doubled the proportion getting four or more O levels. This reflects the increasing confidence of staff, pupils and parents, and a willingness to look constructively at the school's own performance. Where all are motivated to use the results in this way, and have confidence that any comment based on such motives will be received in the right spirit, publication can surely only be good.

We do, however, need to develop all the back-up relationships which make such things possible. Where there is rampant consumerism, a mean spirit between schools, failure to help any in difficulties and, above all, a lack of closeness in the partnership between schools and their parents and governors, the knowledge and trust which ensures that information will be wisely used will not grow.

PARENTS' VIEW OF THEIR INFORMATION NEEDS

The architects of the 1980 Act had a great deal of guidance from researchs of various kinds. In 1976, for instance, the National Consumer Council commissioned a Gallup poll on parents' attitudes to schools, and 39 per cent said that they were dissatisfied with the amount of information they received about teaching methods and subject choices, while nearly a quarter felt that they would be interfering if they went to the school uninvited. A report (5) was prepared in agreement with parent, governor and student organisations called 'Question Marks for Schools' and published in February 1977.

In the following year an investigation took place in Nottingham University which has become a classic of its kind, called 'Written Communication Between Home and School' (6). This was a report of a community education working party, which found that most schools concentrated on purely informative matter, and a limited number encouraged parents to participate, even these often in dauntingly bleak style.

Sussex University published in 1979 (7) evidence that parents 'expressed a strong wish' for information and read avidly all they got, even if it was not adequate, and that they were in fact given very little about the curriculum of a kind which would help them support the children's learning. The researchers also strongly criticised the absence in teacher training of any guidance is assessing and responding to parents' needs.

What all these studies, and many undertaken since, have in common, is the clear distinction between schools telling parents things and using their communications to involve parents in their work. Cambridge University in 1981 studied six secondary schools (8) and found that access was a pre-occupation of nearly all parents. Nearly a quarter in one school had chosen it specifically because head and staff were approachable in matters relating to children's progress. In the wake of the 1980 Act a study of school brochures was made by the Scottish Consumer Council (9). Very very few contained anything on ways in which parents could help or encourage their children, and there was a strong emphasis on what the school thought parents should know.

These are only a few examples from many of investigations all underlining the point that schools do not respond on the whole to the need parents feel for information which would lead them into a dialogue with the school, and this is a factor conspicuously missing from the legal requirements.

The National Consumer Council has become deeply concerned about the adequacy of information given to parents. The Consumer Congress in March 1983 passed by an overwhelming majority the following resolution:

PARENTS: CLIENTS OR PARTNERS?

> This Congress requests the National Consumer Council to urge government and education authorities:
>
> to provide adequate resources so that all children in state schools may receive an education of high quality regardless of home circumstances;
>
> to promote all forms of partnership with parents, including the representation of parents on governing boards - or school councils in Scotland - the right to regular consultation with teachers and the right to form school associations;
>
> to ensure that help in communicating with parents forms part of the initial and in-service training of every teacher;
>
> to research and disseminate methods of communication with parents including the least confident, and to spread good practice;
>
> to develop community schools, promoting the concept of lifelong educational opportunity, and the use of school resources for the community, and community skills for the school.

I have quoted this in full because it is remarkable for a number of reasons. Firstly it puts information for consumers in the context of partnership within a well and fairly resourced service, and there is no mention of choice. Secondly it was resoundingly endorsed and given second priority among a very varied large gathering of consumer representatives from a range of public and private sector activities. Thirdly it inaugurated what one hopes might be a period of continuing commitment by the NCC to the promotion of a higher status and more responsive public education system. I am not criticising its previous activities in this field: what was done was imaginative and useful, but they tended to be publicity-worthy one-off interventions rather than a continuing follow-up of needs revealed. The NCC is funded by the government to care for the interests of consumers in both public and private enterprises, and the resolution above is precisely as a thoughtful state school PTA chairperson or parent governor would see the need, but it has taken a long time to get it expressed. At the Congress, a member of the National Consumer Council spoke strongly against it, saying that what we needed to produce better schools was not more money or more involvement, but more rigour, better value for the money spent, more effective expression of the consumer's high expectations. His intervention was fortunate, since it united behind the resolution many who had not seen the alternatives so clearly before.

That resolution has led to the involvement of the NCC in some useful initiatives on school governor training and information for parents. As a beginning they started in 1984 on an ambitious opinion survey. It began with exploratory discussions, undertaken by a professional agency, of three groups of parents, one in a London borough, one in a shire county, and one in a northern town. The object was to identify issues which might merit further investigation. Enough evidence emerged of parents' concern with access to schools for the purpose of discussing their children's progress to make this the starting point. A structured investigation was then planned, using both group discussions and individual interviews, in an inner city area and a rural county. The parents chosen were those of pupils in the first, fourth, and sixth years of secondary education, to bring in concerns about changing schools, choosing options, and looking at careers. Pupils as well as parents were involved in the second and third groups.

An immense amount of detail is recorded in the NCC report (10) about forms of home-school contact actually experienced, and the degree of satisfaction expressed, with class differentiation where appropriate. Very practical recommendations for improvement are made in the report. For our present purpose, what comes over clearly is the difference between what teachers say is the level of parental involvement and how parents perceive it: the feeling among parents that at times of really critical decisions they had inadequate information, dissatisfaction with the form of consultation evenings, and perhaps above all the impression that communication was one-way, not a dialogue. The parents who obtained least satisfaction from contact with schools were those in semi-skilled and unskilled occupations, and of the pupils who felt that they had not had much help with what to do at 16, nearly two-thirds had solved it by leaving school.

The degree of satisfaction with the straight information provided by schools as an aid to choosing one was much higher than with the contact once the child was in the school, again reflecting very directly the philosophy of the 1981 regulations. It recalls also the observation I made on Page 14 that parents would not be so concerned about choice if they felt they had more say. Over a third of parents in the survey thought they were only consulted 'a little' or 'not at all' by their schools. A third of pupils were dissatisfied with the information they had been given to help them choose their options. Some of the comments made were very revealing:-

You get plenty of communication about fund-raising events ...but I wish you could get some more on what's being taught and how it's being taught and some sort of discussion with them about it.

> Shire, Parent of 4th form pupil

Well, the school I'm at, we have very little communication with the parents apart from formalised parents' evenings and I suppose money-raising functions and therefore the only way of communicating with the parents is by letter.

> City, Teacher

...and then there's a big chop down; 'stop now you're trespassing on my domain' and I think there is this feeling sometimes.

> Shire, Parent of 4th form pupil

Well, you could go to the careers officer but really for that you've got to know exactly what you want to do.

> City, School Leaver

I think we tend to be palmed off with a lot of information that in our heart of hearts we know ...We are just being told.

> Shire, Parent of 4th form pupil

They want you to help with painting the pool or painting the walls or making curtains but ... as far as the actual working or running of the school is involved, I don't think as a parent you are encouraged to have anything to do with it.

> Shire, Parent of 4th form pupil

Although some of what I have said has inevitably been negative, since I am concerned in this chapter to bring out a contrast between the information which parents need as clients of the education service and what they might need to be active participants, I should not like to leave the impression that the effects of the 1980 Act have been bad or even inconsequential in this respect.

The new arrangements will have led many parents to think about their information needs for perhaps the first time. The existence of even inadequate brochures is consciousness-raising. The chance to visit schools is potentially stimulating to thought and relationships. The NFER study 'Choosing Schools' (11) emphasises the scope schools could find in the new arrangements to make positive connections with parents before their children even come, but is disappointed that only a few schools in their sample took full advantage of these opportunities. It looked as if only about half were having open evenings at all, and not all those who did made best use of the occasion. In some, however, headteachers were consciously putting over strongly held philosophies, including the school's efforts to build partnerships with parents. It was reported that where schools were keen to present themselves, parents were correspondingly eager to ask questions. A number of schools suggested that 'one outcome of the 1980 Act has been the enhanced level of questioning by parents.' Sadly, one reason why some schools were holding back, either by not having open evenings in a whole area or by keeping to a standard format (sometimes required by the LEA, it is only fair to say) and providing only the minimum legal information, was a perverse reaction to what they saw as an encouragement to compete unduly. Falling rolls and government policies have indeed encouraged schools to compete rather than co-operate; but it is a pity that their reactions should from the parents' point of view be negative rather than positive. Agreements on voluntary restraint of competition are not the answer.

The NFER survey concludes that if 'open evenings, school brochures, and the act of choosing are seen by schools as a means of increasing parent and pupil commitment and involvement, then many schools and authorities failed to make full use of the 1980 Act legislation to gain this important spin-off.'

There will be many examples in this book of how good results may come from measures of dubious motivation - some would say that the whole concept of the 1986 legislation is in this category, but I still hope its authors may live to be surprised. Similarly the 1980 Act may not prove to be quite the buttress of consumerism it seemed at the outset.

EVALUATION OF TEACHER AND PUPIL PERFORMANCE

No discussion of the 'client' view of the parents' role would be complete without a reference to the growth of interest and experience in the appraisal of teachers and the testing of pupils. Many would argue that if parents are to be assured that the service is sufficiently self-critical to afford their children the best education, there must be formal means for measuring the competence of teachers, which means consequently measuring also the attainments of pupils.

Like most observers of the scene I have been very impressed by the range and quality of work now going on to establish fair and constructive ways in which schools can evaluate their performance and that of their staff as individuals. Nobody who attended the DES Conference on 'Better Schools: Evaluation and Appraisal' in Birmingham on November 14th and 15th 1985, or read the report subsequently published (12) could doubt that the service has advanced in leaps and bounds in recent years both in its enthusiasm for better techniques of appraisal, and progress in developing them. This process seemed to be going on so well without government intervention, that it was regrettable that the government had soured the debate by introducing alien associations into appraisal. For months every Ministerial statement on appraisal of teachers was made in the same breath as a suggestion that there were too many incompetent teachers, with the implication that the only point in more self-critical techniques was to identify and purge the schools of a number of poor performers. It was also unfortunate that the subject was linked with the long teachers' pay dispute of 1985 and 1986, and acceptance of appraisal not only made a condition of pay awards but also linked to incremental progress. It was at that Birmingham Conference that Sir Keith Joseph, then Secretary of State, chose to recant both the punitive view of appraisal and its link with pay, but it was too late to heal all the bitterness.

The Education (no 2) Act of 1986 while not abandoning appraisal, now contains the seemingly innocuous statement:

> The Secretary of State may by regulations make provision for requiring local education authorities, or such other persons as may be prescribed, to secure that the performance of teachers to whom the regulations apply... is regularly appraised in accordance with such requirements as may be prescribed.

Pilot studies were then initiated by the DES in six LEAs, coordinated by the National Development Centre for School Management Training based at the University of Bristol and evaluated by the Cambridge Institute of Education.

What is being developed will be sounder and more durable if it has the understanding and trust of teachers themselves and if it is seen to be positive and constructive in intention and fair and participatory in practice. It is good to see so much emphasis on whole school appraisal, since many of us who have as outsiders become familiar with schools know how much more an individual teacher's performance depends on the teamwork, the leadership, the structures of support within a school than on private talent. This is why the appraisal/pay direct link is so wrong.

This is not the place, and I am not the writer, for expert commentary on the techniques of evaluation and their future, but in any discussion of the part they might play in parents' relationships with schools some very important issues emerge. First, there are some useful benefits for parents and governors. As I noted, parents generally would be very encouraged to know that schools had arrangements for appraising teachers, and even if the information they were given and the involvement they were offered went no further than that it would increase confidence. I see it as essential, as schools introduce such arrangements, that they should describe the system to the general body of parents as well as communicating in more detail with governors. A further benefit is that governors, who often have very difficult staff problems to consider from time to time, would be less likely to be faced with them too late for much constructive action if difficulties were identified routinely in a teacher's early career. At present such issues, by the time they come to governors, are fraught with emotion. Finally in the catalogue of benefits to parents and governors one should mention the help regular appraisal would afford to all those involved in staff appointments. At present much reliance is placed on confidential reports, and all concerned know that they can sometimes be unrevealing and at worst misleading. Those who write them want to support staff seeking promotion, so give them the benefit of the doubt. Occasionally they yield to the understandable temptation to write over-generous comments on one they would like to be rid of. This would be less serious in the context of a properly documented career. Most outsiders know vaguely that there is a code in reports. We are meant to laugh at 'It would be a very fortunate head who got this teacher to work for him', but how do we know the difference between 'worthy of consideration' and 'worthy of serious consideration'? More soberly, a well-documented career affords some safeguard for governors against unhelpful references, but it is also a protection for the teacher against the occasional real or imagined malice or simple human incompatibility. I do not want to suggest that teacher appraisal will solve all the problems of schools, but if we can divest it of some of its dramatic overtones it will surely be a modest help with some of them.

I have heard representatives of the teachers' unions become almost apoplectic about any suggestion that the time might come when governors might take part in appraisal processes. Yet if governors are to have a responsibility for determining a school's aims, and for satisfying themselves as to the methods to be adopted to achieve those aims, if they are to be involved in the appointment and promotion of staff, is it logical to exclude them completely from the school's arrangements for career review? Obviously, if being a governor is not to become a full-time job, there must be limits to the detail with which they can concern themselves, but I suggest that as a minimum they should be thoroughly familiar with the system, should have access to the records, should from time to time have the experience as individuals of observing the process, and should be enlisted to support the head in any particularly difficult or important task arising from that process.

What of parents? I have suggested that it is very important for them to know in general terms what structures exist in the school to review the performance of teachers and to promote their professional development in an orderly way, while supporting any who have difficulties. This is probably all that the majority would wish to know, and I don't think we are yet ready to see teachers' records open as well as those of pupils! The question of parent and pupil input to teacher appraisal is bound to generate heat, but parents and older pupils do have very clear impressions of teacher effectiveness, and I would hope we could give some thought to how we might incorporate them as a part of the total process once it has become routine to have appraisal at all. I should not want to impede such routine acceptance by going too fast, but I do look forward to a time when 'I am not a perfect person' is as unremarkable a statement in teaching as elsewhere.

There are basically two varieties of pupil assessment, the narrow but necessary and the sensitive but slow. The fears which many had about the establishment of the Assessment of Performance Unit in 1974 were that it would lead to a narrowing of curriculum objectives, that it would encourage teachers to teach to the test, and that it would be an instrument of central curriculum direction. As a lay observer I would say that the first two fears have probably proved unfounded but not the third: recent advances in criteria-based assessment, not to mention the attainment of a more streamlined 16+ examination system would not have been possible without the refinement of measurement which the APU have been quietly pursuing in a limited subject field in the decade before those policies surfaced. But limited or not, most of us would agree that such refinement was necessary for a range of purposes, like justifying (maybe of course discrediting), new structures and new methods in education. Croydon LEA has already made a start with giving parents details of the knowledge and skills pupils should have at particular ages. What an explosive weapon in inexperienced hands, many will say, what a stick to beat the teachers with. Again, as with examination results, one can only say that useful information cannot be too long withheld, but it becomes urgent to educate people to use it and to be aware of all the other measures of a school's total influence. I wish this development could have waited just a while until more progress had been made with other forms of partnership with parents and with pupil profiling, to put cruder yardsticks in perspective. With the prospect in the 1988 legislation of national testing at seven, eleven fourteen and sixteen, and possible publication of results, parents will need even more encouragement to judge schools in the round.

Pupil profiling is of course what I meant by 'sensitive but slow' forms of assessment, and all must welcome the blessing now given by the government to the excellent work already in progress in many LEAs before they ever heard of it. As so often I feel the need to say something rarely heard but embarrassingly obvious to the outsider, that the successful development of pupil profiling has wide implications for parents and their perceptions of schools. If the value of what their young people have achieved in school is judged in the most rounded and sensitive way, what an encouragement to parents to judge the schools by a similarly rich and varied set of success-criteria! In the relationships between schools and parents there is one phenomenon to me more significant than all else, and that is people's tendency to say to themselves 'As you value me, so shall I value you.' As my Australian friends often told me, the statement is the same upside down.

CLIENTS CAN TAKE THEIR GOODS AND GO

If you have brought up a family, you can't escape their music. Snatches of it, or telling phrases from the often weak story-line, will haunt you. I actually have to make a conscious effort not to quote them too often. This time it is 'Hotel California' which will not go away: 'You can check out any time you like, but you can never leave'. For in every effort I make to see parents as clients of the education system, I am struck by the total inappropriateness of the term 'client' as a description of a crucial relationship. You do not stop being a parent, as hundreds of thousands collecting the coffee cups from between the sleeping bags, amusing the grandchildren, or listening to the endless Weltschmerz will testify today. Nor can you escape your own schooling, nor can you escape your share in theirs.

It is not just the permanence of the involvement, but its reciprocity which makes it unique. If parents are merely clients of the schools, teachers may be forgiven for seeing them along with the politicians, the press and the Black Paper group as the enemy. It is an image of a cold and demanding face at the other side of a metal grille. Or a white line.

Thanks to the efforts of many visionaries and pioneers it started to be different in the Sixties and went on getting better. Shall we sacrifice a generation of teachers who tried to establish better ways, on the cruel altar of consumerism? I am saying to all the teachers not yet convinced, you can have it the professional/client way if you want, and many powerful forces of our time will be behind you, but it is a chilly and lonely condition, and the price of keeping your territory may be that not much will grow there.

All the discussion of the parent as a client misses one vital point. The relationship is not a passive one, and therefore its requirements are totally different. The Plowden Report (13) in 1967 identified one factor which above all others affected children's success in the learning process, namely the quality of parent support. This conclusion had two contradictory effects. It stemmed the tide of optimism about what schooling alone could achieve, and it opened up a whole new seam of success for those who could read its message and act upon it.

Since Plowden the message has been underlined over and over again. Even in the last few years the DES statisticians have tried hard to read from examination records some evidence of whether one form of school organisation is more effective than another, and have come up with the same conclusion: home background is overwhelmingly the most critical factor. There is no substitute for the support, the help, the confidence of a good home. For 'good' we would of course in most contexts read 'lucky', an identification which we might hope perhaps to change, but very slowly. Simultaneously, however, we have had a refinement of the message, which stops us in our tracks before we too fatalistically link success with social class. From 1978 onwards there has been a spate of researches, discussed in Chapter Nine, which have demonstrated that even the poorest and least educated parents can, if encouraged and motivated, make a significant difference to their children's learning. Even more shattering in its implications, as I shall show, is the recognition that such experience of success can change parents' perceptions of schools and schools' attitudes towards parents.

At this moment, however, I am more concerned about the implications of these researches for the approach we adopt to accountability. If teachers cannot by themselves ensure that children achieve all they are capable of , how can we hold teachers alone to account? We have perhaps done them a great injustice by expecting so much. They have said so from time to time, but perhaps we have dismissed it as an attempt to excuse their own failings.

Surely the logic of all that has been said is that the demands for teachers to be more accountable must take into consideration the overwhelming evidence that successful learning is a shared responsibility between school and home, not a service for which a passive client can look to an active provider? Accountability must to some degree be mutual. Yes, many teachers would tell you, there is a lot we could say on that subject. We would like to throw your words in the teeth of all those who blame schools for the problems of society. We should like to point out that in many homes the quality of parenting leaves much to be desired. We are not speaking, of course, they will say, of the desperately poor and troubled, for whose children we shall continue to do our best, but of many who without such problems do not give their children's education high priority, yet are the first to blame us if things go wrong. Quite well-provided homes, they will say, do not make sure their children have enough sleep, or adequate breakfast. They let them watch all sorts of unsuitable television programmes. They would sooner watch the football than take them to the park to find seed pods. They give them plenty of pocket money, but no time. They do not send them to school with what the poorest once had, learning from songs and stories and nursery rhymes. They do not insist on polite behaviour, and they do not support the school.

It is good to let all this come out, for teachers need to say it. Some of them perhaps do have a romanticised view of the decent poor of years gone by. I am very romantic about my own decent poverty in childhood, so must watch it too. Some teachers do not allow for the effect on people's dignity of the false gods they see in high places. Hardly any have the slightest idea of the power schools have to change things. I do not mean the power unilaterally to transform children's life chances, on which we have all become a little disillusioned, but power to increase families' sense of their own value, while at the same time demystifying to some extent the role of the professional educator. We cannot jump in one joyous leap from a recognition that schooling has to be a shared concern to a golden age in which teachers are free to give parents homework too, and call them to account. Parents will resist attempts to remind them of their responsibilities while they feel, rightly or wrongly, that they are never allowed to tell teachers anything. Furthermore teachers will have to contend, if they try, with the guilty half-recognition many parents have of inadequacies as parents which they may or may not be capable of doing anything about, and the very deep and probably very healthy resistance to the attempts of schools to impose middle class values on themselves and their children. Such reforming zeal will penetrate into some dark and very angry parts of the self.

Are we then to treat the whole subject as too difficult, accept the child as presented to the school with all the gaps in experience which school alone can never fill? Do we go on campaigning for extra resources to help schools in areas where homes have as yet little to offer? Indeed we must; but that is not enough. Nor is it enough to go on lamenting because the parents whose children most need their help do not come. We somehow have to find a way to build new relationships with those parents, arising not from compassion, not from the largesse of our own expertise, but from the belief that they are important.

Schools cannot dismiss the problem as too difficult because they now know, from a wide range of researches, that, even in the most apparently hopeless cases, parents can advance their children's learning. Now that we know it, we have to accept that if we ignore it we are failing to respond professionally to new information affecting the job. For this it is right that schools should be held accountable, a new dimension again. I have said 'we' though I am not a teacher, because as a school governor and a concerned outsider who happens to have read the researches, I feel we share the responsibility for seeking ways forward.

PARENTS: CLIENTS OR PARTNERS?

We spent long enough looking at the market place model of public influence on the education service, only to reject it for its unsuitability, its false hopes and its cruel inequalities. We perhaps concluded that there are no bargain offers or easy terms. We have now looked in detail at another model, that of the expert professional service, accountable to those who are legally responsible for organising it, for the standard of its work for clients. We have seen that most of the rights clients enjoy and the information offered to them presuppose a passive role, once they have exercised that one active responsibility: choice. While either of these models is a determinant of policy, neither teachers nor parents will feel satisfied with its associated accountability, teachers because they know that success depends on factors outside their control, parents because they have been led to expect too much from teachers alone.

There must be a third way. If a child's success requires two active participants, we must somehow dispose of the fears, the misunderstandings, the sensitivities which stand in the way, for from all these the child suffers most. Partnership is a word used loosely and too often, but we can try again. It is at once very abstract, because it is made up of feelings and attitudes, and very practical, in the way it lends itself to check lists and exchange of experience. For the continued existence of those areas of the country where children's needs are most neglected there will be one of two underlying causes. Among the people who live there one will find either a high proportion who do not use state schools, or a preponderance of people who are not very good at exerting pressure. In the latter case, the hope of improvement comes from the possibility that parents will acquire a sense of identification with schools in place of alienation. This in turn can only come from a feeling that in the school, if nowhere else, they matter. We shall see that the sense of their value has been a conspicuous feature of schemes in which parents have been successfully involved in their children's learning. Thus the rewards of the partnership may be not only to the child and the school, but to the service, which so badly needs effective public pressure.

May I use again the words I applied to the effect of good pupil profiling on families' perceptions of the school and its purposes? 'As you value me, so shall I value you.'

NOTES

1. Maurice Kogan, Autonomy and Accountability in Education, paper to the 4th Annual Conference of the British Educational Administration Society.
2. B.M. Stierer, School Reading Volunteers, (Journal of Research in Reading, 3 (1) 21-31, 1985).

3.   Cmnd. 4040, (HMSO, 1969).
4.   DES, Education (School Information) Regulations 1981, (SI 81, No 630).
5.   National Consumer Council, Question Marks for Schools, (NCC, February 1977).
6.   Community Education Working Party, Written Communication Between Home and School, (Nottingham University School of Education, October 1978).
7.   East Sussex LEA/University of Sussex, Accountability in the Middle Years of Schooling, (1979).
8.   Cambridge Accountability Project, Case Studies in School Accountability, (Cambridge University, 1981).
9.   Scottish Consumer Council, The Book of the School, 1982.
10.   National Consumer Council, The Missing Links Between Home and School, 1986.
11.   Andy Stillman and Karen Maychell, Choosing Schools: Parents, LEAs and the 1980 Education Act, (NFER-Nelson, 1986).
12.   DES, Better Schools: Evaluation and Appraisal, conference proceedings, (HMSO, 1986).
13.   The Plowden Committee, A New Partnership for our Schools, (HMSO, 1967).

Chapter Four

'MY DOOR IS ALWAYS AJAR'

From now on I shall be discussing how schools have changed, are changing and may still further change in their relationships with the people beyond those gates. Somewhere a balance must be found between the extremes of professional defensiveness represented by the old white line, and a school like the worst mad open-plan local newspaper office. I hope I have argued convincingly in the early chapters that strong defensive alliances are needed for the child, the school and the service, that the crude accountability of the market place affords no protection, while the concept of a professional/client accountability leaves no room for the active parent support children need for success.

At the same time we have to be realistic about what the majority of teachers can cope with or be trained to cope with. It is reassuring that most in-service courses for headteachers now include a session, sometimes a whole day or more, on relationships with parents and governors. It is worrying that few in-service courses for assistant teachers do so, and even more worrying that as yet there is pathetically little in initial training courses about working with parents. While it is vital that serving headteachers be given some help with this increasingly demanding aspect of the job, it often comes late. Many tell me that, in the early months of headship, they have sometimes felt they would drown in the deep water of the world outside the school, the world of the local authority, the parties, the pressure groups, the governors and parents. It is admirable that most become strong swimmers, but a pity that it is possible to be a deputy head for many years without ever attending a governors' meeting or seeing a headteacher's report to governors.

What is more, whenever one observes a headteacher who is pursuing an imaginative programme of community involvement, there are often teachers in the school about whose commitment to the programme one has doubts. This is not surprising, since awareness of the importance of home links does not come naturally to a young teacher, though it can be taught and it can be a product of experience. After all, newly qualified teachers will not long have shaken off the supervision of their own parents, and they will not normally as yet have had the experience of being parents themselves. Fresh from study, and therefore harbouring as yet no shred of doubt about the efficacy of professional skills alone, but still with little personal confidence, they will tend to be most dogmatic when least sure of their ground - we have all been like that. Parents can be intimidating, especially when successful and confident in their own professions. In primary schools there is a new reason for defensiveness, in that today's informal methods, so much harder to teach well by, perhaps do not look quite as authoritative as standing in front of a silent class and laying down the law. At least a timid young teacher might fear that. If parents come in and at first cannot even find her, then see her stooping or kneeling, talking to small groups, aiding little hands with what look like enjoyable tasks, may they not think this is more like what goes on in the kitchen of a good home than a proper profession?

I did not know in 1967, when we had three children in infants school, that this was the year of the Plowden Report (1). We never entered that school. There was no open day. My children first met their class teachers the morning they were prised screaming from my hand. Once I got a message: 'I haven't read to my teacher for six weeks, but she says my mother can hear me read because we have books at home and some children don't.' So at least we became some of the first parents to help with reading! I asked in writing if the last one could go for a half day with her brother the term before starting, as she was so clinging. They seemed a bit surprised, but they agreed. She still cried but not so much, and they said she would be fine when I had gone. It seems barbaric, but they were nice people and that was how things were then. One child had a reading problem, and he told me he was in a small group with another teacher, but he did not know if it was because he was a good reader or a bad reader. I am glad he did not know: they were clearly both skilled and kind. I am not grumbling. It is just that it now seems strange this was 1967, and one needs one's distance spectacles to look across the years.

Reading glasses are certainly no use for looking at progress: they make it seem too slow. Yet my typical 1967 primary school was a world apart from the typical school of 1977, when the Taylor Committee (2) published what was to be the next episode. Some of the schools we visited as a committee would have been unrecognisable a decade earlier. Whether we have made corresponding advances from 1977 to the present day is more open to question. The most spectacular examples of community-linked schools are certainly another giant stride on, but the typical school? I sense that other forces have been at work. School rolls and budgets were shrinking fast in 1977, teachers felt more threatened by criticism from politicians, industry, press and public. The power of the market place was exercising its souring influence on the generous human spirit. There had been some premature disillusionment with radical ideas tried too half-heartedly and not long enough. The Taylor Committee's message was more difficult to assimilate than Plowden's. Better communication with parents, more welcoming schools, learning which started from the children and their own experience – the Plowden legacy – may not have been easy to achieve, but it was a kindly and benign process, unthreatening to teachers who were still basically in control of it. The hard thing to accept was the idea that the door might really have to be open, not ajar, that schools should share some of their responsibilities with parents and neighbours.

FROM PLOWDEN TO TAYLOR: A DECADE OF PROGRESS

The Plowden Committee visited some three hundred schools and colleges in Great Britain. Their observations led them to make the following recommendations on participation by parents:

1. All schools should have a programme for contact with children's homes, to include:

    (a) a regular system for the head and class teacher to meet parents before the child enters;

    (b) arrangements for more formal private talks, preferably twice a year;

    (c) open days to be held at times chosen to enable parents to attend;

    (d) parents to be given booklets prepared by the schools to enable them to choose their children's schools and to know how they are being educated;

    (e) written reports on children to be made at least once a year. The child's work to be seen by parents;

    (f) special efforts to make contact with parents who do not visit the schools.

2. The Department of Education and Science should issue a booklet of good practice in parent-teacher relations. The Department should inform themselves of the steps taken

by the authorities to encourage schools to foster good relations.

3. Parents should be allowed to choose their children's primary school wherever this is possible. Authorities should take steps to improve schools which are shown to be consistently unpopular with parents.

4. Primary schools should be used as fully as possible out of ordinary hours.

5. Parents and other adults should be invited to help the school with its out-of-school activities. Parents might contribute towards the cost of out-of-school activities, to supplement the costs borne by the local education authority.

6. Heads should have a say in the evening use of their buildings. When buildings are heavily used two deputy head teachers should be appointed, one responsible for out-of-school activities. This would involve a modification of the Burnham provisions.

7. Community schools should be developed in all areas but especially in educational priority areas.

8. As a matter of national policy, 'positive discrimination' should favour schools in neighbourhoods where children are most severely handicapped by home conditions. The programme should be phased to make schools in the most deprived areas as good as the best of the country. For this it may be necessary that their greater claim on resources should be maintained.

Recommendations 9 to 14 set out the detail of the programme for educational priority areas, its time-scale, its provision for experiment and review, and its staffing requirements.

Presumably the good practices set out under the first recommendation above were very far from commonplace when the Plowden Committee made its investigations, and the fact that they have become so is a measure of the schools' success in responding to this mammoth report. They would now be considered to be a minimum agenda for any school's communications system. It is interesting that the recommendations addressed to schools were all followed up, and from contemporary writings one would say very quickly, yet those addressed to local authorities and the DES have met with rather more varied success. We had to wait a long time for the third recommendation, on parental choice, and are still waiting for any noticeable response to the second part of it, namely LEAs taking any systematic action to investigate why some schools did not win parental confidence. And whatever happened to the DES booklet of good practice?

Ten years after Plowden the National Foundation for Educational Research undertook an ambitious survey (3) which took two years to complete and another year to see the light of day. A sample of nearly 1,700 schools was used to investigate the extent of parental involvement in primary schools and the means used to promote it. Thirty five per cent of schools were found to have PTAs (exactly double the percentage at the time of Plowden) and a further 26 per cent had other forms of home-school association; 95 per cent of schools had parents' evenings and open days, with very good attendance levels in many of them; 90 per cent of schools supplemented these formal occasions with informal contact. 65 per cent of the survey schools sent written information about themselves to new parents, and 92 per cent invited new parents to visit the school before their children started. In contrast, less than half provided any kind of written report on pupils' progress, and these were mainly schools for children of seven and over.

In about half of all primary schools some form of home-visiting took place, either by Education Welfare Officers or home-liaison teachers of various kinds. A very high proportion of schools, well over three quarters, organised parent help of some kind, most commonly accompanying pupils on outings, mending books and equipment, helping children dress after swimming, assisting with cooking, music, crafts and so on. The most controversial form of help was clearly with reading, and many teachers were opposed to it. It was taking place under supervision in about a quarter of schools in the sample, but in schools visited by the team, head-teachers frequently referred to it as a very sensitive issue. It is interesting that teachers draw such a clear line between parent help in reading, writing and mathematics, which they may see as an encroachment on their professionalism, and help with art, music, crafts, drama. Yet in other contexts they hotly defend the indivisibility of the school curriculum, the essential nature of all its parts, the equal value they place on children's different skills. I said this kindly to a large group of teachers with whom I was doing some work, and observed that if we were serious about equal valuation of all skills throughout the education process, it must be more than skin-deep: teachers should be just as much, or even better just as little, worried about parents' involvement in art as in mathematics. They were, to do them credit, moved to very thoughtful silence by this idle remark, and most of them later said that they had welcomed being made to think about it.

The schools were asked what problems they had had with parent involvement in school activities. The most common worry was confidentiality and parents gossiping about the work or behaviour of other people's children. Staff resistance to having parents in classrooms was mentioned, and the effect of the presence of parents on children's behaviour. Very few complaints were made about parents being too intrusive or usurping teachers' roles. A high proportion reported concern about the parents who were prevented from responding to the invitation to help because of either circumstances or diffidence.

Finally schools were invited to comment on the benefits in terms of parental attitudes of the closer relationships with the school. Around 60 per cent mentioned parents' greater feeling of confidence in approaching the school when they needed to, their better understanding of the problems of teachers and the aims of the school, and about half saw the benefit in terms of supporting their own children better as a result of the knowledge and interest gained, and finding satisfaction themselves. The degree and success of parental involvement seemed to vary primarily with catchment area and social class, and the researchers leave open the vital question of whether this is due to the lack of interest of working class parents in poor areas, or the school's approach to them, or some other factor. There was a strong correlation between successful parent involvement and the openness of the school's design and the informality of its methods.

Such then was the state of home-school relationships in primary schools in 1980. No such comprehensive investigation has been made since, and evidence of what further advances have been made must be sketchy. We do not even know for certain how many schools have home-school associations compared with the 60 per cent plus in the NFER survey. The National Confederation of Parent-Teacher Associations doubts very much whether there has been any significant increase. The 1980 Act has of course required the publication of a good deal of written information for parents, and there will have been an enormous increase in the quantity if not always the quality of school brochures. My reading of many case studies on parent involvement, my enquiries among the heads and teachers I have worked with on LEA courses over the ten years, some 10,000 of them, and the visits I have made to schools, suggest that there has been some general advance in primary schools but nothing like that made in the previous decade; and that secondary schools, with more natural difficulties and their own pressing problems, have made good progress with structured consultation about pupil progress and information about themselves, but on the whole very little in the admittedly much more difficult task for them of building informal links, sharing decisions and changing attitudes. Overall, the subject has acquired a weary respectability. Most teachers are working very hard to maintain the interest which they know is so important to the school but are making slow headway with the hard core of problems. Where the picture is

strikingly different is in the significant minority of schools
where there is an overriding commitment to success in involving parents, and some vision, despite the rather disillusioning
times we live in, of the difference it could make. In these,
both primary and secondary, there have been some stunning
breakthrough experiences.

LIGHTHOUSES

I wrote earlier that progress is not made by nagging about
bad practice, but by finding a bit of good practice to encourage and advertise. Indeed I often reflect that our education
system, despite recent centralising tendencies, probably still
allows individuals at every level an opportunity to be creative
which most visitors envy. It is the glory of our schooling
system, but its shame it that it has so few efficient mechanisms for spreading good practice. In this respect it is
almost unbelievably weak.

The DES, twenty years after Plowden, has no branch
dealing with home-school relationships or with parents and
their problems. The involvement of parents is sometimes
mentioned in HMI reports on schools, but rarely given prominence or investigated in any depth. As for LEAs, on whom
the primary legal responsibility for delivering an effective
service rests, they can surely no longer doubt that such
effectiveness depends in large measure on the quality of home
support. Yet in their formal relationships with each other it
is not a noticeable subject of debate, and as far as I know
there are no regular arrangements to share experience. Within
their own areas they seem to have no structures for maxi-
mising this vast unexploited resource. I have come across a
mere handful who have an adviser for home-school matters.
Only a few seem to do the simplest and cheapest thing of all,
circulating and regularly updating a list of good practices
found in their own ares, though no doubt where there is a
climate of interest this function is carried out informally by
visiting LEA advisers. Some formally promote and resource
home-link teachers, parents' rooms, mother and toddler clubs.
Others, sadly, are having to take spare accommodation in
schools out of use without regard for its possibilities for
improving parent contact.

Perhaps most important of all, it is rare to find an LEA
in the Eighties extending its nursery provision: most are at
best maintaining what there is and quite a number are cutting
it. Yet there is general agreement that the younger one
involves children in education, the better the chance of
establishing lasting links with parents. The honourable exceptions to these strictures are of course very honourable
indeed. It is just that it is hard to understand how such
generally scant attention to what has long been accepted as a

vital ingredient of educational success can be justified, especially when every week I meet headteachers and teachers who desperately want to improve their practice and will make every effort to get information on techniques which have been found to work.

The most striking of the honourable exceptions are those LEAs which are committed to community education and the growing if still small number who have realised the almost breathtaking possibilities of direct parent involvement in children's learning.

At this point I will describe, impressionistically and with minimum comment, three schools which have remained vivid in my memory as places where minds as well as doors had been opened on the world beyond the gates. It is the only way I know to mark how far, at best, the process has developed. It is not fair, because there must be many schools as or more impressive in this respect which I have not been lucky enough to visit, but I hope that all the heads and teachers who recognise themselves will accept the tribute too. The schools are far apart, and all that they have in common with each other, besides the impression they made on me, is that they are all in areas of considerable social deprivation. All in all a homogeneous neighbourhood, even one with many problems, may be easier to work with.

Concord First School is an EPA (Educational Priority Areas) school in an area of uniformly ugly housing with varied light industrial employment near at hand. There seems to be nothing to look at and nothing to do. My first impression was that this was nowhere. A long time ago the PTA wrote and asked me to talk to them. I dressed up and prepared the sort of things one prepares to say to PTAs. I had totally miscalculated the occasion, for I was to find a packed hall where every parent appeared to have come direct from manual work or cooking the family meal or in a few cases both. The level of interest was intense and the parents seemed very confident. In the years that followed I discovered some of the secrets of that school. I knew that the parents had once successfully fought its closure. They had insisted, another time, on a meeting with the HMIs who, in an otherwise favourable report, had said something critical of the reading scheme, which had been chosen after much discussion by the parents. They were outraged. When I felt I knew her well enough I asked the headteacher whether she thought the criticism had been justified. Well, she said, she didn't think on reflection it was in itself the best reading scheme, but there was nothing like as much to choose between schemes as many people thought. As for us, she said, if the parents chose the scheme it is the one which will work in this school. You should have heard them, she said with delight, telling the HMIs.

One time a high level educational conference was taking

place within ten miles of the school, and one of the working groups decided to visit it. As one of the school's new friends I was invited too. The parents were told and at once they wanted to know what they could do. They could come and have lunch with the visitors, and they could help make something to eat, any who were free. There was a good deal of shift work in the area. Yes of course bring the younger children, why ever not? But they really did want to know what they should cook, so that they all had some assurance that it would fit in. Just make whatever you make the best, said the headteacher, and it will be lovely. In that hall the distinguished visitors could hardly be distinguished at all, for they were swamped with mothers, fathers, teachers, and there were babies, and toddlers all over the floor, all eating this strange multi-ethnic feast. It was so relaxed that the only serious problem was bringing it to a close.

When the 1980 Act came into force, the headteacher told the parents that every school would now have to do what they had been doing for years, so they must keep ahead. Suppose the parents wrote the new brochure? After all they were in on every school decision so it was a logical step. It involved learning new skills of course, but not for the first time in that school. The school had a very thriving club for mothers and younger children of all ages. Many a new baby was brought in on the way home from hospital to be introduced. The most telling thing I heard about the school concerned this club. The headteacher had asked them if they would help her with moving chairs at lunch time. 'We finish at 11.30 now, Mrs Little. Of course you didn't know, but those who can stay will help.' It was the way she told me, laughing but very proud, because they had reached a stage of confidence where they no longer saw any reason why she should be familiar with their arrangements.

I especially liked the way Mrs Little spoke to parents. She did not have a noticeably sweet and reassuring tone. Usually she was equable and smiling with everybody, but you had the feeling that if there was a day when she was a bit irritable with the staff she would be the same with the parents. If she was amused that would come over too because she would not be terrified that they would think she was laughing at them. She was businesslike with those who were partners in the enterprise. Her respect for them was real. Many headteachers would be shocked that I find it necessary to say that.

The second school, Coalcot, was different in that it represented a massive capital investment in an ideal. It was a purpose-built community school in a mining area. It was so sited that you could scarcely go anywhere in the town without crossing some part of it, even though it was very compact. It had its registrar of births, deaths and marriages, its pre-school play group, its youth club, old people's day centre, the lot. It had a three-session day, and I remember being amazed to hear how many school-age volunteers regularly went to evening sessions, as well as adults to day sessions. I have little imagination about space or the layout of buildings, and it was the first time I was personally aware of architecture as an educational concept. It was the way activities were distinct but flowed into the next. I was amazed how ordered it was without any bells or regimentation. I was impressed to hear that the outside doors were never locked, or pupils sent outside at breaks or at the end of the day.

The headteacher took us into an O level maths class, which had in it two elderly ladies, friends. We could have been inspectors for all they knew. One waved to the head. 'We knew 'is moother,' she explained. Then the head had to go to a meeting so he found two fifth year boys, picked at random on their way to the library for the study period, to complete the tour with us. They were of low ability, expecting two CSEs if there were a miracle. Two each, I asked, or between them? They laughed. I asked them about jobs. They both hoped to get jobs in the pit. It wasn't so easy now but they had relatives, one a brother and one an uncle, who would speak for them. Well no, they didn't exactly want to be miners, but it was a real job, not like stacking shelves in a supermarket. I asked them if they'd come back to the school ever, when they'd left. I expected them to say yes, for the facilities for recreation, which were mouth-watering. Yes, they said, of course they'd come back to see the teachers. I found that immensely touching.

That evening I was allowed to see privately three sets of parents who had been violently opposed to sending their children to the school a few years before they reached transfer age. They were prepared to try to move house or keep the children home. The school had at one time had a bad reputation, caused mainly by poor communication about what went on there. They gave an assortment of reasons for changing their minds, but it seemed significant that by chance one of each pair had had a need to undertake an evening course during the period running up to choice, and all mentioned the school pupils in the evening sessions. Community education means a variety of things to different people, from the minimum of the lights being on all evening, through all stations to Coalcot, but the genuine article for me has two essentials. One is that by blurring the distinction between the compulsory and voluntary stages of education you both enhance its value and narrow the gap between the generations. The other is that you respond to community needs without over-interpreting them.

The second requirement was well illustrated in Mill Lane, a primary school in a cotton town with a 97 per cent Asian intake. No one saw this as a 'problem', for the children's homes, though poor, were stable, they themselves happy and industrious. The school was informal in style, but they kept forming spontaneous queues to show me their neat work. They all looked as though they were dressed for a birthday tea. I noted how the headteacher had ventured unafraid into some deep waters, and reflected how on the other side of the Pennines at that time a primary school was getting itself into the newspapers - remember Drummond Middle School in Bradford in 1985? - because of theories. She was intensely practical. She had negotiated with the Muslim community and the swimming baths an arrangement for small Muslim girls to swim in nylon tights. Nobody really wanted to force the school into segregated swimming for infants, so all cooperated. The baths merely stipulated that the school should accept the responsibility for washing the tights between sessions.

The special thing about Mill Lane for me was the presence of large numbers of mothers. They were not washing paint pots - or tights - but learning things. Their younger children played at their feet. There was no programme imposed in fulfilment of some grandiose theory. The school had simply tried to respond to what the mothers wanted, using their own resources, skills found in the Asian community itself, their home-link teacher, their Home Office funding, and much ingenuity. Sewing and English, with occasional richly international cooking, constituted the core curriculum, but no doubt it would develop. As in Concord First School the parent activities had a life of their own, with the minimum institutional intervention. Many visitors came to the school, but for the pupils' impressive work, not the adult learning.

I was shocked to hear a while after my visit that the whole scheme had almost come to pieces. Some well-meaning people had tried to 'regularise' the whole thing as part of the adult education service, for instance trying to introduce courses leading to City and Guilds with no time for sewing sequins on those garments for the birthday tea. When the headteacher returned from a year's secondment she found that the mothers no longer wanted to come. Her own determination, with the support of the LEA, has now restored what used to be, and confidence is slowly being built up again. Recently she told me with great excitement that Mill Lane has just elected two Muslim women as parent governors. I do not need to underline the significance of that.

In all three schools parents were finding it easy and natural to support their children because the school had responded to their needs with respect. Of course behind every encouraging experience one will find an inspired headteacher, and how carefully one should seek out inspiration when appointing. Yet none of these would want to be called charismatic. I deliberately rejected for my purpose several schools more impressive in themselves where I felt the whole edifice might be held together by personal magnetism verging on the hypnotic. These headteachers were modest hard-working people, pragmatic, aware that staff must share the vision if it is to last. What they all had was power to make parents feel valued by the school. It is a different thing from being made welcome. Such a headteacher would not be censorious about parents who never come. Whether or not they come does not affect their value. That headteacher will be sad about lost chances, sympathetic about the circumstances which may have made it impossible, but above all ready to believe that the school itself has not yet found the way to communicate its sense of their value. For schools have a great deal of power.

ARE PARENTS AWARE OF PROGRESS?

That depends on which side of the level crossing you live. Many contrast today's cheerful schools with the walled fortresses of their childhood, relishing being able to walk in, being greeted with a smile, asked to help, encouraged to join other parents in sociable and useful activity centred on the school. They say how in the old days it was very bad news if you had to enter the school. Now it is a pleasant duty for all.

Many parent activists and hard-working parent governors appreciate the opportunity to contribute. They find there is nothing, absolutely nothing, more rewarding than getting properly involved in a school. There is some concern about the immense pressure on parents in some areas to raise money which is not any more used for amenities for the children, but increasingly to make good the deficiencies in public provision, and there is sometimes a little resentment where parents do not have much say in how the money is spent. Perhaps there is even a creeping awareness of how 'political' parent fundraising now is, widening the already yawning gap between the best and worst resourced of our schools, robbing education of the undivided effort of those parents who could be putting the energy into fighting for a better level of funding for all.

What of the feelings of parents about the extent to which schools take their views into account, take trouble to explain their methods and share problems with them? Where schools do these things effectively it is clearly much appreciated and commented on. Once, many years ago, when it was important to me to build up a picture of how a school very dear to me was pulling itself up in public esteem, I got into the habit of listening carefully to what parents said at open evenings, at the school gates, in the supermarket and the doctor's surgery, making a note as soon as I got home to make sure I remembered it word for word.I still do this everywhere I go. The following come from a fairly leafy suburb with some modest private housing and some good quality local authority flats:

> It's really good the way they take the trouble now to tell you how the children are doing and how you can help them. Different from when we had our first lot.

> In our school you feel they are genuinely interested in what you think. It isn't like teachers were gods any more.

> We always go to everything at the school. After all they go to a lot of trouble to put things on for parents so the least you can do is go and take an interest. Anyway, it encourages the kids, doesn't it?

> We even had an evening to show us how they teach maths now, which worried us a lot because it's all different from how we were taught and we were frightened of confusing Mandy. We sat down and used all the apparatus and that, and I don't feel such a fool now when she asks us to help.

> I persuaded my friend to stand for parent governor. She's great at getting her views across, not like me, I tie myself in knots. I said to her I think it's marvellous to give parents a say. It's only right, they are our kids, and we have a point of view.

Sadly, the notebook reveals less happy experience as well. One very noticeable phenomenon is that when people have never been asked for their views they can remain quite passive, but there is nothing like a bit of participation for making them want more, and they react strongly if they suspect it is a sham:

> It's all window dressing. All they really want is to show you what they've done and for you to say it's marvellous, but as for really wanting your opinion, if you dared question anything you'd soon get the cold shoulder.

> It's the same as it always was. What the head says goes.

> Governors are a waste of time. All we ever talk about is the heating in the annexe and how much they made on the sponsored walk, and stuff like that. Just try asking about the standards in reading or whether any teachers have been on courses, and it's like somebody had made a rude noise. If we ask for anything that costs money it comes back there isn't any. Mind you the head's dead

keen on stirring us up to push for more facilities for the school. Sometimes we do get a boring long report from the office to comment on, but by then the time's usually going on a bit, so we just note it.

That lot can probably look after themselves in the long run, because at least they have the confidence to say what they see to be wrong, and it is already one remove from their children. The saddest comments I have heard all come from the other side of the track, and from what I earlier called some dark and angry parts of the self. I know they will hurt teachers, many of whom work very hard to encourage and reassure these parents and their children, but the fact that such feelings still exist, all these years on, from Yorkshire to Wales, from Wiltshire to East London, is something we can't ignore:

We'd put us finger in t'fire, wouldn't we, for us children, but if I 'ave to go oop t'school for owt, I'd as soon 'ave me teeth out. I wait while George is on nights, so 'e can coom an' all.

They're all right if you speak their language, but when I get with teachers, I say, 'This is worris like, mate, bein' foreign.'

If they do well, the kids, it's all glory to the school, innit, but if they're a bit twp [colloquial Welsh for 'thick'] or don't behave theirselves, stands to reason it's our fault.

If you live in a council house they don't expect your kids to get on.

I wanted to say to him, she concentrates very well at home, doing crosswords and playing chess with our Terry, but she's bored out of her mind at school since she went up to the top juniors. Whose fault it that? But then I thought what's the use, I haven't been asked here to answer back.

When I went up there, I intended to say it was just the fractions he didn't understand, because he was away the first time they explained it, but I couldn't seem to stop shaking. All I got was 'I'm afraid your son is very easily distracted, Mrs Johns. Does he watch too much television?'

They have this homework diary now, which is a marvellous idea, because you can put your comments in it, and I put down she'd taken $2\frac{1}{2}$ hours on her French,

was that right, and the answer came back, an average
pupil would take half an hour. So that's it, as good as
saying she's thick. It's the tenses. She was crying over
it last night. I said to my husband, I wish I'd had more
schooling so I could help her. She's such a worker, and
she really loved French last year with Miss Abrahams.

These parents had in theory all had access to the school and
a chance to speak, but how real for them were those opportunities? What comes through is their nervousness, their
sensitivity about their lack of education, a helpless feeling
about contributing, but above all their concern for their
children's progress. I know from talking to thousands of
teachers that they feel intense frustration about being unable
to reach such parents, and I shall return to the subject.
Here the point to make is that there is no real accountability
to parents whose expectations have been stunted by their own
experience. Open doors are indeed a great privilege for those
who have the confidence to come in, but often these are the
ones whose children have many educational privileges. Those
for whom one door after another has closed all their lives may
find it hard to believe that it will ever be different. They
may even see closed doors where none exist, often do,
teachers say. As customers of the educational supermarket in
which some politicians and theorists see them profering their
money-off vouchers and pointing to what they want, if they
do not know the words, as if they were indeed foreign or
deaf and dumb, they would be unlikely to get any bargains.
Not only for all the reasons given in Chapter Two, but also
because no money can buy what their children most need,
namely their confident support. Nor are they likely to have
their needs met in a client role. Neither model of accountability offers them anything. Teachers, knowing there is
another model, namely partnership, will say either that they
are doing it already, or that they are trying their best but
do not know how to make it work for all parents. Schools
need a lot of help with resources and structures, and will
add that education alone will not work the magic. With that I
would agree - employment, housing, health care, all play
their part in giving people a sense of their value. But I
would still say that no agency has quite the same access, on
a very local and human scale, to almost everybody as a
school, or deals with a more vital element in the family's
self-esteem. But no money and no legislation can by themselves create relationships, and this relationship has to be
between equals. That is the hardest part.

NOTES

1. Plowden Report, Children and their Primary Schools, (HMSO, 1967).

2. Taylor Report, A New Partnership for our Schools, (HMSO, 1977).

3. NFER, Report on Parental Involvement in Primary Schools, (National Foundation for Educational Research, 1980).

Chapter Five

THE PARENTS' VOICE

So far all our discussions about home-school relationships have concerned the parent as an individual. We now begin to consider parent groupings and parent representation, joint action, corporate rights, the structures within which schools and parents interact, the ways in which those structures can be developed to promote partnership.

The whole philosophy of a free market in education is an individualistic one, indeed a competitive one. Parents compete to get the best for their children, schools compete to attract custom. The prophets of the market place do not envisage that parents as consumers could unite to improve the quality of what is offered, but believe rather that if choice is given free rein, and schools can only survive by winning support, the cumulative effect of all the decisions made by individuals will be an improvement in standards.

Similarly any approach to accountability based on a professional/client relationship is an individualistic one. It is a direct negotiation between parent and professional on behalf of the child, in which the teacher is seen to be accountable for the quality of the service delivered. No exponent of either philosophy as a model of accountability has suggested that parents' interests might be better served by less competition and more cooperation, and there is a very obvious reason for this. Both approaches are essentially concentrated on the distribution of a finite amount, while combined parent pressures, if effective, might well lead to a higher priority for education with an increase in the money and moral support the community is prepared to give it. Unfortunately there is some identity of interest between politicians and defensive teachers in resisting such combined pressure, for united parents represent more of a threat to the authority of both. I say this in very plain words, because I want above all to demonstrate that the defensive teacher is the worst enemy of a better resourced and respected service, which can never in my view be achieved without massive united pressure by all those who use, work in and value the public education system.

The operation of choice, and to a lesser degree the encouragement of individual parents to become more effective clients, can actually damage the long term interests of parents as a whole in an adequately resourced and more responsive service. Choice divides parents just when they need to be making an effective comment about the schools they have not chosen. It even leads them to say 'I want High Gables because it's the best of a bad bunch,' rather than 'Will nobody join me in saying we all want a better choice?' For those in authority who count the number of satisfied parents do not record the emotions with which they choose. They could have chosen with enthusiasm, satisfaction, resignation or despair, and it would not show in the figures. Many LEAs take great pride in the high proportion of parents whose preferences they have been able to meet. Where this has been achieved through an effort to increase the attractiveness of all the options, to deal promptly and honestly with confidence problems and to build in strong neighbourhood involvement, the pride is justified. Sometimes, however, a high proportion of uncomplaining customers reflects a lazy policy, because it is achieved by leaving a wasteful amount of slack in the system, putting maximum effort into the relatively easy task of fixing individuals up with something acceptable, and very little into the much harder job of responding to what they might in concert be trying to say.

Typically the process of fitting the annual number of the intake into the available schools in an area will leave a hard core of families who have not been given places at the school of their choice. There is often one school that they all definitely do not want, for good reasons or bad. This brings them a temporary unity, which may even last long enough for them to learn a little about how to act effectively in a group and to formulate together a few coherent ideas about what makes a good school. In extremis they may share the experience of withholding their children from school, or even organising an unofficial school. Almost invariably this ends with the LEA finding places for them, a family at a time, in a variety of schools they are prepared to accept, and it is all over. They are all pleased that their protest has been successful, but they have also lost something which could have had a lasting influence for good, namely a sense of common purpose. I have a few times experienced the alternative ending, which is that the arrival of half a dozen families together in a school they did not want had a dynamic effect on them and on the school.

Client pressures, when exercised individually and in an unstructured way, also tend to compete for a scarce resource, namely teacher time. The prizes, as ever, go to the strong, in this case the determined, the articulate, the confident. Even the families concerned, never mind the ones who are not so good at the game, might be surprised to hear that there are better prizes on offer for cooperation than competition.

It now seems to me that no government, of left or right, has so far wanted a strong united parent movement in this country. The contrast with other countries, especially in the EEC and even more so Australia, is striking. The right are very interested in giving more expression to individual wishes, but not in encouraging strong alliances. Such alliances might not only develop egalitarian notions, but could well press for higher public spending. As for the left, they do seem on the whole to fear any kind of democracy other than the political kind, and indeed sometimes seem to fear any challenge to the politician's sole franchise to bestow happiness. Both fear that parents' organisations might be dominated by the 'wrong' people, which is comic when you reflect how very different their conceptions of the wrong people are likely to be.

Increasingly when I talk to headteachers on courses, they ask me whether I agree that most people's opinions fall between the extremes of far right and far left. Why then, they ask, do decisions on education so often emanate from one extreme or another, extremes which may in some areas soon make it very difficult to get and keep good LEA officers? I can only sigh with them, for my own youthful career in the public service was so saturated in Butskellism that, looking back, I cannot even remember by reference to the work I was doing which party was in power, but have to find other ways of remembering. Since then consensus, alas, is hard to find, and as a result the permanent official, at national and local level, has suffered a decline in standing and a loss of independence. Such destructive polarisation is only possible because of the acquiescence, or passivity, of moderate people on both right and left. It has serious consequences of all kinds, including the risk that it will become even harder to recruit and keep the kind of officers, advisers and headteachers who will bring to the service the levels of skill, commitment and integrity we have always expected. Such people will not be prepared to put up with the degree of interference in their work which is not now uncommon, and those who remain may well shrug their shoulders, keep out of trouble and settle for a lower level of professional independence and inevitably performance. The trivia of the 1986 Education Act betray an obsession with the alleged dangers of teachers peddling revolution in the study of sex and politics, and at school level this obsession produces such absurdities as governors turning school libraries upside down to find subversive literature: one example reported to me by a headteacher was the ritual removal of G.D.H. Cole's 'The Common People', of which the worst one could say was that it was a bit old. On the other side I have heard that it is increasingly common for elected members of education committees, presumably not in employment and presumably living partly on allowances, spending all day, nine to five, in the education office shadowing the paid officers concerned with the functions they have taken as their specialism. We are all keen that the bureaucrats should not be all-powerful and that the elected member should exercise proper vigilance, but surely such excesses are incompatible with a quality service?

We have perhaps reached a time when it will be harder to stir the moderate majority into any kind of joining. There has been a massive loss of jobs in those older sectors of our economy in which large numbers of people did heavy or repetitive work together and had common interests. These jobs have been replaced by enforced 'leisure' and consequent isolation for many, and partially, for the lucky ones, by jobs in service or high-tech industries, also often more lonely, and by part-time jobs mainly for women. For many these changes have meant a loss of corporate orientation. The boom in home technology and home leisure equipment has played its part: the centre of many people's lives is not now the trade union meeting, the works outing, the evening class, but the home computer, the video, the hi-fi, the caravan, the barbecue. Wider home ownership, apart from its political significance, also provides pressing - and often very satisfying - alternatives to corporate activity.

Whatever the reasons, education has in a broad political sense suffered, the headteachers I meet are trying to say, from failure of moderate people to get involved in things. Few of those who rightly lament this carry the logic a stage further to ask why schools themselves, as well as the policy-making process, are so often dominated by minorities among their own parents: those who scarcely seem to care at all, even about essential aspects of child support at school, and those who seem to care all too much and get a bit frantic or bossy with it. Between the extremes of what seems near-neglect and what borders on interference, one will find in most schools the majority of parents. I suggest that in education, as in politics, there is only one defence against extremes, and that is to work for the active participation and informed concern of the majority, and engage their interest in protecting the child, the school and the service against destructive minorities. This means a degree of organisation: parents individually are weak and ineffective even in promoting their own interests. Some headteachers fear organised parents, and prefer to see the promotion of good supportive attitudes among individuals as a management role. I can only say that this fear plays into the hands of extremist politicians, who for their own reasons do not like organised parents either, and that experience suggests that it is much easier to cope with problems, to handle conflict, and when necessary to manage change, within a supportive structure, than otherwise. There is no need to be pessimistic about the chances of bringing parents into such structures, provided they get the message that they are partners in an enterprise, since the very social and economic changes which have driven so many people away from corporate activity leave gaps to be filled. Trade union membership has declined and so has the involvement of people in party political activity, but the much greater concentration of interest in things centred round the home could give family and school a new identity of interest, if we encourage it. There are many obstacles in the attitudes of some teachers and some parents, but the first need is to accept that schools and society badly need moderate people to get organised.

Despite lack of official encouragement, parents' organisations at school and national level have been established and have survived a long time. Their weaknesses have been their failure to take over grassroots parent opinion and to campaign vigorously enough for majority parent interests. One or other seems possible, but to combine the two very difficult. Relatively small organisations like the Campaign for the Advancement of State Education have a clear and vigorous message, but find it hard to convince the typically moderate and conventional school-parent that what they are saying is not dangerously confrontational - how ludicrous that promoting a service used by 93 per cent of our children should be seen as 'political'! - but fairly ordinary and obvious. The National Confederation of Parent-Teacher Associations, on the other hand, does have that moderate and conventional school-parent on its books in large numbers, but until very recently has found it hard to promote vigorous messages. Perhaps it is inherently difficult when the very nature of the system creates parental interest which may for a time be intense but which spans only the school life of one family. It is like a hot water tank - every bucket of hot water drawn off makes room for another bucket of cold which reduces the temperature. You get your members warmed up to a campaigning pitch, only to find a new lot as yet unawakened to the need. Perhaps what we really lack is any sense of education as a whole-life activity or a whole-community responsibility, and as so often come back to the true community school as the answer.

NATIONAL ORGANISATIONS

Early Days

'The voice of parents is the voice of God' said the Reverend H. Russell Wakefield, portentously and somewhat obscurely, when he addressed the Parents' National Educational Union in

1899 (1), going on to say that parents entrust their children to teachers only for such specialised instruction as they cannot carry out themselves. This somewhat pious body was founded in the 1880s. Its object was to promote parent education rather than parent participation, which was necessary so that parents could co-operate with schools in their children's interests. There was also, however, a strong teacher-training connection, and sympathetic teacher trainers among the movement's adherents tried to instill in students the need to be open and friendly with parents. It never became a broad-based parent movement.

Under the wing of the New Education Fellowship the Home and School Council of Great Britain was founded in 1930 to promote parent-teacher co-operation. This was unconnected with the organisation of the same name founded after Plowden (2). Its magazine, 'Home and School' (until 1936 called 'Parents and Teachers') had a strong bias towards infant and nursery education. The Council gave advice and support to the Parent-Teacher Associations which were beginning to emerge in the Thirties, firmly stating that the object of such associations was to further the welfare of the school, not to intervene in the running of the school. PTAs remained something of a novelty. The Home and School Council publications of the time made it clear that they were the exception rather than the rule and tended to be suspected by teachers. At the end of the Second World War an enquiry in Nottinghamshire, where the first Federation was formed, showed that only 3 per cent of the county's schools had them. The Council lasted for some years after the war, but seems by then to have passed its peak of influence.

National Confederation of Parent-Teacher Associations

The PTAs which existed immediately after the war soon began to federate. The first Federation in Nottinghamshire in 1946 was closely followed by Derbyshire and Birmingham in 1948 and Cheshire in 1949. By 1950 there were seven, which in that year had a meeting to discuss matters of common concern. In 1954 they formed the National Federation of PTAs and in 1956 this became the National Confederation of PTAs, the name under which we still know it. Lord Hailsham when he was Minister of Education welcomed this development, but with a thinly veiled note of warning:

> I am sure that the National Federation of Parent Teacher Associations respect as much as I do the authority of the headteacher in the conduct of the school.
> Parents cannot run schools. What I hope the Federation is going to do is to encourage the fullest cooperation between home and schools, leaving the precise organisation to those on the spot.

As the PTA movement rapidly grew in the Sixties and Seventies, this warning proved to have been largely unnecessary. Cooperation between home and school was the keynote. Most PTA constitutions had a clause excluding the school curriculum and organisation from their sphere of debate, and the vast majority evolved as supportive, social and fundraising organisations, though in recent years with an increasing emphasis on informative meetings about educational matters. The process by which the Confederation itself became more concerned with national education policy was a very gradual one, but with a very noticeably higher profile on policy questions in the Eighties.

The NCPTA has a membership of some 5,300 schools, some affiliated in their own right, some through membership of affiliated regional and local federations. Not all federations at local level are affiliated. The Confederation offers its members a very favourable insurance scheme for parent activities in schools, and this is one of the big attractions of membership, as well as a source of financial support for the Confederation. Its policies are debated at an Annual Conference, at which its National Executive Committee is also elected. Like most loosely connected national bodies of this kind, it has to respond from time to time to developments and initiatives on which there has been no clear-cut guidance from members, and it is probably true to say that the nature of the movement and the nature of the prevailing policies were in combination such as to make this a relatively uncontroversial matter until the early Eighties. Recently, for a number of reasons, parents in schools have become more conscious of the policy framework within which they operate and aware that life for a typical supportive school-parent can no longer be so simple.

First the squeeze on educational budgets forced many such parents to think for the first time about protesting, as well as provoking questions about the legitimacy of parent funding of increasingly basic requirements of schools. Many PTA members must have realised that in these circumstances being 'unpolitical' was an option not open to them, because the consequences of their activity were themselves political, widening the gaps between the best and worst resourced schools and making it easier for LEAs to go on cutting. They could also not be expected to provide such a high proportion of a school's needs without realising how little say they had in its policies. The 1980 Act with its universal requirement that parents should be represented on school governing boards, and the government's many indications that governors' involvement in the curriculum of schools was meant to be real, must also have led many parents to question the passive part they had played. This growing awareness made it possible for the NCPTA to carry out its survey of conditions in the service and publish the results in its dramatic

1985 report 'The State of Schools in England and Wales' and to do so with widespread grass-roots support. The report was a culmination of a process which had been going on for some time. From the mid-Seventies onwards the NCPTA had had to respond to some major initiatives and policy documents of a serious kind - more than in any comparable period of its history: the Great Debate; the Taylor Report (3); the 1980 legislation; the Green Paper on Parental Influence at School (4); the White Paper 'Better Schools' (5); the 1986 Act and the Education Reform Bill of late 1987. In addition, many developments in curriculum and examinations, the increased vocational emphasis in schooling, the decline in school meals provision, an explosion of ideas for the privatisation of the service, an a few spectacular crises in schools, notably that at William Tyndale which reverberated so long, combined to make this a period of anxiety and turmoil. Parents were sensitised to the importance of what was going on by the rising levels of unemployment among young people, and finally brought to a peak of awareness by the bitter teachers' dispute of 1985-6.

Until recently the NCPTA's capacity to put a radical parent view across was thought to be limited by the inclusion of independent schools among its members and by the traditionally strong headteacher presence in its national affairs. All one can say is that as the climate affecting schools has become harsher, the NCPTA has not failed to make its voice heard on controversial issues, and, as one would expect, this has not been achieved without a certain amount of turmoil within. There was probably more keen debate within the PTA movement in the middle Eighties than at any time in its history, more rapid development of opinion, more questioning of how the movement could organise itself to respond firmly and yet with proper involvement of members to the many burning issues of the day, and how it should be led. It was the teachers' dispute which caused its keenest heart-searching, for that dispute put great strain on individual PTAs and parent-teacher relationships generally, as well as rousing many parents to a realisation that there was a crisis in the funding of education of which the teachers' dispute was but a symptom.

It was indeed the teachers' dispute which caused great soul-searching in the PTA movement in the winter of 1985-6. The strains in the system were becoming acute, though the harsher the effects in schools of the teachers' sustained struggle the more it seemed that parent groups were springing up in their support. One can never know whether these groups were typical of parent opinion, and perhaps for every ten who got together to consider how they could help the teachers' cause there were thousands of silently angry and resentful ones. All I know is that at the time almost every day brought news of a parent group somewhere who had suddenly come to see that their angry feelings about the disruption of their children's education must be turned against the policies which had produced such uncharacteristically dogged and bitter attitudes among teachers. The National Executive Committee of the NCPTA chose that moment to produce a statement urging the teachers in the interests of the children to return to normal working on the best terms they could get. This may indeed have represented silent majorities, as I have said. We have 'no means of knowing. But it created a storm among vocal NCPTA members, and a period of conflict which will almost certainly in the long run lead to greater care about involving member PTAs and Federations in decisions about strategy.

After a period of quiet, the NCPTA again began to cooperate with other parent organisations and teachers' unions in efforts, not only to secure a satisfactory outcome for the teachers, but also to raise consciousness among parents at every level about the deficiencies of state education funding. After months of patient negotiation in small groups, a remarkable meeting was held on June 24 1986, actually hosted by the NCPTA, at which every single national parents' organisation and every single teachers' union was represented, and at which all concerned pledged themselves to work together for certain goals. These were a satisfactory outcome of the negotiations on teachers' pay and conditions; to get state school funding needs discussed at every level; a higher priority for state education in the words as well as the policies of politicians; acceptance for the conviction that it should be possible to secure education of unsurpassed quality in state schools, and that the messages conveyed by shared books, dingy buildings and demoralised teachers must be erased from memory. This meeting was followed by a remarkable sustained effort of co-operation in which all the groups concerned used their facilities and networks to bring the facts to the attention of ordinary parents in all schools and to get them discussed. On 24 March 1986 hundreds of parents came to Central Hall, Westminster to lobby MPs and deliver manifestos. They then delivered to 10 Downing Street wreaths of flowers spelling 'PARENTS'. The co-operation continues.

I have spent some time on this episode because I believe that it is of fundamental importance in the parents' movement, and illustrates that it is not impossible to build alliances even among the excessively numerous, diverse and often irritatingly contentious groups representing teachers and parents. One could not expect to carry such a large and varied and traditionally conflict-shy membership as that of the NCPTA along without great care, and the occasional miscalculation of their mood, and it remains to be seen whether the leadership will push, or be pushed by, its members as education becomes a top-of-the-agenda issue in the late Eighties.

The NCPTA has always, at national and local level, found it easier to make a claim to speak for ordinary parents in consultation about education policy generally than, for instance, the Campaign for the Advancement of State Education or the Advisory Centre for Education which have often adopted more controversial points of view. It had a place on one of the committees of the now defunct Schools Council (though not on its successor bodies), and locally it is common for the PTAs to be invited into consultation and even given a co-opted place on education committees. Both the NCPTA and its Welsh and Scottish counterparts (the Parent-Teacher Association of Wales and the Scottish Parent Teacher Council) have had grants from the government for specific projects, in the case of the NCPTA in the form of help to buy a small house for office and storage space. In January 1985 it appointed a press and publicity officer and has certainly had a higher profile since then, which of course increases the risk that sometimes it will go faster than, or not fast enough for, its membership. My own prediction is that despite the inevitable dilution of reforming ardour inseparable from the annual accession of new parents, the membership will never again be quite as willing to accept the established order as it was before the teachers' dispute and the 1980s squeeze on education spending.

The Advisory Centre for Education

I turn now to the development of ACE, which was founded in Cambridge in 1960 by Michael (now Lord) Young, the Chairman of the Consumers' Association, whose magazine 'Which?', a product of an increasingly consumerist mood, tested products and recommended 'best buys'. The Advisory Centre, and its magazine 'Where' also had in the early years a strong emphasis on choice and the unspoken assumption that well-informed acts of individual choice could improve standards. ACE has changed very radically since those days, and so has the philosophic base of consumerism, and some of the assumptions behind its early policies would not be acceptable to its present Council and staff or to most readers of its magazine. On the other hand its emphasis is still much more individualistic than that of either the NCPTA or CASE, since it has no affiliated parent groups, and is particularly interested in the rights of individual parents and students and of members of disadvantaged groups.

The early Advisory Centre saw its task as to inform and advise parents, and its magazine carried many general articles around various aspects of the subject of what made a good school. There was also already a strong emphasis on parent involvement in schools and the desirability of schools being more responsive and flexible in their working. It even dared publish a 'Good Schools Guide' on the lines of the 'Good Food

Guide', and it did not in those days rule out independent schools as possible choices for discriminating parents. It operated an individual advice service, for which after some time it recruited voluntary correspondents in localities who would be willing to share their experience with newcomers to the area or others who felt inadequate to make the right choice. It encouraged subscribers to contribute to an information bank of reports on schools known to them. In retrospect it seems to have been a highly suspect and dangerous activity, but it was harmonious with much of what was going on then, and many issues concerning individual choice and the erosion of public services did not yet have the sharp edge they have now.

The number of subscribers to 'Where' grew rapidly from 2,000 in the early days to more than 20,000 at its peak in the mid-Sixties. There was then a decline in the Seventies and indeed by the time ACE moved to Bethnal Green in 1977 the Centre had serious financial problems. In Bethnal Green it has operated in a very much more modest style and has strongly consolidated changes first of emphasis and then of fundamental priorities which were already beginning before the move. It is still an information and advice centre for parents and a small publishing concern specialising in leaflets and booklets of interest to users of the education service, but the move to Bethnal Green was symbolic in many ways. The 'club' atmosphere has completely gone, the beneficiaries of the Centre's work indeed are probably seen not as those who regularly read its publications or indeed regularly read anything. There is no suggestion of a cosy subscriber group sharing similar aspirations, who can help themselves and each other to get those aspirations met by the education system. Information is still regarded as the key to progress, but it is needed not so much as an adjunct to choice, but as a prerequisite to playing a supportive role as a parent and to exercising and extending the rights of parents and students to a partnership role. The emphasis now is wholly on majority needs in education, and no advice or support is given to those whose children attend or wish to attend fee-paying schools. Indeed advice about the suitability of particular schools has totally made way for advice on matters of widespread concern. The young staff who work so hard in the Centre - at present only three full-time and two part-time - answer some 100 telephone calls and many letters a month, as well as producing a magazine and a steady stream of booklets and leaflets; responding as necessary to policy developments and important publications in the education field; and supporting parents and parent groups who are campaigning for a more adequate or more responsive service. All the advice given is free, and a high proportion of those who seek it are unconfident people ill-equipped to fight their own causes and often at the end of their tether.

The change of emphasis has brought its problems. There is not such an obvious client group for the magazine. ACE has therefore had to face the fact that the readership of the magazine will be a mixture of sympathetic individuals and institutions who can use the expertise it offers. This can provide only a finite and limited part of the Centre's income. It cannot subsidise the free advice service. The income from publications has soared in the last few years, a fact which is evidence of the quality and relevance of what has been commissioned as well as of the greater complexity of education law and practice which people have to find their way round. Even this increase, however, cannot by itself sustain the other activities.

The Centre has received a number of grants from trusts to bridge the gap. Some of these have been for specific projects, like work in special needs or racial equality. Indeed with statutory services under pressure it gets increasingly difficult to raise funds for the general activity of charitable bodies. In some ways the local education authority is the natural sponsor, and efforts are made to seek LEA affiliations. After all our system manifestly lacks any source of independent support for parents in difficulties, or any bridge between them and a service which to the outsider may to its own great surprise seem closed and unyielding.

Best-selling publications have been those about children with special needs and those intended to improve the effectiveness of school governors. Guides to new legislation and regulations also sell very well. Increasingly ACE's resources have been concentrated on civil rights type issues - open school records, the abolition of corporal punishment, equal treatment for ethnic minorities, girls, and those with handicaps. Often it is seen to be anti-teacher and anti-LEA, since the kind of problems on which it is asked to advise, if not typical, do illustrate the service at its most authoritarian and inflexible. Yet teachers and LEAs are its biggest customers, and often speak of its publications with respect. As a supporter and a Council member since ACE moved to Bethnal Green, I hope that it will not lose its mainstream appeal in its splendid championship of minority rights, since it needs a large constituency to survive, and the constituency needs it if anything even more. I hope more LEAs will support it: a large part of the service is mature enough to recognise its need for critical friends and well-informed consumers.

The name 'Where' proved an encumbrance after the Cambridge era, since it suggested the well-organised chooser as its bedrock. Yet it is hard to find the moment to drop a name, just as it is hard to find a moment to raise a price: anything which makes the apathetic review their standing orders is a hazard; and even an ideological liability can still, through familiarity, have commercial value. The nettle was grasped in 1984, when the magazine was designed in a more business-like format as the 'ACE Bulletin' with six densely filled issues a year instead of ten. The new publication is long on information, shorter on comment, seeming to accept that it had already become less of a 'read' and more of a topical reference magazine. There are several features of proven popularity, notably the digest of publications and the column for parent governors.

The staff work as a collective with equal salaries, sharing decisions and routine chores alike, and worrying away at problems until they reach consensus. They share with the Council in the choice of new colleagues when there is a vacancy. The Centre provides for any student of collectives a very interesting experience, and there is no doubt that such a style makes possible a high level of commitment and morale compared with more hierarchical structures.

Nobody would pretend that this way of working is problem-free. It sometimes confuses enquirers used to hierarchy. Reaching a common view is often hard work; responses to situations have sometimes to be made very quickly and all must be loyal to them; relationships must be able to withstand a very close daily contact in which nobody is entirely out of anyone else's light, in work so intimately shared. The structure does in practice also make the role of the Council as an agent of accountability rather more complex than it would be in a more traditional situation in which the Council appoints the Director and the Director plays a major part in staff selection. It has necessitated a more precise articulation of agreed aims and their translation into long- and short-term programmes of work. This in turn provides a focus for the appointment and induction of staff.

I have spent some time on the working style of ACE, not only because it is in itself interesting and a possible model for other small collectives and parents' advice centres, but also because of its significance as a parallel to the changing style of schools, and the implications of that style for governors and parents. Schools were in the past somewhat hierarchical institutions - some would say many still are. As hierarchical institutions give way to more collegiate ones, accountability must require a good deal more formality in setting out agreed aims and methods.

ACE has obviously done much to increase awareness of parents' needs and to draw attention to the undemocratic and secretive habits still to be found in the education service, despite the progress made in recent years. It has also alerted public opinion to the injustices still suffered by various disadvantaged minorities and helped to increase the confidence of parents and students in dealing with schools and education authorities. Especially helpful are its informative leaflets, written in simple and practical terms, on subjects shown to be of widespread concern. Its activity is only a drop in the bucket of need, and I should like to see an independent parents' advice and resource centre, securely financed, geographically accessible to all parents. The advice calls received by ACE show how often parents find themselves totally in the dark about how their problems have arisen, what their rights are, what sources of help exist, and how they themselves could have averted the trouble.

Campaign for the Advancement of State Education

While ACE was establishing itself in Cambridge, a group of parents, coincidentally also in Cambridge but not connected, joined together because of dissatisfaction with the facilities at their local primary school. They called themselves the Association for the Advancement of State Education, and they began in 1960. Soon such associations were springing up in other places, and in 1962 they formed themselves into the Confederation for the Advancement of State Education. It was not until some twenty years later that, in response to the increasingly bitter feelings of members about the restriction of public spending on education, the more adversarial name 'Campaign' was adopted.

CASE is now twenty-five years old, and has remained in good health as an organisation, but with considerable variations in numerical strength, ever since. Unlike the NCPTA its constituent membership is not school-based, but relates to the area, or part of the area, of a local education authority, and of course it is concerned only with public sector education. Within CASE local groups are autonomous, have varying constitutions, subscriptions, activities and campaign priorities, but the objectives have never varied. They may be summarised as a system of public sector education, from pre-school to retirement, so resourced and respected as to meet the requirements of the most needy and the aspirations of the most exacting of its users; so organised as to afford equal opportunity for all, regardless of home circumstances, ability or disability, sex, race or religion; so managed as to involve parents and the public in its institutions as partners. In pursuit of these goals CASE nationally and through its local associations has campaigned at various times for better pre-school provision; for more generous expenditure on teachers, on books and equipment; for adequate maintenance of school buildings; for a broad curriculum, with no skimping on the arts and recreation; for open access to further, higher and adult education for all who are able to profit by it; for better grants and allowances of all kinds to enable those from disadvantaged backgrounds to take up educational opportunities; for equal opportunities for girls, ethnic minorities, those with special educational needs; and for encouragement of all forms of parental and public involvement in decision making at LEA, neighbourhood and school level. Above all, CASE has campaigned for a fully comprehensive system of secondary education.

In the middle and late Sixties CASE grew very rapidly. The main stimuli were the growing awareness of the importance of home and community to the success of both child and school; the movement towards reorganisation of secondary education on comprehensive lines which encountered political resistance in many Conservative strongholds; and the beginnings of reform in the government of schools, with increasing emphasis on opening up this antiquated system to parents, teachers and community. It is often said that CASE is a middle-class movement which flourished only in leafy suburb and county town, and it is certainly true that the proliferation of CASE groups during those years took place mainly in pleasant neighbourhoods. The unspoken criticism in these comments misses a very important point however. It is in the leafy suburb and the prosperous county town that the majority needs in education are often conspicuously neglected. The vociferous and influential people in that community may buy themselves out of public provision, and their loss is the loss of effective pressure for improvement. CASE in many areas has been an attempt by concerned parents and teachers to redress that balance in favour of majority needs, needs which in poorer areas are often met through the normal democratic processes. After all, it was not necessary to campaign for comprehensive schools in areas where there was an ideological acceptance of the comprehensive principle. It just happened. In an area where the prevailing philosophy favoured a selective system, those who for educational reasons considered selection to be divisive, barren and wasteful of talent had to fight very hard to change things. I joined CASE in Richmond at that time for three reasons. Firstly I was shocked by the low esteem and generally depressed condition of the state schools, and realised that it came about because few confident people were personally dependent on them. Secondly I was saddened by the very limited attempts schools were making to harness the goodwill of parents who did use them, which included some who had ideological commitment to the public sector; some who had awareness and concern about education but no money; and others who had neither but who could have been encouraged to organise if they had come to understand the need. Thirdly I saw the 11+ as an anachronism and a cruelly divisive force among children, families and - not often mentioned - teachers. All in all I thought a prosperous leafy suburb was a rotten place to be poor in, far worse in many ways than places where everybody was poor.

We fought successfully in Richmond for comprehensive schools, properly staffed and resourced; for parent, teacher and community seats on governing bodies; for open access tertiary education; for many other things which seemed unattainable in 1965 when the borough came into being. At the same time CASE groups all over the country were doing the same, and, if the CASE map was pretty blank in the rural areas and the industrial conurbations, associations made an impact where they existed. They were so successful indeed that in many cases they faded away, thinking that they had attained their objectives, and it is hard to keep people joining things when there is nothing to offer but daily vigilance: by comparison blood, tears, toil and sweat seem quite exciting. Even those groups which had diversified their activity and become involved in things other than campaigning found it hard to survive when the big causes were no more. An additional factor in Labour LEAs was for CASE members, who would always include some left of centre in politics, to become absorbed by the local establishment and to lose their cutting edge in a cosy near-identity of purpose.

At its most quiescent CASE could only boast 30 or so local associations, and of these probably only a dozen or so were really large and active. Then came the rude shock that expansion had come to an end. The squeeze on education spending which began in the late Seventies was given the seal of permanence in the local government legislation of 1980 and 1981, and the horrible realisation dawned that not only were the so called big spenders to become smaller spenders but that the small spenders, because of the baseline on which grant-related expenditure was based, were to become very small spenders indeed. Falling rolls, which in innocence some had seen as a promise of small classes and better conditions, brought instead a shrinking curriculum for many schools, as cuts and falling numbers combined to impoverish staffing, and widespread reorganisation proposals. In some areas where comprehensive schools were thought to be safe there were schemes for going back to selection. At national level there was a constant stream of kites flying on vouchers, restoring direct grant schools, and other forms of privatisation. At local level some school ancillary services were indeed privatised, under-fives provision was stopped or curtailed, adult education, discretionary grants, indeed all forms of non-mandatory spending, savagely cut. Parents were known to be funding essentials on a large scale. Finally the teachers' pay dispute convinced many who still needed convincing that state education was again in need of campaigners. As a result new CASE groups again began to spring up: the number of active associations doubled in 1985-87. In this round the geographical variety was greatly increased: Merton, Harrow, groups in Dorset, Cornwall, Hereford and Worcester, Wiltshire, Shropshire, Gateshead, Bristol, Manchester and three in Gloucestershire.

CASE holds an annual conference, which is hosted by a local association and followed by an AGM at which policy issues are debated and an executive committee elected. Importance is attached to a broad representation over the country even though this is expensive in travel to meetings. The committee meets termly, apart from short meetings before and after the AGM. It keeps in touch with associations and national members (who may be individuals or groups) through a newsletter after each meeting, through policy papers for comment and specific questions to answer, and through its termly magazine 'Parents and Schools' which always carries local association news. Any member is welcome to NEC meetings. Every year the NEC arranges meetings with the Secretary of State, the education spokesperson of each opposition party, the teachers' unions, and also meets from time to time HMI, journalists, other groups concerned with education, to keep public sector needs to the fore. It maintains close contact with ACE, the NCPTA, the National Association of Governors and Managers, the All London Parents' Action Group, and indeed seeks to join in initiatives with all these whenever possible. It sees its role as twofold: to represent the whole movement at national level and to support and publicise the work of local associations. Its activity is financed by a levy on local groups who pay £10 in their first year and thereafter £2 per local member of which £1 is for 'Parents and Schools' and £1 for administration.

Local groups vary widely in size. A few might have only 30 members, the largest has 250. The typical group would have between 70 and 150. All keep a close watch on decisions of their LEA, reacting as necessary, and all regularly make proposals for improvements in the local service. A majority do local surveys of some kind and produce various informative publications for parents. Public meetings are held on issues of current concern, leading consultation very often on major reorganisation proposals. From time to time campaigning more vigorous than just transmitting views is undertaken: demonstrations, mass lobbying of MPs, petitioning, and so on.

Most groups combine the inescapable job of protesting against policies which damage education with more constructive activities, promoting various forms of home-school cooperation, running holiday play centres, arranging fun activities for children, and providing training sessions for school governors. Indeed, this may be the secret of a group which lasts. Not only is it less likely to feel that its task is finished when a cause is either won or abandoned, but it is also more likely to keep a broadly based respect among parents than a group which only has time to be against things.

It sometimes seems strange that a voluntary organisation should exist to protect the quality of public sector education: one might be forgiven for seeing that as the role of the Secretary of State. However, there is no doubt that whatever government is in power, or whatever the political complexion of the local authority, both benefit from the vigilance of concerned parents. The potential strength of CASE, compared with an organisation based on the school PTA, is that it tends to attract a proportion of members whose interest outlasts their direct family involvement: the milers, as distinct from the sprinters. Such members, in moderate proportion, act as a repository of the experience which organisations of current parents alone find it hard to make available to future generations. It is vital, however, that the balance is maintained and that the movement continues to attract parents whose children are just entering the system, and also that it watches that its style of communication is simple and direct, to appeal to a wide range of parents. Finally it must keep its rapport with heads, teachers, officers and advisers, whose interests in many ways coincide. Yet it must not lose its independence or its appeal to parents. With its inevitable involvement of many people professionally engaged in education, CASE needs to be careful that its aims extend beyond the attainment of a public education service generously resourced and geared towards justice and fairness. Some members would probably see this as enough, and indeed we are far enough away from that goal of a system based on secure finance and just principles to make it an understandable viewpoint. What that viewpoint means, however, is that professionals say to the public: just give us the tools, work for policies which give us the resources to provide a quality service and equality of opportunity. Even the best alliance between politicians, officers and teachers is sterile unless it includes home and community in its calculations. It is vital for an organisation like CASE to remember that the goal is a partnership of behalf of the child.

We have looked at three national organisations which have survived in good heart for a quarter of a century. Each has a different emphasis. Sometimes it seems a pity that with parents' natural disabilities as agents of change their strength should be dissipated. One needs the hard campaigning thrust of CASE for a properly esteemed, adequately funded service, firmly based on equality of opportunity. One needs the concern of ACE for the rights of the individual, especially the individual disadvantaged by sex, race, disability or diffidence, in a system still strong in bureaucratic, authoritarian traditions and with a pull towards uniformity. One needs the practical, warm, sensible involvement of each generation of school parents represented by the PTA movement, unaware for the most part of the forces stacked against the children, resolutely mainstream in its interests, healthily afraid of people with a light in their eyes. Can these needs be combined? In some countries they seem to have tried it. Perhaps that is an ambitious goal, but at least we should try to keep in step and not compete.

THE PARENTS' VOICE

The Home and School Council

This was set up in 1967 following and in response to the Plowden Report (2). Its aim was to promote the Plowden philosophy of better links between home and school, and it was a combined venture by the NCPTA, ACE and CASE. It originally had a grant from the Rowntree Trust, and in the early days was quite ambitious, even employing a field worker; but over the years it settled down as a publishing concern, supported by all three organisations. The Council commissions small booklets, on subjects of practical interest to parents, selling at very reasonable prices (in recent years 40p, 60p, 80p). Decisions about subjects to be covered, authors to be approached, and editorial and marketing matters are taken cooperatively. At one time all three organisations were responsible for some of the investment finance, but in recent years this has come mainly from the NCPTA, whose members constitute a guaranteed nucleus of subscribers. CASE also includes Home and School Council booklets in the cost of national membership. In 1986 the NCPTA had to reduce its financial backing and the Council has been seeking additional sources of support, with some success. The National Association for Primary Education has become one of the supporting organisations. There is no doubt a market for material of this kind: down-to-earth advice on assistance with outings, helping your children with maths and spelling, transferring to secondary school, children in trouble, children with medical problems, music in schools, being a school governor, to quote some subjects covered in the once-a-term production cycle.

National Association of Governors and Managers

The beginnings of reform in school government which characterised the late Sixties, and went on apace in the early and middle Seventies, gave rise in 1970 to this lively organisation. Its aims have been to improve the practice of school government and enhance its status, to work for governing boards more widely representative of the school's local community, parent body and staff, and to provide individual governors with contact, training and support. Its membership consists partly of individual governors of all types and partly of local associations of governors. It supported the Taylor Committee's formula (3) of an equal partnership in the composition of governing bodies, and has actively worked for the acceptance of that principle. It has organised training courses, both on its own and in collaboration with other agencies, and produces extremely helpful leaflets on various aspects of governors' duties. It has also campaigned vigorously for adequate training and support programmes for governors funded by LEAs and the government, and to this end has carried out a number of surveys of what is actually being done for governors up and down the country.

LOCAL PARENTS' GROUPS

It is invidious to choose among so many. Parents' action groups spring up every day somewhere to fight cuts, to save schools, prevent or promote change. Most if not all are single-issue groups, which either hitch on to a larger organisation or sink without trace when that cause is won or abandoned. CASE particularly has benefitted from the enduring interest of many of them, since they either affiliate in the process of seeking allies or broadening their aims, or else bequeath their goodwill, funds and seasoned personnel to the local CASE group when they disband.

There is a certain sadness about the rise and fall of ephemeral groups, partly because it takes so long to learn one's way round the system, discover how to get information, how to obtain publicity and how to be effective, and partly because for so many it is a period of awakening, self-discovery and comradeship: it would be a pity if both kinds of experience were to die intestate. One of the amazing and in some ways distressing things such brief encounters with public affairs reveal is how much talent for organising, writing, speaking, motivating others, lies normally unused in the community. One wonders whether we have missed opportunities to tap it. I remember when I wrote the history of the Richmond Parents' Association, an enormously successful campaign for comprehensive schools only lightly involved with CASE, and involving thousands in active participation in the late Sixties, that many of the people I spoke to who were not involved in anything before or since told me that it was the most rewarding time of their lives.

One organisation which must certainly have pride of place for the sheer number involved, the speed with which it was formed and the impact which it achieved, is the All London Parents' Action Group, (ALPAG), established towards the end of 1985 and still thriving two years later. It was born of the teachers' pay dispute of 1985-6, which for various reasons affected London more severely than most areas. It began with parents coming together in two London comprehensive schools to discuss the dire effects of the teachers' action on their children's education and the ways in which parents might influence the course of events. It was in these two groups that ALPAG was in a formal sense born, but at that moment there were clearly a large number of parents and parent groups everywhere whose thoughts were moving in the same direction: it is remarkable how ideas will germinate when the time is right. In my own Richmond-on-Thames, where for various reasons there is a particularly volatile parent population, a massively successful movement in support of the teachers had got going some nine months earlier and had resulted in hundreds of parents writing personally to MPs; but attempts to encourage other areas to follow suit had at the time been almost completely unsuccessful.

The aims of ALPAG were simple. They wanted to put the combined weight of a parent group behind a satisfactory settlement of teachers' pay and conditions bringing lasting peace to schools. They wanted to make parents aware that the teachers' dispute of 1985-6 was a symptom of a deeper problem of under-resourcing of education, so that they would be motivated to bring education to the top of the agenda with local and national politicians. They wanted to restore good communication between parents and teachers both on the problems which had caused the dispute and more generally. Their anger about the disruption of schools was not directed at teachers but at those policies which had driven teachers to industrial action, yet they felt that it was a pity that withdrawal of home-school contact had formed part of that action, since it not only gave parents a sense of rejection and exclusion but also made it much harder to put the teachers' case across to those who could campaign with them.

The ALPAG outcry spread like a forest fire. In days they had made contacts all over London and beyond. In a couple of weeks they had an action coordinator in each of the ten divisions of the ILEA, each of the seventeen outer London boroughs, and forty other contacts beyond London. There was no structure of committee with constitution and subscriptions, yet a firm network of support existed from the start. Each local coordinator accepted the job of distributing messages and maintaining contact with all schools. The campaign was to be pursued at every level in the locality and nationally. At school level the task of getting parents and teachers talking was paramount. Two big rallies were held, the second in Central Hall in January 1986 attended by close on 1000 parents, combined with a lobby of MPs. A steering group of open and informal character kept the information flowing, and spread ideas. ALPAG has cooperated with CASE, the NCPTA and other groups and regularly met the teachers' organisations, a process which culminated in the initiatives of June and October 1986 aimed at getting parents in every school in England and Wales talking among themselves, within their organisations, with their teachers and parent governors, about the deficiencies needing urgent action and bringing them to the attention of councillors, MPs and the press. This initiative, publicised on 14 October 1986, was supported by every teachers' organisation as well as the parent groups, and co-operation continued through 1987. I hope that it will go on raising awareness in schools for a very long time, as well as helping to repair some of the damage to trust which the long dispute had caused, and strengthening parent-teacher relationships. In January 1988 the combined groups wrote to all 70,000 parent governors urging them to discuss the new Education Reform Bill.

The best outcome of the 1985-8 developments in CASE, the NCPTA and ALPAG and their co-operation with others would be the birth of some small sense of identity among school parents everywhere. It would perhaps be the first time. Yet in the Fifties, Sixties and Seventies hundreds of local parents' groups had been formed without any awareness that their problems were common problems. Acronyms flash across the screens of memory in bewildering succession: PACE, SPACE, STEP, SAGE, PRICE, PAG. Some of these have joined up with larger groupings, some do not know that their name has been used before, or something like it. Of those which have remained local, and have survived a long time, perhaps special mention should be made of LASPA, the Liverpool Association of School Parents, for they, in a city whose educational problems sometimes seem to be insoluble, have stayed together for many years to try to maintain a steady concern for local children. Their initiative was instrumental in securing a grant from Rowntree for a support service, employing an outreach worker, for parent governors in a deprived area, in the belief that the way to rescue parents generally from despair over the many problems which threatened their children's schooling was to help a few of them to a more confident role within the system. This action seems to have stimulated the LEA to more support for governors.

The causes of parent action at local level are remarkably similar, and this makes it seem very sad that there are few mechanisms for co-operation. We cannot be said to have a coherent parents' movement in England and Wales, but perhaps the events of 1986-8 will bring it nearer. Looking at other countries one is struck by the strength of their parents' voice. Maybe the very complex way in which responsibility for education is broken up is the reason for our failure to find a voice for ourselves. I shall take a brief look at parents' activities outside England and Wales before moving on to the role of school governors as agents of school accountability and a focus for home-school relationships.

NOTES

1. H. Russell Wakefield, The Parent in the Educational System, (Parents' Review 10, pp. 502-13).
2. The Plowden Committee, Children and their Primary Schools, (HMSO, 1967).
3. The Taylor Committee, A New Partnership for our Schools, (HMSO, 1977).

4. DES, <u>Parental Influence at School</u>, (HMSO, May 1984).

5. DES, <u>Better Schools</u>, (HMSO, March 1985).

ADDRESSES OF PARENT ORGANISATIONS

National Confederation of Parent-Teacher Associations
43, Stonebridge Road, Northfleet, Gravesend, Kent DA11 9DS. Tel: 0474-60618.

Advisory Centre for Education
18, Victoria Park Square, London E2 9PB. Tel: 01-980-4596.

Campaign for the Advancement of State Education
The Groves High Street, Sawston, Cambridge. Tel: 0223-833179.

All London Parents Action Group
23, Alverstone Road, London NW2. Tel: 01-459-3405.

Home and School Council
81, Rustlings Road, Sheffield S11 7AB. Tel: 0742-662467.

Parent Teacher Association of Wales
Talgoed, Pen-y-lon, Mynydd Isa, Mold, Clwyd CH7 6YG. Tel: 0352-4652.

Scottish Parent Teacher Council
30 Rutland Square, Edinburgh EH1 2BW. Tel: 031-229-2433.

National Consumer Council
20, Grosvenor Gardens, London SW1W ODH. Tel: 01-730-3469.

Welsh Consumer Council, Castle Buildings
Womanby Street, Cardiff CF1 2BN. Tel. 0222-396056.

Scottish Consumer Council
314, St. Vincent Street, Glasgow G3 8XW. Tel: 041-226-5261.

Chapter Six

PARENTS IN OTHER COUNTRIES

Can you guess where it was that a national education Minister said that he needed the support of a parents' organisation to do what he had to do? Where the leader of that parents' organisation some years later, arriving as an honoured guest at a new President's first address to the nation, was cheered by the great crowd? Where a commentator said apologetically that of course only between a quarter and a third of families were paid-up members of a national parents' organisation? You will at least be sure that it was not London. It was Paris.

Can you guess where three leaders of a national parents' organisation reached positions of great influence within less than a decade? Where one became a member of a state Parliament, another became national Minister of Education, and a third became a member and for a time acting chairman of a central policy-making body on education? Where they were all women? That was Australia.

In the USA, Canada, New Zealand, Australia, nearly all the member countries of the EEC, there are arrangements firmly based in law which give parents substantial representation as of right on school level and sometimes higher decision-making bodies. In many countries, including Australia, France, West Germany, Belgium, Luxembourg, Denmark and the Netherlands, parents' organisations are subsidised directly or indirectly, in cash or in kind, by the government. It is perhaps significant that in all the countries mentioned above with the sole exception of Denmark the curriculum is government-prescribed. This works two ways: it encourages parents to put their pressure where policy is made, so that their organisations are likely to be strong national ones, but it may also make teachers more willing to share power than they are in the UK where traditionally teachers have more power over what is taught. By the same token, in countries where parent involvement at school level is on paper considerable, there is evidence of some dissatisfaction that in practice that involvement is peripheral, given the narrow range of issues where policy is determined at that level. In a number of other countries also the relationship of church and state in education is very different from our own, and there is nothing which corresponds to our uneasy but lasting marriage of religious and secular education within the state system. In most countries, and especially those with a large Catholic population, the education provided by the state is strongly secular, and denominational alternatives are usually funded in some other way. This is almost always a highly political issue, and unites parents in central organisations where they try to influence government policy in the direction which favours their interest group. The outstanding example of this is France, where the Catholic lobby is identified with the right in education and there is an equally powerful secularist parent lobby with considerable trade union and party allegiance.

This is not the place for a detailed account of how parents and the public influence education policies in other countries, but I do want to mention some interesting features of other systems, with rather more detail for obvious reasons on the French experience and a fuller commentary on the extremely interesting state of affairs in Australia.

In the USA a huge number of citizens' advisory councils of various kinds function in the different states, some under federal law, some under state law, some under local bye-laws, but all with the role of bringing parent and other lay influence to bear on the decisions of educationists and education administrators. It is estimated that at the very least a million citizens participate in such councils. The federal provision is aimed at making better educational facilities available in disadvantaged areas. The other councils scattered through the 17,000 school districts are the result of state or local initiatives, and tend to be concentrated in larger towns. From time to time reports on the effectiveness of this activity are produced by the Institute for Responsive Education in Boston as well as by researchers elsewhere The consensus seems to be that the councils are not very widely representative, being largely white and middle class; that there is a high turnover; that their remit is often confused; that they find it hard to make an impact on the entrenched policies both of administrators and teachers; and that they are ineffectively serviced. There are shining exceptions, as everywhere, particularly among the federally established councils. Their purpose is to further compensatory resourcing in disadvantaged areas. As in Australia the federal support given to schools in such areas is conditional on the involvement of parents and community in the enterprise, and the council's responsibility may extend to the authorisation of spending. In some cases the role of the councils will also have been negotiated in advance to some extent with teachers' organisations locally. Over the country as a whole it is rare for members of parents'/citizens' councils to be elected or for any proper constituency to be identified and protected, and they are either volunteers or appointees of the providing authority. This is unlikely to produce effective participation. On the other hand there is plenty of evidence of successful relationships of a less structured kind between parents and their schools. The trouble with unstructured participation, as many an American teacher will testify with feeling, is that unless it is unselfishly motivated and unless it is handled by teachers with enough confidence to make relaxed and open behaviour effortless, it can be threatening to professional morale.

In CANADA also we are dealing with a number of separate systems, but the structures of school governance are similar throughout the twelve provinces and territories. In most there has been a steady development of Parent Advisory Committees, but the most comprehensive as well as the longest established system is in Quebec. The committees have been established on the initiative of the providing authorities with the object of encouraging parent cooperation with educators to improve education at school level. The committees are composed solely of parents, and they have the dual role of advising schools and promoting parental support. The emphasis is strongly on cooperation and communication, almost to the point of making the parent bodies part of the system. In the Seventies there was some disillusionment with them mainly for this reason, and in Quebec at least the government has tried to give the committees a stronger role in recent years. Evidence that the committees were failing to express parents' concerns is provided by the proliferation of protest groups to fight reorganisations caused by falling rolls, protests for which the traditional home/school associations had also failed to provide a channel. Support and cooperation dominate the ethic of the Canadian Home and School and Parent Teacher Federation, so much so that in one case the PTAs had played no part at all in a disputed school closure to which 90 per cent of all local parents were opposed.

NEW ZEALAND has on paper one of the most highly developed systems of parental participation in school decision-making. Every primary school has a school committee with between five and nine elected house-holders and most secondary schools have a governing body with five parent members. What is more, the school level bodies are the constituency for the Education Boards which administer the local service. The organised PTA movement also has a very large membership. In practice the influence of the school level committees/ governors, despite high-sounding intentions that they should be the agencies of school accountability to local parents and citizens, has been reduced by a progressive centralisation of curriculum and resource decisions, with consequent popular frustration about 'sham' participation. There seems to be a remarkably high level of public interest: in the New Zealand equivalent of our Great Debate in the early Seventies, a very ambitious enterprise in six regions with many distinguished visiting experts from other countries, some 60,000 New Zealanders took part, and in one region there were 680 group reports and many from individuals. The demand for more devolution and user participation was the dominant theme. Yet the process of centralisation has continued almost unabated.

In NORWAY and SWEDEN we have examples of strongly centralised administrations which, like so many, attempted some devolution in the late Sixties, and in which the schools shared to some extent. They both have participatory councils for schools, but in Sweden the main emphasis is on secondary schools, and with a stress on pupil rather than parent participation. Norway has parents', pupils' and teachers' councils in all schools, with a 'collaboration committee' to unite them, but their effect seems to have been largely to strengthen the position of principal and staff.

DENMARK has strong legislation on parents' rights. Parents may choose between a state school and an approved independent alternative. They may also choose which subject options their children study. They are the only voting members of school boards, which are established by law in all public sector schools, and their national organisation is strong and well-respected. But it is not a client-dominated system. There is a strong emphasis on the responsibilities of parents, as well as their rights. Partnership between school and family is underpinned by requirements about good communication by the schools and encouragement to parents to play a supportive role. This structure is embodied partly in legislation and partly in Ministerial guidelines. The school board has considerable influence on school rules and organisation and general oversight of its performance, but it is clear that, in curriculum and curriculum-based resource decisions, its role is to consider what the professionals propose rather than to initiate. Consent, rather than intervention, is the word. The Danish model is baffling. It has been praised by visitors from the educational left and right alike. The choice between state and private alternatives does not seem to cause much commotion or to have very divisive consequences. All that parent influence seems to exist without noticeable teacher stress. I suspect that one must look beyond the relationship between school and family for the reasons: to the values conveyed by government policies as a whole; to a society much less class-conscious than ours; to the pay and status of teachers; and the character of the independent schools, which seem to have an 'alternative' rather than an elitist flavour and are often set up by parents. Perhaps because parents have influence in schools they are less obsessive about choice, or rather see choice as just a part of a system which is basically designed to meet their needs and in which they are participants. As for teachers, perhaps parent influence is easier to live with in a framework of mutual responsibility for the child in a clearly defined partnership. Whatever the reasons, Denmark stands out as very different from all the other countries studied.

In ITALY, as in other countries, the structures of school democracy were formed as a result of the student uprisings of 1968. Before that there had been strong parents' organisations and even two parents' newspapers, one Catholic, one secular, but only fragmentary forms of involvement. The events of 1968-9 went far beyond the expression of student aspirations for more involvement for themselves: they were also a revolt against an elitist and rigid school system scarcely reformed since the Fascist era, with the consequent alienation so poignantly described by peasant teenagers through Lettera a una Professora (Scuola di Barbiana 1967). Parents joined in the expressions of discontent, and so did the unions, reacting to unemployment, inflation and an oppressive and unjust state. The outcome was a system of class, school district, provincial and national councils to make decisions on education policy. Professionals were represented at all levels, and parents and older students at all but the national level. This elaborate system, with every step set out in incredibly tortuous detail - until it came to the actual functions when a familiar vagueness took over - was superimposed on an administration as highly centralised and cumbersome as that which had produced the unrest; and with all curricula and timetables emanating from Rome it was not surprising that frustration followed the initial euphoria. The pay and status of Italian teachers is not high, and at times they have been suspicious or even obstructive, though as the councils have developed they have begun to accept them. Although the extent to which education is government-controlled has set limits on progress, the councils have had some success in democratising schools, extending scientific and cultural provision, improving libraries and integrating pupils with special needs. These advances have been made despite the overwhelming load of trivia and procedural tussles with which the councils have had to contend.

In spite of the difficulties, parent interest has been remarkable. The 70 per cent turn-out in the first round of elections has not been sustained; but, through all the frustrations which have beset the councils, parents have worked very hard to make something of them. About half a million Italian families belong to a parents' organisation. These operate without government subsidy. The participatory structures may have brought disappointment, but those who have taken part seem to have learnt a good deal from the experience.

WEST GERMANY affords another example of a federal system with a guiding philosophy but considerable differences in the practical application of that philosophy in different areas. Over most of the country a system of participatory councils operates, but details vary between the eleven Länder. The framework is one of general principles and rights embodied in the Grundgesetz or German basic law. The state is the guardian of the quality of schools, but the Länder are the legally sovereign providers. The Grundgesetz is the explicitly moral statement of a new democratic state trying to obliterate fifteen years of its history, but echoing finer days. There had been participatory structures as early as 1919, destroyed by the Nazis, and in Hamburg especially a strong parents' movement, with an emphasis on social reform, and in the Twenties even its own newspaper. Among the most highly developed systems are those in Hamburg, Bavaria, Hessen, North Rhine Westphalia and Baden-Württemberg. Some consultative education councils were introduced in the early days of the Federal Republic, but as elsewhere the main period of development was the late Sixties following the student demonstrations. Most structures provide for class and school and in some cases higher-level committees involving teachers, parents and students, typically separate from each other but coming together for issues of mutual concern. Since there is almost no power over the curriculum at school level, there must in the nature of things be limited scope for debate, but on issues of budgeting, school and class organisation, social and cultural activities, discipline, one forms the impression of a dialogue conducted with some dignity and mutual respect among the various participants. All observers comment on the excellent quality of information provided for parents. Parents' organisations are well supported, and most receive some form of public subsidy to carry on their affairs. In contrast to France, German parent activity remained for many years apolitical, its institutions representing a search for consensus. This situation was disturbed only by the moves to introduce comprehensive secondary education, and in many areas bitter controversy raged on this issue, controversy in which the official organs of parent involvement were sometimes bypassed as the initiative passed to associations of parents fighting change, most dramatically perhaps in North Rhine Westphalia, where a people's petition achieved the 20 per cent support necessary in their law to have the proposals referred back.

BELGIUM allows parents free choice of schools and schools have to adapt to take all comers. There are no legally imposed participatory councils, though they are encouraged on a voluntary basis and some interesting experiments are going on, especially in the Catholic sector. Parents' associations at school level are encouraged, and so are national parents' organisations which are subsidised. Better home-school communication and co-operation are being promoted by advice and encouragement.

In the NETHERLANDS parents also have a free choice of

school, including independent schools which are fully financed by the government. There are school councils and municipal participatory councils with strong representation of parents - this under very recent legislation. Parents' organisations have indirect government subsidy through the schools.

The organised parents' voice in SCOTLAND has similarities to some of the continental and Commonwealth models as marked as those to the arrangements in England and Wales. It has its own Parent Teacher Council, corresponding to the National Confederation of PTAs in England and Wales, and the Scottish Consumer Council has a tradition of strong support for the concerns of Scottish parents. There is nothing in Scottish education law to correspond to the ancient institution of the school governing body, but since 1918 Scotland has had community councils exercising functions on behalf of schools. The present system goes back to 1973 when the Local Government (Scotland) Act required school councils to be established with mandatory representation of parents and teachers. The proportions and detailed arrangements were left to the twelve education authorities, but only a tiny minority of the 3,000 odd schools have councils of their own: most are related to quite large groups of schools. Although they have very broad representation of local interests, their role has been largely confined to minor aspects of school life, with scarcely any involvement in the curriculum. There is strong pressure for individual councils with a more substantial function, having decision-making powers in matters where school and home touch closely (home-school communication, discipline) and advisory functions only in relation to the curriculum.

At the time of writing, consultation has taken place on radical changes, parallel to those in the Education Reform Bill of 1987 for England and Wales, giving Scottish councils parent majorities and more teeth.

We come now to the two countries which I have chosen to look at in more detail, partly because of their intrinsic interest, partly because they illustrate some general features of parental involvement beyond England and Wales in particularly clear ways. FRANCE and AUSTRALIA both have a politically vocal Catholic education lobby, both have their Catholic schools outside the government system, but with heavy direct subsidy, and in both countries recent moves by left-wing governments to integrate, or remove financial support from, the church schools led to such violent protests that they have had to be abandoned. In both countries there is a strong secularist parents' lobby, and both have powerful central determination of the curriculum, though in Australia this is in the main the function of the state, not the federal government. Both have statutory school-level councils with parent representation, though in Australia they are not yet mandatory in all states.

The fascinating feature of the parents' movement in France is its extraordinary rhetoric, only credible because it is clear that nationally parents are a political force of some importance. The opening paragraph of this chapter described how the crowds cheered Jean Cornec, the head of the left-wing parents' federation when he arrived as a distinguished guest on the occasion of M. Mitterand's first Presidential address to the nation. Jean Cornec had already referred in euphoric public terms to the importance of the change of government, with recollections of Victor Hugo and descriptions of French parents as soldiers of a new age. This moment seems to epitomise the drama associated with parents' activities in France.

In a highly centralised system the feelings of parents about education policies can be concentrated on visible targets. When, after the fall of the Fourth Republic, it was proposed in 1958 to provide government subsidies for the Catholic schools, eleven million people signed a petition in protest. The policy was nevertheless carried through in 1959, and the battle between denominational and secularist interests took on a more bitter and inevitably more highly organised form. There was already a strong left-wing federation of parents and teachers linked to the primary teachers' trade union (SNI), but after the events of 1958-9 it reformed its organisation and broadened its base, swallowed up some smaller sympathetic organisations, encouraged school level groupings, and had strong separate sections for primary, secondary and technical interests countrywide. Under the presidency of Jean Cornec from 1956 to 1980, this Fédération des Conseils de Parents d'Elèves became the largest parents' organisation, with the equally vociferous organisation of Catholic school parents, the Union National des Associations de Parents d'Eléves and the Fédération des Parents d'Elèves de l'Enseignement Public, a moderate-right small organisation of the lycée parents, joining in the national debate.

There was a thriving system of parent councils in the Catholic schools before the events of 1968 brought in their wake a national participatory structure. The student riots of that year sparked off a general strike and a deepening political crisis. After the general election the chosen policy was a move to ordered participation, not what de Gaulle graphically called the chienlit of violent protest. The outcome was the Loi Haby, which in 1975 consolidated and refined a series of earlier measures designed to provide participatory councils, at first only in higher education and secondary schools, but in 1975 extended to the whole education system. Secondary schools each have a council with equal representation of staff, parents, students and community, while primary schools have elected parent councils and teachers' councils meeting in joint session. All schools also have a system of class councils, a feature of continental structures which seems to have been on the whole very viable.

The new system was intended to establish harmony, not institutionalise conflict. The councils have concentrated on pastoral matters and school clubs, transport, health and safety, and so on. With only 10 per cent of the curriculum under school control, the scope for discussing educational matters is very limited. Between 1975 and 1981 this led to a certain amount of frustration, with familiar talk about the system merely strengthening the position of heads and giving the councils rubber-stamping functions, preoccupying itself with trivia. One recurring grievance was that parents could not get paid time off to attend meetings, and this was one genuine reform to come out of the euphoria of 1981, since M. Mitterand redeemed a pledge to fund parents' attendance. Whether any other lasting improvements have emerged from the activity of the early Eighties remains to be seen, but there has certainly been a great deal of rhetoric about decentralisation and curriculum reform to overcome the alienation of young people. As I have already observed, the plan to integrate the denominational schools was frustrated by passionate protests from the Catholic lobby, and tension between the contending parents' groups remains acute. One source of conflict, as in Australia, is that denominational schools appoint their own staff, while government schools do not, and in both countries this not only sharpens the envious feelings of the secularist lobby, but inhibits the evolution of a school-level partnership. But the parent voice remains a powerful one in French politics.

In AUSTRALIA perhaps the first thing to note is that a country-wide organisation of state school parents is given considerable financial assistance by both federal and state governments, and as already stated three of its prominent campaigners have reached high office, one as Minister of Education in the Hawke government. The Australian Council of State School Organisations, being like the NCPTA school-based in its membership, but having a feeling much more like CASE in its strong campaigning thrust, its ideological commitment to the public sector, and many of its daily preoccupations, has the use of premises in Canberra rent-free, and a grant sufficient to employ an executive officer and an information officer. Communication over such vast distances would not be possible at all without assistance: internal air fares are high in relation to other living costs. ACSSO produces impressive publications, comments promptly and pertinently on events and organises communication among its affiliates in the states. It is represented on a number of important national bodies. Its freedom to comment on government policies seems, to say the least of it, to be in no way inhibited by its dependence on government funding. Every state has a corresponding organisation, Victoria and South Australia two each, and one soon gets used to VICSSO,

WACSSO, and similar acronyms tripping off the tongue. Everywhere the local organisation of state school parents' organisations or clubs enjoys some support from the state government. At the very least it is the cost of a part-time organiser, and at best - in Western Australia - it is a suite in the modern Department of Education building with staff, postage, telephones and even transport on the house.

Parents' organisations at school level often seem even more 'domesticated' than ours, with strong social and fund-raising emphasis, sometimes a three generation flavour even, a lot of cake-making and, since there are no officially-provided school meals, often heavy involvement in lunchtime catering. Their influence in curriculum matters is rarely great, yet they feed into a state and national level network which has a strong sense of commitment to government schools, campaigns vigorously against government subsidised alternatives, and fights the same market-place philosophy as besets the UK. There too one hears talk of vouchers and other forms of privatisation, of excessive reliance on parent funding, and other divisive policies and how parents can fight them. Even more remarkable, parents participate in large numbers in training programmes financed by the government but organised by parents' groups and designed to help parents play a more effective role in support of their children at school. It was striking to meet many quite ordinary parents who had come a thousand miles or more to attend such a course at the weekend, as I did in the Northern Territory for instance, and I also participated in such courses in Canberra, in New South Wales, in a steel community in South Australia, a brown coal producing area north of Melbourne, and in Queensland.

Supporters of government schools in Australia have formidable barriers to the high-status public service which is their objective. Only 75 per cent of Australian parents use the state system, but of the 25 per cent in non-government establishments, only 5 per cent are in what we should in the UK regard as independent schools, the rest being denomi-national schools, some of them poor both materially and in their curriculum range. Like the North Americans and French, the Australians have started from a strongly secu-larist standpoint, and do not feel that it is right for govern-ments to get involved in religious education. The one subject UK state schools must by law teach is the one theirs may not.

Yet it is clear from the experience of France and Australia that if in a democracy a significant number of parents want this dimension in education, the state will end up funding it in one way or another, and the way in which those countries have done this divides ordinary parents and teachers, removes church schools from normal public account-abilities, and forces government schools to fight some very hard battles. Firstly they must contend with falling rolls when there is no public constraint even on the opening of new private schools with guaranteed government funding. Secondly they must defend the broad curriculum against competition which panders to all the pressures for basics, uniform and punishment. Thirdly they must suffer the demands made upon their own parents to supplement what public funds provide, asking them for money for books, paper, art materials: payments which often, with all the other calls made on parents, come to more than the fees of a subsidised private school offering a very limited curriculum. They are not helped by the fact that in general the basic law of education in the Australian states guarantees parents free instruction, not education, so it is not illegal to charge for certain extras. Above all, the system of appointing teachers in Australian government schools, by the stateload as I unkindly used to describe it on my visit, offers the opposition a present on a plate, since what uncommitted Australian parents will fight to maintain, and sacrifice to buy, is the option of schools which choose their staff and whose staff choose them, with the stability they think this brings.

Who can blame them? I must return to this theme because of its relevance to the effective participation of parents, but here it is merely one more way in which parents and teachers in government schools fight with one hand behind their backs for the prestige and health of the public sector.

The arrangements under which parents share in decisions at school level vary from state to state. There are systems with statutory councils in all schools in the Australian Capital Territory, in Victoria and in South Australia. In Queensland, the Northern Territory and Tasmania legislation provides for school councils but they are not compulsory. Development of participatory structures has been more patchy in Western Australia, while in New South Wales, where the teachers' unions are particularly powerful and the state government highly centralised, there has been a history of resistance to devolving authority to schools and, where decentralisation has been attempted, a favoured model seems to be top-down rather than bottom-up form of participation.

However, over most of the Australian schools' system there has been a strong movement towards school councils with representation of parents, teachers and older students. The councils have a mixture of advisory and decision-making functions. In the Australian Capital Territory they have been part of the system ever since the ACT acquired its independence and its own Schools Authority in 1973, and this is a most interesting example of a structure created rather than evolved, where the councils have some decisions devolved to them in a rational sequence by a Schools Authority which itself has representatives of teachers, parents and the public. In Victoria where there has always been a particularly strong parents' voice, there is a long-established structure to which the state Department of Education has also been strongly committed and which has been promoted even more vigorously since the Labour Party won the elections of 1982. In Victoria too parents are involved in education policy at state level.

A visitor hears all the familiar complaints all over Australia about devolution to schools working mainly to increase professional authority, about lack of effective curriculum discussion, about parents being poor relations in a participatory structure. Yet I believe they have made great advances there considering that there is no tradition of devolution, in a vast country with large empty spaces, and at least there is acceptance of responsibility by government for parents' need to organise and to have help in becoming better informed. There is no doubt where one should look for the two biggest obstacles to further advance: to the government funding of private schools, which creates so many difficulties for state schools in the competitive situation, and divides parents and teachers; and to the way in which teachers and for the most part principals are appointed. The system started with the best of motives, that of ensuring that a reliable and fair supply of teachers reached remote areas. The good results of taking the needs of these areas seriously are plain to see in the lack of great differences in accents and the apparent confidence of country children in their comparable life chances, though I realise that the reasons for this are more complex. However, the tail has now been allowed to wag the dog, and many people have, or think they have, vested interests in maintaining the central state direction of teacher supply. The teachers seem to think it is fair that they should occupy a numerical place on a list related to their qualifications, length of service and competence, but that in return they should have little or no choice of where they go. The needs of remote areas could be safeguarded by a much less rigorous degree of direction combined with incentives.

I have already spoken of the effect this system has on the competitive situation of government schools, but it also seems to me to have a major inhibiting effect on educational advance by the lighthouse method and on the development of school partnerships. Until recently it was generally the case that a principal would not be selected at school level and would normally have little or no say in the choice of staff. This seems to make it very difficult for a school to develop a distinctive style which is reasonably durable and which if successful can influence others. Heads doing something special, of whom I met many, live in daily fear that staff changes will bring unsympathetic elements. One head in Queensland was breathing a sigh of relief the day I was there because 21 pupils had been added to his roll the day after rather than the day before the annual census, since they would have taken the school into a higher group to which his place in the pecking order did not entitle him, and he could have been on his way, with his school-age family, anywhere in that huge state. Yet his school was a model of everything I admired, all the relationships right, a sense of unity and purpose for which he had no doubt worked a long time, especially with a staff he had not chosen. I became acutely aware, while I was there, of how much it had meant to me as a school governor that there was a mutual commitment between chooser and chosen, and how responsible I personally felt for supporting and defending against all enemies a headteacher who had wanted to come to us and whom we had wanted. When a school was working very hard at partnerships, it seemed especially important that there should be a chance to recruit like-minded colleagues, so that it could develop steadily and be seen to work. I suppose I felt this especially in the schools which had been assisted under one of the Commonwealth Government schemes for direct funding to achieve certain goals. Following the critical Karmel Report on Australian education in 1973, the Schools Commission was established with massive funding to support a number of objectives, including innovation, overcoming disadvantage, community involvement; and the support which was given to a deeply disadvantaged school, for instance, was conditional on the involvement of the community in the project. These were some of the most striking schools I visited, an interesting parallel with the federally assisted schools in the USA which commentators say display the best participatory councils. How hard it must have been for a head to maintain the quality of what went on with so little chance to influence staffing. Yet things are slowly beginning to change.

School councils, as they inevitably develop greater curriculum involvement, find the logic of having a part in staff appointments inescapable. Indeed in the last few years, there have been some welcome moves in some states towards school level selection of headteachers, with predictably a growing interest by those headteachers in having some say in staff selection, a development which has been resisted by teachers on the whole. As one might expect, these developments have taken place in areas where school partnerships have been furthest advanced.

Conclusion

I have tried in describing what happens in other countries to record what seem to be significant facts without attempting to see too much of a pattern. One obvious comment is that where there is strong central control of the curriculum, school level councils will suffer frustration about the limits of debate, but parents' organisations are more likely to develop some national political influence through their pressure on government policies. Teachers may be more willing to accept partnership at school level when they have themselves little curricular freedom, and the results can be quite good in pastoral areas. Any devolution of power to schools may well in the short run benefit professionals more than parents. Where there is a substantial denominational sector under different control, parent activity is likely to be more political and to exhibit stronger conflict.

If schools are to be more accountable, parents must be helped to self-confidence. The symbolism as expressed in legal rights, both individual and corporate, in government support with the practical tasks of organising, communicating and educating, and in good habits of consultation on education policies, is itself very important for establishing such a basis of confidence.

No single country displays all these good features. Denmark is distinguished by its firm foundations for partnership between individual families and their schools; France and West Germany, Australia and New Zealand, the USA and Canada, all have substantial, if not universal legal provision for parents to be represented as of right in school level councils; Australia is perhaps most outstanding in the assistance it gives to parent organisations to run their affairs and particularly in the support it gives to parent education; France above all displays how parents can become a force with which all national governments must reckon in framing and implementing education policies. In most of the countries we have looked at there are structural barriers to an effective whole-school partnership, whether in the form of strong central control of the curriculum, or in the arrangements for appointing staff to state schools, or in the very bitter conflicts which can arise from a large denominational sector only partially under public control.

In the face of such major problems one might conclude that there were good foundations in the UK with schools which still enjoy some independence, with its decentralisation of staff appointments, and its integrated dual system - for a genuine dialogue at school level involving all the partners in the process. One could even hope that in time the parent voice might acquire in this process a confidence and maturity which would win a hearing in national debate. The chapters which follow, with their emphasis on parents' role in school government, may promote consideration of such possible developments. It is by no means an easy road, nor is success a foregone conclusion, but I think that in our circumstances it is the most hopeful way forward.

Chapter Seven

AGENTS OF ACCOUNTABILITY: GOVERNORS BEFORE 1975

It was, of course, in 1975 that the Taylor Committee was set up to look at the arrangements for school government, and I intend to review the period leading up to that event. First, however, to help with the perspective, I want to look at one day a decade later, when history, like a drowning man's life, was reflected in some deep and dangerous waters.

A LONG TIME GETTING IT RIGHT

It was autumn 1985, and the first ever governors' training day in Manchester, first ever school governors, indeed, in the accepted sense, for until the 1980 Education Act required them, Manchester had no individual governing bodies. The LEA had resisted all but the letter of previous Education Acts by making a sub-committee of the Education Committee the governing body for all the city's schools.

At lunch time a single line of participants queued patiently around the hall to ask me things too private for the questions session. This in itself was a novelty, for normally at these affairs people push in, talk at once, don't mind who hears the most intimate details of their battles with the established order. One of them, when his turn came, only wanted to make a comment:- 'I'm glad you said there had been school governors around for six hundred years, because we've got some of them on our board.' Oh dear, so new, and already so familiar! To be fair to the LEA, the whole occasion exuded conscientious enthusiasm. Manchester, coming to it late, seemed keen to make it a success.

It was hard for them to have to baptise their new governors in the fires of Poundswick. That, you will remember, was the school where staff had been on strike because some teachers were suspended for refusing to teach a group of pupils who had defaced walls with obscene graffiti. The governors had supported the head in excluding the pupils, but the LEA had ordered reinstatement. As I was looking for the course venue, I met a parent governor from that school. Her daughter, only 11, was a totally innocent victim, and had scarcely attended school that term. That's really tough, I said, mother to mother. Yes, she replied, it was very tough, but we must support the teachers, mustn't we? Inside the hall where the course was beginning, feelings ran high on this issue, which had been widely misunderstood. Manchester, starting late, had learned from the experience of others, and in its Articles of Government had given the LEA the last word on exclusions. Those governors, however, said that they saw in Poundswick evidence of what they had already suspected, that as soon as a really big issue came up they would be ignored. In that moment I realised not only how fast these new governors were making up for lost time, but how far we still had to go.

EARLY DAYS

I remember being astonished, doing my homework for the Taylor Committee, to discover that there had been governors for six hundred years. Winchester School dates back to 1382, and to provide for some independent oversight of its affairs, the Warden and two Fellows of New College Oxford were to visit annually 'with not more than six horses' (splendid that vulgar display was not encouraged!) and were charged 'to scrutinise the teaching and the progress in school of the scholars ... and the quality of the food provided for the same ... and shall correct or reform anything needing correction or reform.' (1)

By the fifteenth century laymen were commonly involved in the establishment and management of schools, and it was not unusual for schools to be founded by wealthy individuals or guilds, and the management to be shared between laymen and clerics. A good example was Oswestry School, founded in 1404. A more radical departure was marked by the foundation of two schools (one by John Abbott in 1443 and one by John Colet in 1512) for which the Mercers' Company were made trustees. Erasmus referred to this decision by his friend John Colet, saying that 'there is no certainty in human affairs, but for his part he found less corruption in such a body of citizens than in any other order or degree of mankind.' (2) The next step was to make an assorted group of laymen trustees, and this was the form adopted for the grammar school founded in Macclesfield in 1503 by Sir John Percyval, a Merchant Taylor, moved to action by the fact that 'God of his habundant grace hath sent and daily sendeth to the inhabitants there copyious plentye of children, to whose lernynge and bryngyng forth in conynge and vertue right fewe teachers and Scholemaisters be in that contre.' (3)

Many schools were founded from the proceeds of the

expansion of industry and commerce which followed the Reformation, and a few with a mathematical bias emerged to meet the needs of navigation. Towards the end of the seventeenth century a number of Nonconformist dissenting schools were founded in response to a demand from the emerging middle classes for something more practical than Latin, Greek and ritual, while a century later a huge variety of private schools were founded in London and the large industrial towns. Thus over four hundred years a wide range of schools for older pupils had grown up, most exhibiting in some degree the principle of trusteeship. The geographical pattern, however, now bore no relation to the need, following the great movement of population as a result of the Industrial Revolution. The quality of the schools varied enormously, and in many cases the intentions of their original founders or benefactors had become obscured by time and the neglect, it seems, of uninterested and absentee trustees.

Anxieties over these issues led to two major Commissions of Enquiry, the Clarendon Commission on the nine public schools in 1861 and the Taunton Commission on the grammar, proprietary and private schools in 1864. The reports of both Commissions resulted in legislation before the end of the decade, the Public Schools Act and the Endowed Schools Act. The Taunton Commission especially found evidence of how time and changing circumstances had caused schools to drift away from their original purposes and uncovered many abuses, particularly that of the missing trustee. The Commissions both produced the recommendation that all schools should have governing bodies, and the pattern they established is the one which was later taken as the model for the public sector, unchanged in essentials. They went into considerable detail about the functions of governors and their relationship to the headteacher. They attached importance to having governors who lived reasonably near the school, who were interested and who had no pecuniary involvement.

The reports (4) of these Commissions make extremely interesting reading for any student of school government today. The Clarendon Commission described governors as 'the guardian and trustee of the permanent interests of the school' who should include 'men conversant with the world, with the requirements of active life and with the progress of literature and science.' Their powers should include the management of school property and the appointment and dismissal of the Head Master. On discipline and teaching it was recommended (5) that the Head Master be given as much freedom as possible, and in particular to have charge of 'the division of classes, the school hours and school books ... the measures necessary for maintaining discipline and the general direction of the course and methods, which it is his duty to conduct and his business to understand thoroughly.' On the content and balance of the curriculum, however, the Commissions gave clear responsibility to governors:

> The introduction of a new branch of study, or the
> suppression of one already established, and the relative
> degree of weight to be assigned to different branches,
> are matters respecting which a better judgement is likely
> to be formed by such a body of governors as we have
> suggested ... than by a single person, however able
> and accomplished. ... What should be taught, and what
> importance should be given to each subject are therefore
> questions for the Governing Body; how to teach is a
> question for the Head Master. (5)

These quotations are from the Clarendon Commission's
report, but the principles were later followed closely in the
report of the Taunton Commission. In fact they had infinitely
more significance in relation to the Taunton field of enquiry,
since, quite apart from the much larger number of schools
covered - a thousand perhaps - and the greater variety, it
was here that the problems arising from the haphazard development of schools and the great changes in the character and
needs of their users had become acute: not only their geographical pattern but crucially for this purpose their curriculum had become inappropriate. There was thus a real job
for governors to do if they were to determine 'what should be
taught and what importance should be given to each subject',
since as the Taunton Commission put it, there were schools
which 'give undue prominence to what no parents within their
reach desire their children to learn.' The task was 'to adapt
the schools to the work which is now required of them, by
prescribing such a course of study as is demanded by the
needs of the country.' (6)

Some of this sounds very modern. Two things stand out.
The first is that the current concern about governors'
'intrusion' into the curriculum, and the presentation of the
1986 Education Act as daring and revolutionary, rest on the
assumption that the teacher's territory is sanctified by history and law. That assumption is unfounded. The convention
that the curriculum is a professional preserve is a recent
development and arises from the neglect of that responsibility
by those who are supposed to exercise it, and who have been
responsible since the earliest days and through a steady line
of legislation. The second is that the notion of public
responsibility for education goes back much further than
public education itself. In the period we have been considering, only a tiny proportion of the population received
schooling, yet there was intense concern about how the
communal interest in an activity of such manifest importance
could best be safeguarded. Nobody ever spoke of it as a
transaction, no suggestion was ever made that its well-being
could safely be left to those who freely embarked on it, or

that threats to its quality and suitability were not of concern to all. In this respect, as I have suggested in an earlier chapter, perhaps some of our ancestors were wiser than our present rulers and leaders of opinion.

As we leave the Taunton Commission, we are close to the time when our lawmakers were beginning to consider how schooling could be extended to all the people and how the gaps in provision could be filled. Before going on, however, we must step back a few years to look at the somewhat different history of elementary education up to this point. This also demonstrates the continuity of the trusteeship idea, but not in quite such a long or straight line as the public and endowed schools, which is why I took these first.

Chaucer tells of the song schools, and a few of the early grammar schools had small schools for the younger children attached to them, but until the eighteenth century there was no elementary education on a significant scale. A great many schools were founded during that century as charity schools, which owed their finance either to endowment or to private subscription. Their aim was to instil God-fearing attitudes in little children before they all too soon entered the rough world of work, thus protecting them against the sinful tendencies of the urban poor and incidentally also against the blandishments of Rome. The trustees of one of the most famous, Grey Coat Hospital School, met weekly on a routine basis, and at quarterly intervals tested the standards of work in the school. They personally supervised the tailoring of the grey coats, gave the mothers the yarn to knit stockings, and cajoled their wives into making the caps. Such dedication!

The charity school movement eventually lost its momentum: a feature of its decline, alas, was mismanagement and misappropriation. The responsibility for providing elementary education was taken up in a renewed outburst of reforming zeal by the National Society and the British and Foreign Schools Society, who embarked on their educational activities in 1811 and 1814 respectively. The National Society's aim was a school in every parish. Between them the two Societies provided schools and trained and paid teachers. There was a huge expansion in the number of children in school; indeed, it doubled between 1818 and 1828, by which time the Societies were coming to realise that the task was too vast to be accomplished by voluntary effort alone and were exploring the possibility of government aid. In 1833 Parliament voted the first grant from public funds for education, a sum of £20,000 to be disbursed through voluntary agencies. The conditions of grant were stringent and a Committee of the Privy Council was established to oversee the arrangements.

This Committee of the Privy Council on Education came into being in 1839. It was the forerunner of the Board of Education, which in 1944 became the Ministry of Education and in 1964 the Department of Education and Science. The conditions of grant aid were (a) that the school should be open to inspection and (b) that it should be conducted in accordance with an approved scheme of management (7). Both conditions were the subject of some resistance from denominations, who saw them as interference.

Thus from the beginning there was firmly established the principle that public funding demanded accountability, locally through boards of managers, centrally through inspection. Indeed in the public and endowed schools, as we have already seen, the idea of trusteeship was so strong that these were required to have governors from the 1860s even though no public subsidy was involved.

In very small parishes the parson was to be sole manager of the new grant-aided schools, unless and until the Bishop directed the election of a committee of subscribers. In other cases there were three management models, each giving the managers oversight of the conduct of the school, care of its premises, responsibility for staff appointments and trusteeship of its funds. The parson was always a manager, and others were elected or co-opted from those church members who also lived locally and subscribed to funds. The electors also had to be subscribers. Similar models were evolved for the Roman Catholics and the Wesleyans.

No account of the period leading up to the introduction of universal free elementary education would be complete without a reference to the infamous system known to most people as 'payment by results'. There had been some dissatisfaction with the standards of the grant-aided church schools, varying degrees of acceptance of any kind of government intervention, and suggestions that some managers were not carrying out their duties very conscientiously. Following an enquiry by the Newcastle Commission in 1858-61, the system of paying grants was tidied up and all payments went to the managers - previously some grants had gone direct to teachers. The managers had control of the finance, and its release was dependent on pupil attendance and tests of pupils' basic skills by HMI. Local fund-raising was encouraged by relating grants also to the school's success in attracting subscriptions.

These arrangements were very unpopular and did not last long. It became increasingly clear that the improvement of education needed more radical approaches.

The Education Act 1870 (the Forster Act) aimed to provide elementary schools for the whole population. Where the voluntary schools were insufficient to meet the need, school boards were to be elected with power to raise local rates, supplemented by government grant, to fill the gaps in provision. School boards were to delegate to school managing boards all their functions except that of raising funds.

In 1886 the Government set up the Cross Commission to review the working of the 1870 legislation, and it devoted a whole chapter in its report of 1888 to school management. This stressed that education was concerned with character formation as well as passing examinations, and that therefore managers had a role beyond that of oversight 'inasmuch by their active sympathy with, and kindly influence over, individual scholars, they may do much to mould their character, and help to make them good and useful members of society' (8). The report emphasised the need for frequent visiting and personal involvement. Among qualities important in a school manager were interest, some knowledge of education, sympathy, breadth of view and ability to work with others harmoniously. Enough leisure was also thought vital (9). The report criticised those school boards, mostly in large cities, which had resisted delegation to managers. The Commission found the board school managers more efficient in the narrow managerial sense but those of voluntary schools more committed to the school and harmonious with those in it (10). There was a preponderance of the leisured and moneyed classes among both groups as the Commission found them. Women were under-represented (11). The Commission thought parent managers would be a good idea as long as they were not preponderant (12), but there was no great support for this recommendation and an amendment to secure parent representation was defeated during the passage of the 1902 Act.

The Bryce Commission of 1894 was set up to consider how best to improve provision of secondary education. It also looked at the governors of secondary schools, recommended their continued existence with a general supervisory role and with representation of the local authorities in future - there was as yet no government funding of secondary schools. It considered that in schools attended by girls the governing body should include some women.

THE FRAMEWORK OF EDUCATION 1902 - 1980

1902 - The Growth of Local Responsibility

The 1870 Act was of course the foundation of the partnership between central government and locally-elected bodies in the provision of schooling. It placed upon local people the responsibility for determining the needs of their area. It gave them the power to raise money to meet those needs and established the principle that central government would honour those judgements by augmenting local funds from taxation. On these foundations the Act of 1902 was to construct a national education system already recognisable as an ancestor of our own. It established local education authorities - a rather larger number than today - with responsibility for both elementary and secondary education, including the

105

provision of new secondary schools. Secondary school pupils' numbers quadrupled in the twenty years which followed. The new authorities took over the old board schools provided under the 1870 Act, and were made responsible for the secular curriculum of the voluntary schools. The managers of the voluntary schools continued to appoint the teachers but the new local education authorities paid them. The authorities also took over the maintenance of the buildings of voluntary schools, though the managers continued to be liable for improvements and any repairs not attributable to fair wear and tear. Although managers selected the teachers, their choice was subject to a veto by the local authority on educational grounds, and no teacher could be dismissed without the local authority's agreement save for a teacher specifically appointed to give religious instruction.

Public elementary schools were to have managing bodies consisting of four local authority and two minor authority nominees. Voluntary schools were to have two-thirds of managers representing the foundation and one-third representing the public, these to be appointed by the local education authority and the minor authority. Secondary schools were to have governors (the different terminology persisted until the 1980 Act) appointed according to schemes approved by the Board of Education, following very closely the pattern established in the public and endowed schools by the legislation of the 1860s. A recurring theme in the words of Board of Education spokesmen was the responsibility of the managers or governors to protect the individuality and variety of schools against too much bureaucratic interference - how modern that sounds! Sir Robert Morant, the first Permanent Secretary to the Board of Education, described that role as to 'ensure living interest in the school' and provide 'a real supervision of the conduct and progress of the school.'

Several large city authorities defied the requirement that they should delegate functions to local managers and governors: Leeds, Manchester, Birmingham, Bradford and Hull. They were in dispute with the Board on the matter for many years, and hostilities even at one time reached threats to withhold grant. As we have seen, it was to take two more major Education Acts to resolve the issue in at least one of these cities.

1944 - A Vision for Reconstruction

At the end of the Second World War the education service, despite massive practical problems, nurtured some shining new ideals. The task of reconstructing the system in the most simple operational sense - roofs over heads, enough teachers to fill the heads - was big enough. It is worth recalling that for a time a new school was opened every day. Yet in retrospect even this enterprise is dwarfed by the less visible one of establishing an education service as broad as it was long, providing appropriate opportunities throughout life, removing old inequalities and opening new horizons.

To understand the drive behind such a major endeavour one must think of the way people had lived for five years. A significant proportion of our people had left their homes and their class, and many for the first time in their lives had had the chance - whether through effort or boredom, proximity to others or loneliness, dull tasks or danger, fear, pain or the daily presence of death - to think about what had been and what might be. Evacuees left inner city slums for comfortable county towns, or prosperous homes for mining valley and mill lane. Public school boys worked in the mines, and girls from finishing schools on the land. Those who had known no hardship shared discomfort, squalor and danger with those who could not write, and some who had been at the bottom of the heap found themselves with authority to command people and events. Women worked, and not just in sections of society where women had always worked. People from all walks of life huddled together in shelters, lay in neighbouring hospital beds, or together mourned their sons. The comradeship of the barracks or the queue, the equality of the ration book or the graveside, the sharing of soap, the borrowing of wedding dresses, extra clothing coupons for tall children, and the special care of babies, all combined to push down the walls of the tidy compartments in which we had lived. Can one wonder that some emerged with a desire to change the world, and that the first requirement of the new world was to accept that we might have enhanced aspirations for our children? It is scarcely remarkable that it took more than a quarter of a century to come within sight of those great, but then uncontentious goals. Nor should we be surprised that the full realisation of their significance has been slow to dawn, and that in our time we are seeing in some quarters a determination to retreat.

Remember that before 1944 most people had only elementary education to 14, with a fairly rigorous grounding in the three Rs and religious observance, a bit of history and geography, and some practice in filling inkwells, which at least was preparation for repetitive jobs to come. These were the children. The only adolescents and young adults to receive full-time education were volunteers, given the opportunity to volunteer either by reason of their ability or their parents' ability to pay. In either case they were likely to understand what it was for, to be motivated to succeed, and to have home support.

The 1944 Act not only established universal free secondary education to 15 and later 16 - though not yet for all abilities under one roof; it also invented primary education. This sounds obvious, but we often forget, not only for how short a time in the perspective of history we have had all young adults to educate, but also how recently primary education has emerged with distinctive aims, its search for a relevance of its own scarcely begun. These are important factors in the task of winning public understanding of the nature and needs of the service.

In structural terms the 1944 Act laid the foundations of the 'national service locally administered' as we know it, and the partnership between central and local government as we may soon cease to know it. In fact we have seen that some of the essentials of that partnership, the duty of locally elected bodies to determine their own needs, their right to raise and spend local rates to meet those needs, and the general intention of central government to accept those judgements and assist that expenditure, were established as long ago as 1870 and not disturbed until the Local Government Acts of 1980 and 1981. But the 1944 Act brought both primary and secondary education under the same management for the first time, and also established a harmony if not an identity of purpose between the county and voluntary sectors of education.

The role of the Minister was to maintain the loose legal framework within which education was provided: to establish duties and responsibilities for the various parties concerned with its provision (parents, LEAs and school managers and governors); to regulate the size and shape of the service in a very broad sense through the approval of local development plans (now defunct), through control of capital expenditure, and through planning of teacher training capacity; to exercise judicial functions in respect of certain defined disagreements; to bestow powers (as distinct from duties) on LEAs and others; to provide educational services, or assistance to individuals, over and above what was required by law; and finally to promote the quality of the service, through inspection of schools, through the support given by HMI not only to schools but to general ideas and policies, and through the promotion of research. No more direct influence over what was taught in schools was vested in the Minister by the 1944 Act, and the only subject which schools were legally obliged to include in the curriculum was religious education.

The Act placed upon parents the duty to see that their children received efficient full-time education suited to age, ability and aptitude, and placed upon LEAs the duty to ensure the provision and maintenance of schools sufficient in number and facilities to meet the needs of their area. No charge was to be made for any education provided in schools maintained by LEAs. Theirs was also the responsibility for the curriculum of county schools and the secular curriculum in voluntary primary schools. In voluntary aided secondary schools the curriculum was determined by the governors. The LEA appointed and paid teachers in county and controlled schools (the latter retaining some say in appointments of teachers for religious education), but in voluntary aided schools the teaching staff, though paid by the LEA, were appointed by the managers or governors. LEAs were required to delegate responsibility for individual schools to boards of managers or governors.

Before considering the detail of such delegation, it is worth noting that the balance of responsibility for the education service described in the two preceding paragraphs has remained virtually undisturbed since 1944, despite subsequent legislation, including that of 1980 and 1986. This makes more dramatic the proposals in 1987-8 to impose a national curriculum; to remove certain functions from LEAs; to allow schools to detach themselves completely from LEA control, and to legalise payment by parents for certain educational services which under a strict interpretation of the 1944 Act should have been free.

School Government from 1944 to 1980

We now come to the framework within which schools were governed for forty years - the 1980 Act only took full effect in September 1985 - and the experience which still shapes the attitudes of most LEA officers, heads, teachers and parents now involved in the service. They are important attitudes: it is as well, as the surgeon might say, to identify that which we have to remove.

The requirements of the 1944 Act on the government of schools are contained in Sections 17 to 21. All primary schools had to have boards of managers, secondary schools boards of governors. Their constitution was to be set out in Instruments of Management and Government, which in the case of county schools were made by the LEA and in the case of voluntary schools by the Minister. Primary schools had to have a minimum of six members, but not even a minimum size was laid down for secondary schools. In county primary schools where there was a minor authority, one-third of the managers were to be appointed by that authority and the remainder by the LEA. Otherwise all county school boards' members were appointed by LEAs. In voluntary aided schools two-thirds of managers or governors were appointed by the foundation and one-third by the LEA (with again a share for minor authorities, if any, in primary schools). In voluntary controlled schools these proportions were reversed, one-third foundation, two-thirds LEA (with minor authority representation in primary schools).

The responsibilities of managers were to be set out in Rules of Management (made by the LEA) and of governors in Articles of Government, made by the LEA (but subject to the approval of the Minister) in county secondary schools and by the Minister in voluntary secondary schools. Functions were not covered in detail in the Act at all, but in 1945 the Department of Education and Science issued a model (in the form of a schedule to Administrative Memorandum No. 25 of 26 January 1945) which served as guidance to LEAs in making the Rules and Articles for which they were responsible. These model Articles suggested that governors be required to inspect the school premises and report on their condition to the LEA; that they share in the process of budgeting for the school and, jointly with the LEA, in the selection of the headteachers; that they be responsible, with the headteacher, for the selection of other teaching staff; that they have power to grant occasional holidays; and that they have 'the general direction of the conduct and curriculum of the school'. Local arrangements did of course vary, but most kept close to the general lines of the model.

In voluntary aided schools the nature of the settlement with the churches on which the 1944 Act was based gave their managers and governors an essentially different role. They were - and still are - the employers of the head and staff, though the LEA are paymasters, and formally at least it is still governors who appoint and dismiss, subject to certain LEA vetos. (In voluntary controlled schools, where the foundation has no financial liability and all costs are met by the LEA, the managers and governors retained rights only in respect of the appointment and dismissal of teachers appointed to give religious instruction.) Managers and governors of voluntary aided schools also had, and continue to have, more control over the admission of pupils and the use to which premises are put outside school hours than those of county schools.

Section 20 of the 1944 Act allowed the grouping of one or more schools under a single body of managers or governors.

The Act gave no guidance as to the kind of people whom the LEA might appoint as managers or governors. Perhaps, with hindsight, one would say that this was its greatest weakness. The Act's provisions on school governance were an attempt to graft firmly on to the state system of education a model which had been devised for the public schools, and in which the Victorian figure of the 'local worthy' loomed large. Perhaps this model was unsuitable for a service in which very large numbers were compulsorily involved. Perhaps it was unrealistic to think that a few hundred thousand well-motivated and suitable citizens could be found from outside the schools who would with a minimum of guidance offer the kind of oversight and support which would make them, in the sense intended by all those who thought about the matter on and off for centuries, agents of the schools' accountability to society. Perhaps it was inevitable that managers and governors either became meaningless appendages of the schools or mere tools of the providing authority, site agents, as it were, of the contractor. One thing is certain: they were incapable, as organised in the Sixties, of responding to a new

awareness of the importance of parental support to the success of children and of schools or to the increasing emphasis
placed on the rights of the consumer in all aspects of our
lives. They had no role in the growth of partnership between
teachers and parents, chronicled in earlier chapters, in which
one can find the embryo of a new mutual accountability for a
shared process. Whatever model of accountability one chooses,
the market place model, the professional/client model, or the
partnership model, the 1944 structures proved quite incapable
of adaptation to changing needs.

A MORIBUND SYSTEM

Whether there was ever any life in it, even at the very
beginning, is open to doubt. During the late Forties and the
Fifties the main emphasis was on rebuilding the service for
greatly increased child numbers after wartime destruction and
neglect. The years more people remember, when we think of
school governors, whether as teachers, parents or pupils, are
the Sixties, when the system reached a low point in public
esteem.

The period 1965 to 1969 is in fact chronicled in a
detailed study financed by the Department of Education and
Science, and undertaken by Baron and Howell of the Department of Educational Administration in the University of
London (13). The study, which covered only England, revealed a sorry state of affairs in the 78 county boroughs and
45 counties which there were at that time. The concession in
Section 20 of the Act, which allowed grouping, had been used
to an extent which went far beyond what one presumes to be
its authors' intentions. In the boroughs only a quarter, and
in the counties just under half, of the authorities had individual boards for their schools, and in a quarter of the
boroughs a single body acted as managers for all the primary
schools and a single body as governors for all the secondary
schools. It was quite common, in urban areas particularly, for
all the members of managing and governing boards to be
councillors, or at least party activists. The boards had some
involvement in the appointment of heads and senior staff
almost everywhere - horrifying when one considers the limited
knowledge of individual schools many must have had. Generally their involvement in financial matters was slight:
confined to formally receiving and approving estimates drawn
up elsewhere. As for the 'general direction of the conduct
and curriculum of the school', this was a dead letter almost
everywhere. Headteachers maintained that they had sole
responsibility for what was taught, though some reckoned to
keep governors informed. Even this was a farce where schools
were in large groups. Heads would queue up outside to
present reports, often were not allowed to stay for the dis-

cussion (if any!) or even to see the minutes. One can imagine that this was not conducive to quality in report writing.

Most professionals probably considered this sometimes comic, occasionally contemptible travesty of school-level democracy totally irrelevant to the education of children. Some were perhaps content to be undisturbed by any kind of external oversight, and the only complaints one heard were of political influence or incompetence in interviewing for appointments. One cannot blame teachers at the time for taking little interest in a system so lacking in life or relevance.

CHANGE IN THE AIR

By the late Sixties there were signs of ferment in this discredited system. The reasons were fairly easy to identify. The importance of parent support to the child in school was increasingly stressed. The Plowden Report (14), which appeared in 1967, incorporated the best-known research on this theme, but in fact the contemporary air was heavy with it. Indeed the recognition of the vital role of parents as individuals broadened naturally into the advocacy of parent help in and support for schools, and in turn into an increasing acceptance of the school as a community resource and responsibility. The PTA movement, already chronicled in Chapter Five, was growing in strength. Groups of concerned parents already active locally came together in 1962 as the Confederation for the Advancement of State Education, and by this time the Advisory Centre for Education was also thriving. The National Association of Managers and Governors came into being in 1970 with the express purpose of revitalising the ancient structure of school governance. Although it was not a year in which any dramatic national change in education law took place, 1969 seems in retrospect to have been an important year. In many countries there were student uprisings in 1968-9, followed by reforms of varying kinds in participatory structures. These were a response to impatience with authoritarian and paternalistic ways of thought, and to pressure for people to be more actively responsible in their own institutions. In our own country in that year the Maud Commission (15) reported on local government reform. Many LEAs were beginning to appoint parent governors, and Sheffield to reform school government radically in a way which was to be influential.

Comprehensive reorganisation was also a powerful agency of change. The concern of individual parents about their children's progress, at its peak in the secondary years, had been scattered to the four winds, geographically and socially, by the 11+. The 'chosen' might even have felt it was safe to relax, believing that their young would have the best, that they were safe in schools where the objectives were clearly understood by all concerned and where high motivation could be taken for granted. The parents of those who were not chosen often tragically lost heart and felt that no amount of support on their part could now make a difference. But when it came to pass that nearly all the youngsters in one neighbourhood went to the same school in these vital years, it seemed to parents much more important to make it their own, to be both vigilant and supportive. When even the illusion of choice had gone - and it always was illusory, of course, for those whom the system did not choose - influence suddenly became a lot more important. Thus many reforms of school government followed local reorganisation.

Although the restructuring of local government did not take place until 1974, the Maud Commission (15), which led to all those changes, reported in 1969, and had already stressed the importance of sound and community-based school government within authorities which would be fewer in number and in many cases much larger and more remote from their institutions. Indeed the stimulus to reform came not only from the fear of size and remoteness, but also from the catalytic process of merging authorities which had already begun to make some changes in school government with others which had not. The process was aided by a rising awareness of consumer needs and rights in all aspects of our lives, and a climate in which individual participation was a natural growth.

LOCAL REFORMS 1969 to 1975

The Baron and Howell survey already referred to was not published until 1974, a year in which the National Association of Governors and Managers was beginning an investigation, published by them in 1975. The changes which had taken place even while the earlier survey was being written up and printed were remarkable. By 1975, when the Taylor Committee began its work, at least two-thirds of LEAs had provided for some representation of parents and teachers on governing bodies. This was a very rapid response to some of the factors we have identified. In most cases the changes appear to have brought about only token involvement, and it would be quite misleading to suggest that there was any widespread development of school democracy or active redefinition of public trusteeship. Nevertheless in all nineteen LEAs visited by the Taylor Committee (See Annex B to Appendix A) there was evidence of fresh thinking about the role of governors and a conscious defence of the particular local interpretation of that role.

I shall look in some detail at Sheffield, which was one of the earliest LEAs to introduce reform, and which was a kindly light of leadership to me when I first became interested in the subject, and at Richmond-on-Thames, where a similar reform was achieved in response to public pressure rather than consciously planned. First, however, it is very interesting to look at how reform came about in Sheffield, not only because, in relation to the 1986, Education Act and its intended complete implementation by 1989 Sheffield was almost exactly twenty years ahead of its time, but also because events in Sheffield seem to give us the concentrated essence of that late Sixties ferment of thought about people and their institutions.

There was nothing to distinguish the Sheffield system from others until 1968. It produced its share of school governor horror stories: grouping, party political control, trivial rubber stamping operations. The Labour party had retained power, with only one short break, from 1926 to 1968, and in that year lost control of the city council, a dramatic event which to those concerned was the first indication that the old solid working class vote could not be taken for granted. Simmering under the surface there appears to have been widespread dissatisfaction for some time with the tight party management and paternalistic style of the Labour administration, particularly in the matter of housing policy and the management of local authority housing estates. There had been resentment about rent increases imposed without much explanation, about a system of rent rebates involving the hated means test, and about a general tendency to discourage any kind of questioning of council policy. People's limits of tolerance had been dangerously miscalculated. Indeed tenants' associations openly hostile to Labour had been appearing, but it took the crude shock from the ballot box to make the point that the workforce was changing, and the technician, the draughtsman, the instrument maker, would have to be wooed back if Labour was again to speak for organised labour in the city. It is incredible that all these years later there are so few signs of this lesson being learned in similar areas, and as yet little evidence that even the clear message conveyed by the outcome of the General Election of 1987 has been read by the Left nationally as it was read in Sheffield that year. Labour support has been sustained in the areas where the nature of employment and the class structure have changed little, but in more diversified working communities it has been a different story.

There was deep heart-searching in the Labour Party in Sheffield during its period out of office, and contemporary local newspapers contain evidence of much imaginative leadership. They went to the electorate in 1970 pledged to work for a more participatory style of local democracy, with encouragement to tenants' associations, consultation with these and other non-political support groups, and community-based individual governing boards for all schools.

As far as schools were concerned the new council certainly did a proper job. The grouped governing boards which

114

had existed up to 1970 had involved only 100 governors, all party activists, for all the city's schools. By the time the reform was complete, there were 5,000 school governors, of whom only a minority were LEA nominees. There were places for elected parents, teaching and non-teaching staff, and older pupils, while the wider community was represented through a broad range of organisations of a voluntary kind. Governors were encouraged to become actively involved in their schools, they were given clear and admirably vivid informative material, and their status was recognised by the way in which the LEA consulted them. They were offered an ambitious training programme in collaboration with the extra-mural department of the university. The political will to make it all work was luckily matched by the commitment of at least three enthusiasts among the senior staff of the education department and at least two at the university.

Many other LEAs began to initiate reforms involving the inclusion of some parent, teacher and sometimes pupil representation. Hardly any went about it in the same radical fashion as Sheffield, but there were on the other hand a variety of schemes in which some worthwhile individual point was made. Gwent, which eloquently defended grouped governing bodies during the Taylor enquiry, had set great store by the association of a comprehensive with its feeder primary schools to strengthen neighbourhood feeling. Birmingham similarly defended the grouping of secondary schools comprising a consortium under one board (with primary schools also included, but this was beside the main point) on the ground that, having deliberately gone comprehensive on a consortium basis so that schools with varying facilities and reputations co-operated instead of competing, it was logical for governors to be encouraged along the same lines. Those LEAs which had made advances in community education, Nottinghamshire and Cambridgeshire, for instance, both visited by the Taylor Committee, used governing bodies to bring the community users of schools within their management structure. Harrow, with its three-equal-shares boards (LEA, teachers, parents) consulted governors to identify the least harmful ways to effect economies - cynics would say to legitimise economies - in the service. The ILEA, while it was slow to give up its majority, was first in the field with supportive structures for parent governors to maintain contact with each other. All these variants, though they may have stopped short of wholesale partnership and involvement, were at least a recognition that governors had potential, and they were part of the process of change.

I intend to spend a little more time on the reforms in Sheffield and Richmond-upon-Thames, Sheffield because it has been reviewed in detail by a major local participant as well as being the first, and Richmond-upon-Thames because I have been a participant myself for some twenty years and believe that it demonstrates how setting governors free from political control can produce better education.

SHEFFIELD: AN ENCOURAGEMENT FOR OTHERS

A most interesting study of the Sheffield reform was undertaken by William Bacon, one of the distinguished academics involved in the training of governors at the university (16). It was published just ten years after the traumatic Labour defeat which precipitated the reforms, and it was based on extensive enquiry into the practical consequences of the changes and the attitudes of various groups to them. The study seems to have led the writer to some rather disappointed conclusions, but I have chosen a positive title for this section because my reading of his admirable analysis leads me to be anything but disappointed. It depends on one's expectations, and some perhaps expect too much too soon from changes involving people's attitudes. What the study accepts as the solid achievements of the reform I would consider very remarkable in the time. These are outcomes which, if they could have been foreseen, would have greatly encouraged the officers who introduced them, and would have made many educationists feel that the effort was worthwhile. Indeed, in the harsh climate in which we live another decade later, those solid achievements may seem beyond price. It is worth remembering that the quality of Sheffield's schools earned high praise from HMI a year or so ago, and this has not always been the case with other LEAs who have similarly egalitarian aims, similarly generous resourcing, but not similarly participatory structures. I will come back to the achievements, but what of the disappointments?

William Bacon's main source of disappointment was with the extent to which the reforms had opened up decision-making within schools. The hopes of the visionaries who planned the scheme seem to have included the prospect of schools being more democratically run, with teacher participation a strong feature. Instead he found that headteachers, though displaying a much more open style of leadership in relation to governors, parents, the community at large and exhibiting the confidence which came from a broader base of understanding and support, operated with no serious challenge to their authority from teacher governors or teachers generally. The preoccupation which governors still had with peripheral aspects of school life - which broadly speaking was also found among consultative bodies in industry - tended also to leave unchallenged the real power of heads and officers in important matters, so that governors would only be absorbed into the existing structures of authority, rather than replace them. It would, in Bacon's view, take more than a restructuring of school government to undermine old patterns of working, and he saw no evidence of any robust grassroots demand for power-sharing either by teachers or parents.

Bacon even dares predict that the democratisation of school government would be a passing phase in the movement towards a more prescriptive educational programme, nationally monitored, based on a broad political consensus, rather than a school-level process of negotiation and consent. He wondered whether school board democracy would even before then produce socially divisive curricula which will 'provoke a counter-reaction leading perhaps to the reintroduction ... of tighter, more centralised systems of control and the consequent downgrading of democratised school boards.' After all, he concluded, such centralised systems 'have typified much of the English urban educational system for much of this century'.

We must take these prophecies seriously. In a few hectic months of 1987, the philosophy of the 1986 Act, with its emphasis on debate and consensus, its apparent desire to underpin the real authority of the head teacher through the sharing of difficult decisions rather than the exercise of muscle by the LEA on the one hand or the individual on the other, was suddenly dragged in a completely different direction. The initiatives of 1987-8, whatever their outcome, pull away from the notion of locally-delegated responsibility towards a national curriculum delivered under customer rather than community control, and schools competing in the market place rather than developing a common voice through co-operation and rational debate.

Yet the causes are surely not as simple or the outcome so predictable as Bacon suggested, though his prescience about politicians' intentions was remarkable. There has been no disillusionment with school level democracy - in most places it has not even been tried. The source of the alternative proposals has been rather a burning political desire to create a free market in education, which, by segregating the aspiring minority from the needy majority, at once would make education cheaper and less subversive. Nor is it inevitable that the people will in the end prove to be such feeble adversaries.

To return to Sheffield and its disappointments, I would totally agree that the impact of teacher governors has been disappointing, not just then but even now after all these years. Their difficulty in coming to grips with frank discussion about schools in the presence both of outsiders and their headteacher is understandable, and there are not enough of them. But there is a deeper problem in the low priority which I believe teachers now give to internal democracy in schools. A senior spokesman of the NUT said, in a totally different context in July 1987, that among teachers' priorities, democracy in schools was last out of five items, well below pay, contracts and working conditions. I believe this is true: I make a point of asking teachers on in-service courses whether they wrote to their MPs or made any other representations about their inadequate number of seats on governing boards, and I have not yet found one who did so. The result of the teachers' withdrawal of goodwill in 1985-6 has in some schools been a return to more autocratic styles of leadership, with little teacher protest. Indeed had they valued the consultation process more, they might not have included meetings of this kind in their sanctions. We must work to raise awareness of the importance of teacher-governor input and to get their numbers increased.

When one comes to other aspects of Bacon's disappointments, many are the reverse side of enormous advances. Headteachers may still feel in charge, but this is a reflection of their widespread acceptance that governing bodies are not a threat, and that reasonable decisions will be supported by most reasonable people, provided they are properly debated. It is a vital step in the development of governing bodies that initial professional fears should have been overcome. It is an even bigger advance if headteachers recognise that they can stand more firmly on decisions reached by consent, and this recognition is expressed by many of those questioned by Bacon. Indeed he repeatedly gives evidence of more confident promotion of school policies when they have been explained, justified and accepted by governors, surely a process which not only changes for the better the whole style of leadership, but also helps schools to operate on a surer basis of community support for what they are trying to do, more vital today than ever. When the book accepts that there have been gains, they seem to me to be enormous gains, particularly the stronger voice the individual school has acquired in the local system, the better image of schools in their communities, and the habit of widespread consultation with governors now automatically pursued by the LEA in managing its local affairs. This is a situation which governors in many areas would envy. In a society which only changes slowly, these are considerable achievements in less than a decade, and what I have heard about Sheffield from those closely involved since the book was written suggests that the evolution of the system has proceeded along the same sound lines, with much involvement of a wide range of ordinary people in school government, healthy debate about school and LEA policies, and above all communities understanding and valuing their schools in a way which must be a strength to the service as a whole.

ANOTHER WORKING MODEL: RICHMOND-UPON-THAMES

That is just how we hoped it would be in Richmond-upon-

Thames when we modelled our scheme largely on that of Sheffield. Like them we had all the worst abuses of the old regime in the Sixties. I have told in Chapter One how shocked I was to come with three under-fives to such a well-endowed riverside town, so rich in civic self-expression as well as blessed by nature and inhabited by so many people whose work and/or talent seemed to be in one way or another well rewarded, only to find state education a soup kitchen service, poorly resourced, little respected, and not chosen by 30 per cent of local parents, the highest proportion opting out in the whole country.

I have also told how in such a situation I was sad to find very little home-school contact, and no organisation of parent support for the service. When I stumbled over the typically moribund system of school government, I could scarcely believe that it could survive at all. Our primary schools were managed in groups in neighbourhoods roughly corresponding to electoral wards. In both primary and secondary schools members of boards were councillors or nominees of the political parties. There was no other way in which one could become involved. They were not bad or neglectful people. They did the job expected of them. They went to the harvest festival and the carol service. They would pat a child on the head if they could find a fairly clean one. They took part in the appointment of headteachers, and they granted occasional holidays. Otherwise their involvement in school life was slight. They took note of matters needing attention in the buildings and reported them, but as they were only in effect site agents of the contractor, so to speak, this was a formality.

I had already joined the local Association for the Advancement of State Education, not then very large, mainly because one of its members had asked me to help with a survey of home-school contact - 'That's easy,' I said, 'there isn't any' - in the infants school where my children were, just at the time when I was beginning to reflect how sad it was when schools, which had nothing going for them, were not drumming up support. I was also very anxious to help in their campaign against the 11+, which we had then. I was pleased to discover the AASE were also interested in working for a better system of school government, since I was already beginning to believe that we might find in this ancient and neglected structure a valuable agency of change.

It was hardly a campaign, compared with other things we did: no stopping the traffic or getting turned out of the public gallery or anything like that. Just a sustained polite correspondence, that is all, not attacking the present incumbents but merely stressing what opportunities were missed to involve people who might not be so important but who had time and personal commitment. I do remember that we sought support from Toby Jessel, then and now one of our MPs. He

119

wrote rather a bewildered letter, saying that he had never been unsympathetic to our aims, but thought our present request had little to do with education. The problem, he said, was 'giving an outlet for the aspirations of those who would like to become governors ... a purely social demand'. He did not see how LEAs could be expected to appoint governors who might disagree with their policies, and it was so convenient if governors were known to councillors because there was no waste of time finding out about likely candidates. I found this letter delightful, probably because it was such an innocently perfect description of what we were complaining about.

Within months of the receipt of that letter, our Conservative Council had responded decisively and positively to this gentle pressure for reform. It followed hard on the heels of a much more dramatic decision, to introduce comprehensive education, and as I have suggested earlier in this chapter, it had something to do with the recognition that popular involvement would help to build confidence in the new system. Indeed the 11+ was abolished in 1973 and the new governors took office a year later.

There were undoubtedly one or two councillors who embarked on this reform with very positive feelings, those who had also had the vision to accept the demise of selection as an opportunity to create something better, rather than a mere capitulation to public opinion. Most of their party colleagues, however, probably acquiesced in the reform of school government because they thought it was unimportant. If it was a charade, did it matter who wore the funny hats? Some of these would probably have given a great deal to put the clock back later, when it became clear that the new governors were capable of independent thought and that nothing would ever be the same again.

I had no idea at the time that what Richmond did was so radical. Now, fourteen years later, there are probably no more than five LEAs which have no majority of their own nominees on governing bodies - though the 1986 Act will make this state of affairs universal - and Richmond, all those years ago, gave away its control. All schools were to have their own governing boards, with four representatives of the LEA in secondary schools and three in primary, two parents and two teachers in all types of school, two students in the 16-19 colleges, and community governors, two in primary and four in secondary schools, chosen by the other three groups, as later recommended in the Taylor Report and as required by the 1986 Act. The headteacher had the option to be a governor. It is interesting that in the first round, when nobody could visualise what non-political boards would be like, the local Association of Head Teachers recommended their members to refuse this option. Four years later, they professed themselves so delighted with what the new governors had achieved for the schools that they warmly recommended their members to be governors.

Recently the system has been revised to provide exactly equal representation of the four groups, three of each interest in secondary and two of each in primary schools, with power to co-opt older pupils and non-teaching staff in secondary schools. The LEA nominees have always had to be councillors or members of the Education Committee (this is only possible in a small LEA), and wherever possible they are councillors for the ward concerned, whatever their party. The strong local emphasis of the structure has been vital from the beginning, since it was considered that real accountability was provided by the presence of the locally elected member, whether or not s/he was of the ruling party. Community governors are also offered on a very local basis from volunteers responding to public advertisement, or from nominees of community organisations of various kinds, or from governors' own suggestions.

Amazingly, with so little to go on, the LEA got much of the vital detail right first time round. For instance we always had parent elections with provision for a secret ballot which had to include the opportunity to vote in private at home and to return forms by post or by child as well as at the school in person. For something like ten years it remained necessary to tell most LEAs that a school meeting was not the best way to achieve high participation or wide social spread, and now of course the 1986 Act imposes on all exactly what we do. We have been lucky to have an officer in the schools section of our education department who was enthusiastic in introducing the scheme and who has remained enthusiastic over the years about improving it. I was delighted to find that he could even get excited once again about helping to make statutory annual meetings effective and improving training, as well as about many enterprises on the way.

But the main object of this section is to give some evidence of how the system has worked for schools and for children, since I have to justify the claims I so often make about the structures we now have to build everywhere. In particular, I have to provide the back-up for the thousands of answers I must have given to questions in what I call the 'What if?' department on headteachers' courses and the like. What if few parents come forward as governors? What if they do come forward but only from the ranks of the privileged? What if they are, in educational terms, reactionary, harping on basics and petty aspects of discipline? What if they show no care for the broad curriculum or the disadvantaged in schools? What if parent governor elections become politicised? What if they gossip? What if they go in for trivial interference with teachers' work? And so on. I deal with some of these issues in Chapter Nine, and all I will now say is that we have been working this way for a long time, these things have not happened, so look at the benefits.

We used to be exporters of children in the days when nobody seemed to care about the schools. Even the Council worried about young families moving away. Now we are heavy importers, and out-borough fees bring in some £2½ million a year, a lot for one of the smallest LEAs in the country. Our schools have an enviable reputation all around us. We haven't had any serious cuts, and we are still undertaking modest all round improvements despite having to finance them largely from rates alone. Attempts to impose cuts have encountered fierce public resistance, from a public now very sensitised to the needs of state schools. Only a year after the new system came into being, there were massive parent and teacher demonstrations against proposed cuts in primary school staffing, demonstrations in which some three thousand parents turned out more than once to say peacefully that teachers in local schools were a top priority with them. Councillors had to enter by back doors because of the crowds, and it was rumoured that the majority group leader slept in the town hall overnight to be sure of going to the meeting.

I shall never forget the atmosphere in the public gallery the night of that Education Committee meeting. At least three thousand townspeople were in the forecourt, and only chosen representatives from each school left the crowd to claim the small number of places available inside. But there was already a whole row of parents from one primary school, who must have been waiting all day for seats. They had never been in the council chamber before, they said. They had come to see the chairman of their governors vote against the cuts. They were of course political innocents, and they gasped in unbelief as his hand went up in support of the cuts package. How could he, when he had seen how they were going to affect our school, brought our petition this very evening, sent the governors' resolution a week ago? He was not very happy either, and neither was a small group of his colleagues who were also chairmen of primary school boards. Before the main Council meeting, they had wrested permission to abstain, from a leader whose discipline had been iron. It was not a charade any more, you see. Next time there was a big argument on education, it was not a matter of a handful of abstentions, but of a dozen or so members of the majority party voting in opposition. What this illustrated was three-fold. Firstly that the new governors could act as a focus of parents' feelings. Secondly that they could make a reality of hitherto barren democratic rights, since although anyone could listen to Council debates and read their minutes and budgets in the library, there had been no means of decoding and transmitting the messages in time for parents to understand and act. If you did not know how pupil-teacher-ratios were worked out, you might think that a worsening from 25.1 to 26.1 just meant one more child in each class. If you knew in time that it actually meant the loss next term of three mornings of a music teacher or five of a remedial teacher, it was real. Thirdly, the new arrangements brought political nominees into close contact with infectious commitment, and that made party discipline very difficult. The school where I once stood outside the white line booked coaches to take its parents and teachers to the demonstration. I have described these events in detail because they were the first fruits of the new system. I could go on and find dozens of examples of how the new governors and the new awareness they promoted – how quickly most headteachers learned that it was wise to allow them the means to communicate – prevented the implementation of policies which harmed education. Perhaps the most remarkable was when an unwise young Conservative councillor tried to argue that we should go back to the 11+. Like another such in Solihull, he thought mistakenly that Richmond was just the sort of place where the public would love it. The opposition forced a vote of confidence in the comprehensive schools, and the majority party went to pieces. In a recorded vote one-third – the older members who had been around long enough to understand their public – of the majority party voted for the system we had. One-third, younger and more right wing, voted against. One-third abstained. The Richmond Association for the Advancement of State Education took five minutes to decide what to do and not much longer to do it. They merely sent every secondary school governor and PTA the voting details without comment. The resulting row went off like a jumping jack in every governing board in turn, and the LEA nominees who had voted against comprehensives or abstained were under enormous pressure to resign from their school boards. The leadership did not want resignations, because there were critical by-elections pending, so most of them had to play it all down and strive to retain their places even if this meant taking a lot of stick: in two schools the entire staff also called for governor resignations. Incidentally the majority party lost those by-elections, and began a process in which they not only lost the Council but were reduced to three councillors, where once they had had 100 per cent of the seats. I am not presuming to explain this, but it would be a very interesting study for a political writer, especially as education, which had never even been an issue, played a part in almost every crucial confrontation.

Even more remarkable in a way was the part which the new governors played in the implementation of major un-popular decisions. Our Council, under both parties, had consulted the public really efficiently about proposed changes, giving all the facts and involving not just parents and governors of the affected institutions but all. We had the extraordinary spectacle of governors voting sadly but firmly for their own schools' demise, as we closed a couple of non-viable schools, amalgamated a number of small infant and junior schools and established a tertiary system whose success is nationally famous, but was very painful to achieve. Finally there was widespread public support, to counter a passionate save-our-school campaign, for the LEA's decision to merge a heavily over-subscribed girls' school with the best examination results in the town with another, also over-subscribed, and halve the provision for single sex education for girls. I won't go into detail, as it was a complex issue, but will only say that in my view it was a correct, though hard, decision, and has been vindicated by events. The point is that there were enough people who saw the sense of it to help the LEA to get a difficult decision through the Council and the Secretary of State, and I have no doubt that our lively governors and the sophisticated public opinion they have helped to create were a critical factor.

I spoke of a sophisticated public opinion, and that is the most difficult thing to prove. I used to joke about Richmond, a community with its share of educational greed as a place where, if you wanted to have a meeting on remedial education with standing room only, you would have to call it something like 'Are slow learners holding your child back?' Now you could have a meeting on special needs any night of the week and call it whatever you liked, and you would have a good audience. I am not saying you can't still find greed, but there is a forum in which the point that the quality of education is indivisible, and that we neglect anybody's need at our peril, is at least understood. The most striking thing of all is that the new governing boards not only brought in the total range of our social variety, though of course I would not pretend that this latter is as wide a range as the average, but that they did not produce reaction against modern methods or egalitarian habits in education, but a considerable number of supporters of them. I could write a book just about those decisions of governors which reflected majority needs in their schools and it would bring a wan smile to the sad faces of all those teachers who expect the opposite.

Three further points must be made. One relates to the widespread acceptance by professionals of the system we have, so that there has been no drama about the 1986 Act or about annual meetings with parents. There is very little drama about anything to do with governors. Obviously some approach it with more positive feelings than others, and have seen the full scope it gives for increasing the acceptability of their decisions, even in the odd case improving their decisions, for tapping community resources for the school and increasing the school's self-confidence and clout. Few who have been here all the time would deny that it has transformed the outlook for state education by organising its unpowerful friends into powerful agencies of support. The second point is that a few governing boards have played a courageous and effective part in carrying through those decisions whose stories can never be told: the ways in which governors have helped to deal with unsuccessful leadership or professional misdemeanour, a tiny number anywhere but needing great patience and skill. Finally, one must note that the LEA has been very conscientious about consulting governors on everything, not just changes in their schools, not even just changes in the local administration of the system, but about major issues in national debate. The Green Paper 'Parental Influence at School' (17) was not only the subject of consultation with individual governing boards but of a Saturday conference of all governors, whose views, rubber-stamped by the Education Committee, instead of vice versa, went forward to the DES. The proposals floated for consultation by the Secretary of State in the summer of 1987, despite the horrifying difficulty of organising anything at such speed and such a time of year, were also communicated to governing boards' chairpersons at least, and later summarised for all parents.

The Richmond Association for the Advancement of State Education provides opportunities for governors to meet and talk of matters of common concern from time to time, and also, before the 1986 Act, arranged, with LEA support, one training day a year. Now that day is organised by the LEA with RAASE support, and the LEA is also trying to encourage governors to form an association. RAASE is the largest CASE group in the country, and for a long time has had one member for every eight children starting school in any one year. There is no doubt that they have been a great source of support to governors, without ever knowingly trying to indoctrinate them. If there is one thing we have achieved in our town, it is to generate pride in the local state schools, and in that process governors have played a decisive part. Such an example must surely encourage those who feel nothing but fear in the presence of the 1986 Act and at the prospect that governors everywhere could take on such a role in school life. We have also brought about a very practical working partnership between parents and teachers, and in this too the existence of balanced governing bodies has played a major part.

We have been lucky in our elected members. During the period covered, control has passed from Conservative to Alliance in a dramatically fast and wholesale way, but both parties have supported this school democracy and tried to make it work better. We owe a tremendous amount to the imaginative, fair-minded and patient Conservative education chairman who was in office for the crucial years in the Seventies when this system was built, and he played a decisive part. Our current Alliance chairman is equally determined to maintain it.

NOTES

1. A.F. Leach, <u>Educational Charters</u>, Statutes of New College Oxford, p.363.
2. J.H. Lupton, <u>John Colet</u>, p.166-7.
3. A.F. Leach, <u>The Schools of Mediaeval England</u>, p.284.
4. Report of Clarendon Commission, 1864, p.5.
5. Ibid, p.6.
6. Report of Taunton Commission, p.576.
7. Committee of the Privy Council on Education, <u>Minutes and Correspondence</u>, 1848-9
8. Report of Cross Commission, 1888, Ch. 3.
9. Ibid, p.65.
10. Ibid, p. 69.
11. Ibid, but for more detail see P. Gordon, <u>The Victorian School Manager</u>, (Woburn Press, 1974).
12. Cross, p. 67.
13. Prof. G. Baron and D. Howell, <u>The Management and Government of Schools</u>, (Athlone Press, 1974).
14. Plowden Report, <u>Children and their Primary Schools</u>, (HMSO, 1967).
15. Report of the Commission on Local Government, chaired by Sir John Maud, (HMSO, 1969).
16. William Bacon, <u>Public Accountability and the Schooling System</u>, (Harper and Row, 1978).
17. <u>Parental Influence at School</u>, (DES, 1984).

Chapter Eight

MOVING TOWARDS PARTNERSHIP IN SCHOOL GOVERNMENT,
1975-86

THE TAYLOR REPORT

Chapter Seven described a near-moribund system of school
government, displaying stirrings of life in a few areas. This
was the situation in 1975, when a Labour Government set up
a Committee of Enquiry under the Chairmanship of Councillor
Tom (now Lord) Taylor, then Leader of Blackburn City
Council. The Committee had the following terms of reference:

> To review the arrangements for the management and
> government of maintained primary and secondary schools
> in England and Wales, including the composition and
> functions of bodies of managers and governors, and
> their relationship with head teachers and staff of
> schools, with parents of pupils, and with the local
> community at large; and to make recommendations.

I have provided in Appendix One a fuller summary of the
Committee's Report, 'A New Partnership for our Schools' (1)
than exists to the best of my knowledge anywhere else, with
details of the composition of the Committee and its work. I do
urge that this be read carefully, since the Report has become
in the late Eighties a document of crucial importance in the
development of school government, and is indeed almost a
handbook for those concerned with the implementation of the
1986 Education Act.

We have seen that the attempts made in the legislation of
1870, 1902 and 1944 to graft on to the state schooling system
a model of school government devised for the public and
endowed schools were on the whole a miserable failure. There
was a coherent philosophy of school government in Victorian
times and indeed a clear line of thought from the earliest
days to justify the involvement of the lay public in the oversight of schools. When only a minority of the population
received schooling, and it was a voluntary activity, one could
say that there was an implied contract between the individual

127

family and the school, providing the personal accountability of professional to client, as well as the market relationship of buyer and seller. The governing body was not a forum within which those directly concerned debated their policies as participants, but rather an agency through which the school remained true to the intentions of its founders and accountable to the wider public. As such it made an important and still relevant point, namely that education had a significance far beyond that of a transaction between individuals. Because education bestowed power and influence, because it shaped opinions and values, because it contributed to the quality of professional services available to all, and to literature and the arts, it was important to those who did not receive it in a sense which demanded some public oversight. We should not forget this conception of education as a community purpose, a threatened species in our time.

Yet we must also accept that by itself this model of accountability was inadequate for a major public service in which every family was compulsorily involved. There were not worthy, detached people available in the numbers required to ensure the responsiveness of thirty thousand schools in which this compulsory activity took place, or to provide the degree of personal support and interest which those schools needed.

When people have not the choice of accepting or refusing a service, they become much more concerned about how far it is open to their influence. This legitimate aspiration became more important as the period of compulsory education became longer. It acquired a sharper edge as the education process became more complex, and its aims and methods for various reasons less and less a matter of consensus or even understanding. Above all, the late Sixties and early Seventies brought a widespread recognition that home support was vital to the success of the child, community support to that of the school and public understanding to the protection of the service. The traditional model of the detached guardian of the public interest offered no framework within which that support and understanding could be fostered, in which aims and methods could be debated. The model became increasingly unsuitable also to express the living concerns of those compulsorily involved. We should have to try again if what we sought was an agency of that mutual accountability of home and school which was becoming an accepted goal of the thoughtful teacher and the concerned parent. The widespread dissatisfaction with the moribund system of school government, and the patchy efforts to reform it, reflected these concerns. It is also true that the less suitable school governing bodies became for the real job to be done, the less useful they seemed for anything at all, the more peripheral to school life, the more open to corruption. For institutions don't stand still: if they do not advance with the times and the needs, they decay.

These factors, the growing dissatisfaction with the old system and its abuses, and the upheaval caused by local government changes in 1974, provided the stimulus to the setting up of the Taylor Committee, representing all sections of the education service and with a wide-ranging brief.

In this chapter, since I have summarised the Taylor Report so exhaustively in Appendix One, I will only pick out its dominant themes. Firstly, members were convinced that schools needed more than ever a body of concerned local people to ensure their responsiveness to those whom they served, to provide guidance and support, and to keep under review their progress towards agreed goals. The importance of protecting a school's individual character within the local system was also stressed - 'within the framework of national and local policies, however these may change with time, the special character of the individual school is precious to most people and should be protected' (Preface to the Report, 6i).

Secondly, the Committee condemned the domination of school governing boards by LEAs, and wished to see an equal partnership of the four main interests (LEA, staff, parents and pupils, and local community). The principal of equality was very important to the Committee, symbolically and practically: it was a formula which was easy to justify, it promoted the idea that a successful school depended on proper status for all the partners in the education process, and it produced the right environment in which matters could be debated, not on a basis of power but with a will to consensus.

The stress upon consensus was indeed a marked feature of the Report. The role of the governors was to 'discuss, debate and justify the matters which any one of them may seek to implement'. (6.21)

The Committee rejected any concept of territory in school affairs. Equality of representation was echoed in equal rights to participate in decisions, with a strong sense of the totality of a school's activity, and indivisible nature of responsibility for its success:

> Nor can we see any logical way of dividing responsibility by defining different sets of functions at different levels of generality, for which final decision-making might be assigned to the local education authority, the governing body and the headteachers respectively. We have concluded that there is no aspect of the school's activities from which the governing body should be excluded nor any aspect for which the headteacher and his colleagues should be accountable only to themselves or to the local education authority. (6.29)

A substantial chapter in the Report deals with communication, and it actually precedes the chapter on the curriculum and all other functions of governors. A strong theme is that of the governing body as a guardian of good relationships and good communication, both within the school and between the school and its community. More specifically, the governors were to have the duty to oversee the arrangements for headteachers to involve their staff in internal policies, the school's involvement of parents, its proper attention to the views of pupils and its relationships with the wider community. (Chapter 5)

Two major recommendations of the Committee not implemented both concern teachers, their equal representation on governing bodies and the governors' duty to make sure that they were properly consulted within schools about policy matters. There has been no loud protest from teachers about either of these omissions, which perhaps reflects the small importance they attach to the whole subject of governing bodies, as well as the waning relative importance of school democracy in their negotiating objectives.

I have already reported that a spokesman of one of the major teaching unions expressed the view at a conference I attended that industrial democracy was last in a list of teachers' priorities, way behind pay, promotion prospects, conditions of service and working conditions. I have no means of judging this, but the teachers' action of 1985-6 certainly set back democracy within schools very significantly, and many headteachers, some sadly, some gladly, have said that as a result they have reverted to more authoritarian styles of leadership. Teachers presumably would not have included meetings for the purpose of discussing school policies in their sanctions if they had attached greater importance to advancing democracy in schools. It seems a great pity from many points of view. Advances in teacher appraisal, school-based in-service training and professional development, strong participatory structures of management, will all suffer as a result and governing bodies will be the poorer. The Taylor Committee certainly attached great importance to this subject, and indeed even debated seriously, at the request of the Secretary of State, whether consultation with teachers should be mandatory.

Communication with parents clearly occupied a great deal of the Committee's time, and they set out what in their view a good school would do to inform and involve parents and enlist their support. As Appendix One shows, seven members of the Committee were not satisfied that this went far enough, and asked that parents be given rights in law to the information they need to perform their statutory duty responsibly, with properly structured access to teachers for the purpose, and the school's protection against abuse of that access safeguarded by the governors. The whole Committee wanted parents to have a right to form associations and reasonable facilities to run them: this has not been implemented.

The Committee spent a great deal of time discussing the question of parents' responsibilities, and its teacher members naturally wished to register the importance of parents' support for children's learning, the difficulties teachers experienced with the minority who did not take their responsibilities seriously, and the truism that rights must carry corresponding responsibilities. Indeed they explored the idea of some kind of home-school contract, a discussion actually instigated by the Committee's parent members. We all knew, in fact, that an unenforceable contract was a non-starter, but the discussion was very helpful, partly because it contributed to closer understanding among Committee members and a better appreciation of the problems of teachers, secondly because it led to discussions which were more profitable. Members felt that schools might usefully bring a little more formality to enrolment by sending parents a letter of welcome in which the school made certain promises and reminded parents of ways in which they could help (annexed to Appendix One). This was as far as they felt one could go: parents are sensitive about being lectured on their duties, and some, for reasons they cannot help, find it hard to fulfil them. We thought it was tactful to make the school's promises the heart of the letter. The device of two copies and 'recorded delivery' invested it with as much formality as was practicable. While the Committee was still sitting, Mrs Shirley Williams, then Secretary of State, aired at a conference of Education Welfare Officers the idea of a rights and responsibilities contract.

The Committee wished governors to work as openly as possible (most of their detailed recommendations on procedures to this end have been incorporated in regulations either in 1981 or 1987) and to have training.

Finally one should perhaps emphasise the importance the Committee attached to the place of the school in a firm structure of local administration: the governors' powers derive directly from the LEA and are exercised on their behalf. The Committee would have been shocked by the prospect of governors being encouraged to take their schools out of the local system as is now under discussion. There is not a breath of 'consumerism' in the market place sense in the Report, and indeed governors are seen not merely as the agency of the school's accountability to its transient clientele, but also, and crucially, as guardians of its distinctive place in the local system and participants in a healthy local system meeting the needs of all its children.

Nor was the monitoring aspect of governors' work stressed at the expense of the supportive. Governors were certainly seen to be there to protect the rigour of the learning process, but in partnership with professionals and in warm understanding of the difficulty of their task in present conditions. To give the Committee the last word, as I gave it the first:

A school is not an end in itself: it is an institution set up and financed by society to achieve certain objectives which society regards as desirable and it is subject to all the stresses to which society itself is subject. It is vital therefore that teachers have the support of people outside the school in the increasingly difficult task of attaining those objectives and dealing with those stresses. If ordinary people do not, as some teachers suggest, understand what schools are trying to do, it is in part because they have traditionally not taken an active part in determining the educational policy of the schools. Certainly there are substantial difficulties involved in fostering such participation, especially in the early stages, but we think that it will eventually promote fuller understanding, better relations and a wider knowledge and appreciation of the education provided by schools and of the skills which teachers bring to a difficult task.

(6.14)

REACTIONS TO THE REPORT

Opposition to the Taylor proposals came from two quarters: many LEAs resisted the equal partnership formula because they wished to retain their majority, and the main teachers' unions saw in the total sharing of responsibility by lay people a threat to their control of the curriculum. In fact they had in some ways misunderstood the legal and historical foundations of that control. As Chapter Seven shows, it had been accepted for hundreds of years that decisions about what was taught was a matter for determination by lay persons, teachers being responsible for how the curriculum was delivered. At the time the legalities to me, as a member of the Taylor Committee completing the agreed task by speaking about the Report all over the country, though relevant, were secondary. It did not seem to me to be as important to argue whether the public had a right to comment, when they were commenting all the time, mostly in an unhelpful and ill-informed way, as to ask whether we were prepared to accept that quality of comment or try to change it. I was also becoming acutely aware, as I am sure every member of the Taylor Committee was, of a colder climate, more pressure for central control, shrinking resources and a strong pull towards a two-tier system of state education, the quality depending on where you lived, how good you were at getting information and making choices, how skilled and confident at playing the system, and how deeply you could dip into your pocket for extras. It was very frustrating to believe that a strong alliance was within our grasp, and that those who had most to lose from letting the opportunity pass were actually hostile to it.

THE 1980 ACT

This was a delayed and diluted response to the Taylor recommendations. It dealt with a number of issues besides school government: removing the statutory framework for school meals and milk, except for the very needy; ensuring that all parents were able to have the maximum choice of school compatible with efficiency and effective use of resources, even across LEA boundaries; and giving parents rights to information about schools. It also simplified the procedures for closing, contracting and changing the character of schools, which changes, with the extension of parental choice, were intended to enable LEAs to respond more effectively to contraction.

The provisions on school government did little more, in county schools, than extend the best current practice. It is true that it reduced grouping of schools to pairs of related primary schools, that it provided for two parent governors and one or two teacher governors elected by secret ballot, plus the head if (s)/he wished, and this was above all an advance for voluntary aided schools, which had previously not been legally able to have full voting governors representing either parents or teachers. These schools still retained a majority of foundation governors, slightly reduced to two over all other interests' in boards up to eighteen members and three in larger boards (previously the foundation group had been two-thirds of the total).

Nothing was said in the Act about functions, so these continued to be subject to the Model Articles of 1945 as adapted to local preferences.

Probably the most significant changes brought in by the Act, at least in county schools where parent and teacher governors were not a novelty, were not contained in the Act itself but in the regulations about governors' procedures brought in as Statutory Instrument No. 809 of 1981. These set out to open a few windows on a musty old system. Governors had to elect their chairperson annually, and any governor was eligible other than a paid employee of the school. This was an advance, since in many areas local rules provided that an LEA nominee should be in the chair. No governor could serve on more than five boards, in many areas a big improvement on what had gone before. Any three governors could request a special meeting, and governors' minutes and agenda had to be available in the school to parents, staff and pupils, save only such items as the governors ruled confidential. This was a big advance, as it knocked on the head that common assumption of the bad old days that one contracted out of confidentiality rather than the reverse. Finally, the regulations made it clear that governors should only be constrained from taking part in any discussion by direct pecuniary interest. This was very important to teacher governors whose role many LEAs and heads had sought to limit, but who were now clearly intended to participate in all governors' duties, including appointments, as long as there was no possibility of direct personal gain. It was made clear that the Department of Education intended these to be maximum restrictions, but they were not tightly enough drafted, and the DES, who had supported the National Union of Teachers against the London Borough of Croydon in claiming the right to take part in staff selection, was overruled on appeal. It was left to the 1987 regulations to tighten this up.

The Act and the Regulations were clearly intended to bring in a more open and participatory style of school government, and there is no doubt that there was an increase in awareness of the ways in which things were done and a certain amount of fast learning among new parent governors particularly. It is common to find that giving people some involvement stimulates a demand for more, and I could quote many examples of new governors who had never expected to be in that position at all, but who were nevertheless outraged by any limitations placed on their participation or by any efforts to suppress debate. On the whole, however, the possibility that governing bodies could still be dominated by LEA nominees put a brake on further development, and from discussions I had with many headteachers it was clear that parent and teacher participation was limited by a feeling that the amount one could achieve as a minority group was small. This is not to say that the LEA appointees were anything but good and caring governors in many instances, but only that, as I said in Chapter Seven, having one dominant group changed the nature of debate.

An important study of the operation of the new governing bodies was undertaken with government financial support at Brunel University by Professor Maurice Kogan and colleagues (2), and published in 1984. They studied in depth the operation of governing bodies in four LEAs, a shire county, a city and two contrasting suburban LEAs, following the progress of governors' business, studying relationships, and exploring attitudes. No simple patterns emerged but there were common themes. Role confusion seemed to be very common and governors were seen by the researchers to be choosing from, or moving uneasily between, four main views of their function. These were the accountability model, the supportive model, the advisory model and the mediating model. I am not suggesting at all that the authors thought there ought to be only one: I too think a governor's function contain elements of all four, and I think the researchers were concerned only that governors should be more sure-footed in managing the different approaches. They discovered that governors, especially parent governors, found it hard to work out a properly independent relationship with either the LEA or the professionals in the school or both: it was all too easy to become overwhelmed by such a powerful interest group, dependent on them for information and access, even though other governors had something distinctive to contribute.

THE GREEN PAPER: PARENTAL INFLUENCE AT SCHOOL (3)

Even before the 1980 Act was in full operation, the Government was looking at more radical changes in school government. The Green Paper, which appeared in May 1984, is very interesting in the light of what has happened since. It said, simply, that the 1980 Act was a start, but that it would help schools to be more effective if parents had an even bigger say than the Taylor Committee envisaged and if governors had more real power. The proposal was that parents should have an overwhelming majority on governing boards, ten representatives in the largest schools, with LEAs and teachers alike having only a small minority of seats. Governors were to have complete control of school spending and substantial involvement in appointing and dismissing teachers. This proposal found favour with scarcely any of those whose views were reported. Most people thought that it was ludicrous to believe that such recruitment of parents was either practical or desirable. The National Confederation of Parent-Teacher associations, the National Association of Governors and Managers and the Campaign for the Advancement of State Education all said firmly that it was partnership, not power, which interested them. As for representatives of LEAs and teachers, they found a sudden passion for the Taylor Report and its prescription for equal shares and sharing of responsibility.

Sir Keith Joseph, then Secretary of State, was bitterly disappointed that no one liked his Green Paper. A few saw in it a major step towards a consumer-led education system, even perhaps towards privatisation or hybrid schools. I remember asking Sir Keith Joseph what had become of the idea of partnership, when LEAs and teachers were so miserably represented, and he was genuinely bewildered: the partnership was, he said, between the governors and the LEA and teachers, who had such power anyway that one must provide a countervailing force. In other words it was to be a sort of consumer council. This was certainly not the Taylor philosophy: partnership for them was symbolised within the governing body.

THE WHITE PAPER: BETTER SCHOOLS (4)

This appeared in March 1985, and foreshadowed the 1986 Act. The proposed balance on governing bodies was greatly improved, with equal numbers of LEA representatives and parents, two to five of each according to the size of school. The functions were to be more or less as suggested in the Green Paper but the new document also spelled out the ways, now familiar to us in the 1986 Act, in which governors would communicate with parents.

The White Paper covered a number of other subjects and has some sensible statements on the nature of the curriculum, statements with a much more up-to-date feeling than the national curriculum proposals consulted upon during 1987, and some helpful comments on viable sizes of schools. There were even some genuflections towards pupil profiling, towards measures to deal with underachievement among ethnic minorities, and towards better provision for special needs. These got lost on the way to the statute book, but in broad outline the White Paper foreshadowed the legislation which was soon to be published.

THE EDUCATION (NO. 2) ACT 1986

We now come to a substantial and coherent piece of legislation, concerned almost entirely with the structure of the education service rather than any educational entitlement, and so in no sense comparable with the visionary 1944 Act. Its passage through Parliament - it was introduced in the Lords in fact - was fairly stormy, and took all the summer and much of the autumn of 1985. The debates were characterised by tremendous confusion about objectives; by a hopelessly disunited opposition in both Houses, putting paid to any chances of getting just a few worthwhile improvements such as better teacher and student representation; and by a determination of many extreme right wingers to ride hobby horses.

THE IMPORTANCE OF ATTITUDES

The first campaign I took part in was nothing to do with education. It was about children in hospital. I now know that there is a very effective pressure group concerned with their well-being, and it has transformed children's wards as surely as our primary schools have been transformed since, over twenty years ago, I first viewed one from the wrong side of a white line. I only knew then that I had moved to a modest house on a modest new estate with three under-fives, where everybody else was new and had approximately three under-fives. One of our number had been badly treated by a hospital. She had a child of two who was dying of leukaemia, and she wished to spend what might be his last days and nights with him. She sat many days and nights on a hard chair, and she was not offered a bed or a meal or even a cup of tea, and she was told many times to go home and leave the job to the professionals.

We raised a bit of money in our street, and we sent a cheque to the hospital, asking them to buy a folding bed for the children's ward in the name of our street and that little boy. It was returned with a polite letter saying that it was not the policy of the children's ward to allow parents to stay. So we bought the bed and we sent that, a technique I would now recommend. Our small stone started a landslide and some time later that hospital built a permanent parent and child unit. Perhaps the sister in charge of the children's ward was moved after a decent interval to the geriatric ward, where the presence of parents was unlikely to be such a nuisance. But our action brought to light that there were already four folding beds exactly like ours in the children's ward, donated by the Friends of the Hospital for the same purpose, locked in a cupboard and never referred to.

I might have included this homely tale to show that it has taken professionals in health, education, architecture and many other fields a long time to decide that sometimes the best professional job needs a little help from outside. That is true, but my main interest now is in those beds in the cupboard. The best structures in the world will not work when human beings do not want them to work, and even quite imperfect structures can work very well when the spirit is right. In the hospital a mattress on a floor with a welcome to go with it would have been gladly accepted. Many sound legal structures may well remain locked up because of negative attitudes.

THE 1986 ACT IN PERSPECTIVE

A careful reading of Appendices One and Two will show that almost all the Taylor Committee's recommendations have been implemented. (The exceptions are interesting and I have already mentioned them.) Yet the overwhelming majority of heads and teachers, and many LEA officers, are victims of an optical illusion. They see the 1986 Act as part of the series of attacks characterising the period to which it chronologically belonged: attacks on local authority independence, teacher status and morale, and free and fair schooling for children. I have found it almost impossible to convince them that the Act on the contrary affords opportunities to strengthen the concept of local responsibility, enhance teacher status and morale and restore free and fair schooling for children. I

137

suggest that despite its poor timing, despite its minor accretions of ideological nonsense, the 1986 Act is a culmination of a very different series of events which had their origins in a long history of noble intention, if sometimes ignoble usage. Chapter Seven traces that history, and shows that the advocacy of more public involvement in school government was never a political issue, and the more effective involvement of the public is now an aim of every major party. It was a Labour Prime Minister - James Callaghan at Ruskin College in 1976 - who opened the critical decade. It was a Labour administration which had set up the Taylor Committee, and if you read through the list of its members you can only conclude that at least one-third were open and active Labour politicians and several more were supporters. Among the rest there was one Conservative elected member. I either do not know the politics of the rest or suspect that, like me, they were members of no party. I can say confidently that there were no centralists, no Black Paperites, no free market enthusiasts. The background to everything we discussed was a belief in the continuation of the partnership between central and local government in the provision of an improving public education service, caring, just, and in the future perhaps more responsive to its users.

The Committee reported to a Labour Secretary of State, Shirley Williams, who had taken more interest in its deliberations than any Minister before or since. The 1980 Education Act was a somewhat altered version of a Labour Bill which fell with the Labour Government in 1979, but the sections on school government were not the contentious ones, and the reasons why they failed to go further in the direction of a Taylor partnership had nothing to do with national politics, but merely reflected the reluctance of local authorities and teachers' unions to accept any more. Shirley Williams herself had believed that it was unnecessary to be any more explicit about governors' powers, since if you got the right people involved they would soon find their way to a meaningful reinterpretation of their ancient role.

I totally accept the prevalent belief that there is indeed a firm if unwritten agenda for a programme of action to reduce the involvement of local authorities in education; to bring teachers' pay and conditions and ultimately the content and process of teaching under government control; to question the sanctity of free education; and above all to create, in the name of choice and freedom, a situation in which children's chances depend much more than formerly on their parents' living in the right places, knowing how to get and use information, making good choices and being able to pay a bit more for a full curriculum. I also accept that there is a lot of rubbish in the Act. I likened the Bill, as it went through its parliamentary processes, to a skip standing overnight outside the Department of Education and Science, which in the first light of morning was suddenly full of old mattresses, battered prams, tin cans and whalebone corsets. Many a passing MP and peer used the opportunity to turn out the contents of his or her ideological attic.

Yet in essentials I maintain that the Act is nothing to do with the hidden curriculum of LEA and teacher-bashing, or with the establishment of a free market in education. It was certainly preceded and followed by many moves in this direction, but I wish people would read it and think about it with uncluttered minds, and see the historical genesis of it. I wish they would consider how it can be used to build a whole-school partnership which will help to restore local freedoms, release teachers' creative energies and uphold their professionalism, a partnership within which we can fight for the right of all children to the best we can offer, whatever the circumstances of their homes. I have often heard teachers say that the Act is a minefield, I can only think they would not know a minefield if they saw one. The resistance of some to sharing any real responsibility with parents and governors, at a time when explosive charges are being laid under the foundations of the service in which we all have hostages, looks like building toy forts all over the real minefield. We could have had our partnership ten years sooner if they had been willing, and I do not believe that we should then have had to face the present series of enactments which has nothing to do with partnership, but only with power: the power of government, the power of business, the power of money, the power of the market place, and the power of greed.

Between the 1986 Act and the legislative measures of 1987-8 there is an ideological gulf. Whether the opportunities afforded by the soundly restructured and redirected governing bodies can in time be used to reverse or at least mitigate what I consider to be a wholly evil and destructive process I cannot say, but I do know that it depends more than anything on whether headteachers, teachers and LEA officers take positive attitudes to the opportunities.

As for the ideological rubbish, one should not take it too seriously. It is of course absurd that an education service which is run on the whole by moderate and non-violent people should be turned upside down for the sake of curbing a few extremists, and it has led to the inclusion in the Act of some clauses totally out of place in my view in an Act of Parliament at all. The best hope is that they will not be workable. I refer in particular to the sections giving governors responsibility for sex education and for ensuring balance in political education, clearly designed to frustrate certain extreme left councils and teachers ostensibly seeking to indoctrinate pupils and promote positive images of homosexuality; and the one requiring governors to make every effort to ensure freedom of speech on college campuses. It is interesting that the

first governors to use their power to direct balance in political education were complaining about a government defence
film, and insisting that a peace film be shown also! I have
so often in my own town seen the outcome of politicians'
actions confound their intentions that I am not at all surprised. I am sure that many noble Lords who voted to give
governors and parents jurisdiction over sex teaching did so
in the belief that it would lead to less sex education, not
more. Yet as I have seen parents and governors with sensitivities a generation old swallow hard on some of the explicit
material they have had to confront, I have also seen them
driven inexorably towards a vote for maximum information
with only a passing sigh for innocence. As for requiring us
to ensure that such teaching is given in the context of moral
values and family life, who can be against that? Yet when we
have to confront the stark question 'whose moral values?' we
shall better understand our teachers' dilemmas in seeking
among the cultural differences of our society such underlying
values as we share, and that will be good for us.

The best comfort for anyone who does not know whether
to laugh or cry at the naivety of putting such things in
legislation would have been to sit with me through some of
the long debates in the House of Lords and hear how much
worse it nearly was.

But these are peripheral issues. Let us look now at the
essential provisions of the Act, not line by line, for we have
a detailed summary in Appendix Two, but in the context of
my claim that it could 'furnish all we need to ask'.

WHAT THE ACT SETS OUT TO DO

The first thing to say is that for the first time we are to
have a national system of school government, not one hundred
and four variations on a fairly thin common theme. The
Taylor Committee had concluded that what was left at local
level of the rather grand designs of earlier legislators was
scrappy and confused, and full of abuses. It recommended
that the new partnership it advocated should in essentials
follow a common pattern: the flexibility and responsiveness
which were its aims were to be in the deeds of the new
governors, not in the structures to which they must conform.
The effect of Sections 1 to 10 of the Act is that the role of
the Secretary of State is confined to the settlement of the odd
dispute arising from the construction of school governing
bodies. But this is possible because the Act itself sets out
with so much greater precision how governing bodies are to
be constituted and what their responsibilities are to be, that
LEAs can be left to make local arrangements to give effects to
the new rules.

The second, and to me overwhelmingly important feature

of the Act is that it brings to an end the dominance of governing bodies by nominees of the LEA. By making the representation of LEA and parents exactly equal in county and controlled schools, and by providing that co-opted governors to represent the community should be freely chosen by the rest of the governors, a group on which parents and teachers will have a majority, it also makes it impossible - provided members of that group do not take too long to find their glasses - for co-opted governorships to be a back door for party faithful either. I am not saying that all LEAs used their right to appoint a majority of governors for party political ends in all cases - the links were often benignly tenuous, especially in rural areas - or that many governors appointed in this way were not conscientious and caring. I am only briefly reiterating that the practice found in many areas of making governing bodies a mirror of the local pattern of political power had, over the years, brought the system into discredit. Even more important, however, all my experience has convinced me that the creation of a balance in school government changes the whole nature of the debate. While some members can wield power - however little they use it, or however benignly they use it - merely by being there and putting their hands up you have one kind of discussion. When no group can prevail except by the wisdom of its arguments and its demonstration of loyalty and commitment to the school, you have a completely different kind of discussion. It also changes the people.

The third effect of the Act - and I emphasise this particularly for those who see it as part of the process of undermining local government - is that it firmly restates the responsibility of the LEA for the determination of the curriculum of its schools, a responsibility largely neglected for forty years. Yes, it is inconsistent with later moves to introduce a national curriculum, but you cannot point to this inconsistency and still maintain that the 1986 Act has the same ideological parentage. In fact the inconsistency is not total, because there will still be a great deal of space for local decision. The greater significance of the Act for local government, however, is the scope it offers for strengthening the voice of the individual school, an effect noted in Sheffield, where the first experiment in balanced school governing bodies took place (1), and certainly my own experience in a town where it has over fourteen years so increased the power of individual schools to articulate their needs that the status and strength of state education itself have been advanced. What is a local system but the sum of its schools? I believe that effective school-level democracy can defend the interests of local government in a way it has proved incapable of defending itself.

Finally, the Act at every turn emphasises debate and consensus, an emphasis which in retrospect seems to have been the hallmark of the Taylor Report. You will see in the summary in Appendix Two a quotation from the Report which unusually - the bulk of it bears all too painfully the scars of committee drafting - we eagerly plucked straight from the lips of one member: 'so that they can discuss, debate, and justify the matters which any one of them may seek to implement'. It is fashionable to look for clear unquestioned authority again, and I have heard many teachers complain that the Act is a recipe for indecision and time-consuming negotiation. They are in many cases the same people who rage rightly against the denial in 1987 of their own negotiating rights as employees. I believe there is only one way to lasting harmony, and it is the tedious one of negotiation. Surely it is debate, and out of debate consent, which makes the difference between authority and authoritarianism?

Take the process by which a school's curriculum is determined: the LEA to set out for all to see its curriculum policy; the governors to translate it, with modifications to take account of school circumstances if necessary, into curricular aims for the school; the head to choose, reconcile, express as a learning programme, his or her preferred themes from this debate, again to seek consent (Sections 17 and 18). How strong the product will be.

Another prime example is in the choice of a headteacher. There is no longer to be a casting vote. Governor and LEA voices are equal. At every stage they must strive for consensus, repeating certain processes until they attain it. Either side may add up to two names to the short list, if they cannot agree (Sections 36 and 37). Slow perhaps, tedious perhaps. Maybe not in itself enough to guarantee the right choice; but almost as important as the right choice is the way people feel about it once it is made, the time taken and the effort to agree. The same process seeks to take the bitterness out of the exclusion of pupils. At every point there must be discussion, with headteacher, governors and LEA taking the lead in turn, each checked by the pressures to seek agreement, each contributing from a different point of view.

In disciplinary matters the rules are also geared to debate. The objectives are clear: to secure justice; to get the pupil back into school as soon as possible; to ensure that parents are informed; to involve governors constructively; and to introduce an appeals procedure to take the sting out of final decisions. The involvement of the partners in discussion at so many stages is a warning to all concerned not to adopt hard positions, not to get so committed that it is difficult to negotiate.

Indeed much of the clever detail of the Act is designed to take the hard edge off so many typical and inescapable confrontations in schools: for example, the one already mentioned on shortlisting; or the provision that governors may write a job description to guard against a total mismatch in a redeployed teacher, and that if they are still not satisfied the matter must be referred to the Education Committee. All these clauses are designed to make people more careful.

The regulations on governors' procedures (5) make them more open and participatory. The provisions of 1981 on chairperson elections and on calling a special meeting are repeated, but some rules are much strengthened and some are new. Governors may not now be on more than <u>four</u> boards. <u>All</u> governors' non-confidential papers may now be seen by <u>anybody</u>. The rules about when governors must declare an interest make it absolutely clear that they are exhaustive: that is, local restrictions may not be more severe. Another meeting must be fixed if scheduled business is not completed. Each of these thoughtful measures reflects careful DES reading of earlier cause célèbres. I read through the text and keep exclaiming 'Croydon!' 'Weymouth!' 'Poundswick!' 'Shropshire!'

The arrangements for governors to report to parents and meet them are in my view very important, and so is the greater openness about money. I have made some comments on parents' meetings in the next Chapter, and also about the many ways in which heads can ensure that all the new provisions in this Act work well for schools and children.

GREAT EDUCATION REFORM?

It is not right for a Minister to prejudge the view of Parliament by calling a measure a reform until they have pronounced on it. It is also not right to receive 16,500 letters and take no heed of them, since most must have had reservations about the word 'reform'. Finally it is not right to proceed with measures which do not have the support of those who provide, work in and use the service.

There is an ideological gulf between the 1986 Act and the proposals of 1987-8. I do not consider the latter a step on the road to partnership, but there are those who do and one cannot ignore them.

The proposals making up the 'Great Education Reform' hang together. They diminish local authorities by taking power away from them in every area of work covered. The national curriculum takes away from them their main responsibility, while open enrolment removes the power to plan their space effectively. Delegation of financial power obviously robs them of such flexibility as they now possess. Opting out forces them to pay for schools lost to the local system and under no quality control locally. Polytechnics and colleges, including those training teachers, will be taken away from them.

Teachers similarly are robbed of much responsibility by this tinkering with the partnership. As for parents, they may come to realise that it is a cruel game in which schools compete for custom, and parents compete for the best chance, and children compete in all too obvious ways. Which of the partners gains by these moves? The one not mentioned yet, obviously, the one who is gaining so many new powers over what is taught and how it is tested, who is appointed and who is dismissed in some very key positions, not to mention so much more of the money.

I believe that these so-called reforms have emerged from three little publicised propositions. One is that the way to remain powerful is to control teachers and what is taught. The second is that there is not, because of financial policies, enough good education to go round, so it has to be rationed, and the market place does this effectively. The third is that good education is dangerous. It gives people ideas. None of this is anything to do with partnership.

We still have many choices: not the choice being offered in the Great Education Reform, but the choice of whether to go on fighting for partnership or to simply fight each other, whether to seek the best for our children or the best for all children.

NOTES

1. Taylor Committee, A New Partnership for our Schools, (HMSO, 1977).
2. Maurice Kogan, Daphne Johnson, Tim Packwood, School Governing Bodies, (Heinemann, 1984).
3. DES, Parental Influence at School, (HMSO, May 1984).
4. DES, Better Schools, (Cmnd. 9469, HMSO, March 1985).
5. Education (School Governing Bodies) Regulations 1987, (HMSO, 1987).

Chapter Nine

MAKING PARTNERSHIP WORK

We must clearly take very seriously indeed the clamour for
schools to be made more accountable to their users, either by
enforced exposure to market forces, or by more direct professional answerability to client and employer alike. I have
not underrated the political imperatives attaching to such
ideas, or the ease with which they could be made attractive.
Hence the space devoted to their appeal and their inherent
fallacies in Chapters Two and Three.

What is amazing, given the strong institutional resistance
and the practical obstacles, is the speed with which these
ideas were pushed up the agenda following the return of a
third Conservative government in the summer of 1987. The
long-drawn out teachers' action of 1985-6 provided fertile
ground for the opportunist, and it was easy to play on public
weariness. Parents, who on the whole knew pathetically little
about what schools were doing and what life was like for
teachers, had long been sitting ducks for the hostile propa-
ganda of press and politicians. Now they became even more
remote from schools. I always thought, even when campaigning actively on teachers' behalf, that they were ill-
advised to include contact with parents in the voluntary
duties withdrawn. Relationships can only be sustained
through routine contact, especially in a service with an
annual 10% client change. This made it very hard to sustain
sympathy for teachers over so long a period, and played into
the hands of those whose plans required that parents be set
against them. During the worst of the disruption, parents
understood the withdrawal of teachers' labour better than the
cessation of home-school contact. Children being sent home
had an immediate impact and made people angry, but some
were able to turn their anger against those who had driven
teachers to such uncharacteristic behaviour. As term followed
term with no chance to discuss one's child with a teacher,
parents became hurt and bewildered by what they saw as
rejection.

A large parliamentary majority was also a factor. It was

often claimed by Ministers that, whatever the outcome of the direct consultation on their proposals in July–September 1987, they had a clear political mandate for what they saw as necessary reforms in the education system. There had been a manifest commitment to creating wider parental choice and providing escape routes for schools dissatisfied with local council policies. These plans, it was claimed, had been given a thorough airing in an election campaign culminating in a resounding victory for their sponsors. People were thought to be dissatisfied with a monopoly provider spending a lot of money and failing to deliver the goods; with militant teachers; and with extreme left-wing councils.

Nevertheless the entire education service was stunned by the speed and ruthlessness with which plans long regarded as belonging to the crackpot fringe of Conservative ideology were translated into a precise legislative programme. The ideas, as Chapter Two demonstrates, had been around a very long time, shunned by permanent officials, educators, and the many Conservative moderates who in forty years had not as a group strayed far from consensus politics in education. Suddenly those ideas broke away from all such restraints.

I hope I have argued convincingly that the 1986 Act was very different in its ideological parentage, its motivation, and its essential philosophy from the measures which followed it in 1987-8. Yet many teachers find it hard to see it this way, and some even confuse the two. The 1986 Act gives us a logical and coherent structure for school-level debate within a local system. It provides a framework within which the individual school may seek accountability of the partners to each other. Remember how, in Chapter Eight, when I was talking about Sir Keith Joseph's Green Paper, 'Parental Influence at School' (1), I made a distinction between his notion of partnership and that of the Taylor Committee? The Green Paper saw the partnership as one between the governing body on the one hand and the LEA and the teachers on the other. There was no need to have more representation of LEA and teachers because they already had so much power. In other words the school governors were a sort of consumer council to which the school was answerable, and the power residing in the governing body was that of customer or client. The logic, which is now emerging, is the partial privatisation of the service. The Taylor Committee, on the other hand, envisaged a governing body symbolising within itself the whole-school partnership, and thus embracing that ideal of mutual accountability to which I tried to beat a path in the early chapters. Such a body derives power from consensus, and its concern is with the success of the school within its permanent context of a sound local system, community support and the diversity of children's needs: it is not just the voice of those presently favouring it with their custom.

It is vital to make this distinction, around which indeed

this book has been written. It is particularly important to make it when considering the ideological divide between the Green Paper and the 1987-8 proposals on the one hand, and the Taylor Report, the White Paper 'Better Schools' (2), and the 1986 Act on the other. Few streams run entirely clear and unobstructed from their source, and the waters of the 1986 Act have been polluted in one sense only by the spite against the teachers which was the contemporary mood: the logic required that it give teachers equal representation on governing boards, and governors the trusteeship of teachers' rights to a say in school policies. But spite prevailed over logic.

PARTNERSHIP AND POWER: WINNING THE RACE

I now come to the very practical reason why I have insisted on distinguishing between the 1986 Act and the 1988 sequel, which will almost certainly be on the statute book soon after these words are written. It is because I see the immediate future as a race to the winning post between the two competing ideologies. One is of education as a community service meeting needs, the other of education as a market responding to demands. The 1986 Act has time on its side, not much, not enough perhaps to make victory certain, but enough, if we use it well, to raise awareness, to help people realise that they do not have to behave as programmed, that they do not have to send off their order form now for the great prize draw or the never-to-be-repeated bargain offer. They do not actually have to participate at all in the evil game from which in the end we all emerge losers. Anybody is free to put the junk mail in the bin.

I spoke of an evil game. It leads to a world in which, in place of debate, in place of a search for mutual accountability, we have the crude morality of the market place, a cold accountability for services exchanged between people who have no relationship, the brute power of buyer or client over deliberately crippled providers. How can we be so foolish as to think there is any point in giving us our freedom to buy, when all that's left to buy is made without imagination or joy?

We can imagine a world in which parents compete for what should be their right, and in which schools compete for the means to provide it.

An education service meeting all needs (after all, it spends our money) should be an entitlement and not a prize. Must we set school against school until the blood runs, and the strong run off, clutching their confidence and their money and their children, leaving all the problems to be tackled with ever-declining resources?

It's healthy to look at what can happen, as long as you go on to say that only people can let it happen. People can

say that competition between schools doesn't solve the problems of a chronically underfunded and undervalued service,
but merely assists the rationing of opportunity. People can
expose the fraud of choice for what it is, demonstrate that a
good school is a school in a good local service, reaffirm their
belief that whatever an individual child can achieve is value-
less unless it can flourish in a world where all children have
the means to achieve. People can even say that education is a
community purpose not a transaction. People, especially head
teachers, can flaunt their wounds instead of hiding them,
share their problems instead of pretending there aren't any -
a particularly unhelpful effect of market place mentality - and
press their needs in unison, refusing to believe that because
there isn't enough for all they have to outwit each other to
get any.

Parents need help in perceiving these verities. They
don't have enough access to the system and to schools to see
them with consistent clarity, and they are still very timid
unless they are sure that their teachers are on their side. We
desperately need our partnership in good working order, and
we have all the structures already on the statute book. There
is one thing which gives me enormous hope, and that is that
Saturday after Saturday, when I meet new school governors,
I realise how much they care and how fast they learn, when
they are given leadership and encouragement.

Our time is short. We first have to shake off the associations of a corrupt old system. We have to dismantle
defences, establish a common language, open all the doors
and windows, celebrate children and their learning with all
those who will join in. The only time I feel bitter is when I
realise that we could have had our partnership years sooner
if teachers had been willing. They are so busy defending
themselves against the wrong people. I myself wrote in 1977:

> I fear that if the rigour of a proper management struc-
> ture is not accepted at school level, we may find there
> is an overwhelming outcry for a different and much less
> desirable kind of rigour, in the form of more central
> government prescription, which would not only damage
> something we have traditionally valued greatly, namely
> the independence and variety of our schools, but would
> not, I fear, even achieve its aim of making them more
> effective. (3)

If these words were prophetic, it was not because I was wise
but because at the time I was rarely privileged to wander
among professionals as a stranger, and I could see things
which they were too close to see.

The rest of this chapter looks at some of the practical
problems of making the 1986 Act a living reality in schools.
No matter that it may have undergone changes before you

read this, no matter that some of its detail has been swallowed up in new provisions. No matter even if you have to take your pencil to some of the references and words used and bring them up to date. I should not go on writing at this time if I did not believe that in essentials it will not become out-of-date. As long as there are schools, and as long as teachers, parents and community have something to say to each other about children and their learning, there will be a need for structures within which that debate can take place. As long as there are competing ideologies - and even in my darkest moments I don't think the concept of education as a community purpose pursued in partnership will be that easy to destroy - there will be choices to make and those choices will have to be made by people. No law can make us fight each other. No law can totally control the agenda of our debate, and if the agenda is partnership, no government can make that illegal. But if people are to make wise choices, they have to have information and insights. Barriers to their effective communication and obstacles to their productive joint action must be removed.

All the partners have contributions to make. The government have a responsibility to underpin the legislation we already have, before they embark on any more. LEAs can and must prove that they are the best agencies to provide for the varying needs of local children, not just the most responsive, caring, experienced and flexible, but also the most cost-effective. Most important of all, they must demonstrate that they see the positive contribution of parents, governors and community as the very foundation of an efficient service, and take steps to facilitate it. Governors must accept a difficult role and be prepared to fulfil it with tact and patience as well as commitment. Above all, however, since in any system head teachers are the people whose skills and attitudes create the climate for advance, it will be they who with other members of the senior management team in schools will have the greatest scope for creative and wise initiatives. Their attitudes can promote partnership or stifle it; they have the power, the opportunity and the skills to build structures of involvement, and their expectations can release the energy of others. Any management training for head teachers and potential head teachers which in future takes no account of this dimension will at best be limited and at worst dangerous.

THE ROLE OF GOVERNMENT

There is as I said earlier, no branch of the Department of Education and Science concerned with home-school relationships, or with the country-wide development of working partnerships between the education service and communities.

This statement alone is a telling indictment. In all the guidance which they issue to LEAs year in year out, it is rare to find any references to the relationship of parents to schools except as customers exercising choice, still perhaps the only form of influence recognised in high places. The law and regulations on the information schools must give to parents (notably the 1980 Act, with SI 630 of 1981) have a strongly consumerist flavour, concentrating almost wholly on the information parents need to help them choose, not on that they require to be effective partners in the process afterwards. For instance schools have to tell parents about their curriculum and organisation, about their rules and their exam results, but not about their arrangements for informing parents about their children's progress, involving them in their policies, enlisting their support or encouraging them to join together in parents' organisations. One would like to see the government taking a lead and at the very least endorsing the best practice.

Many government reports, most recently and cogently the report of the Select Committee on Education, Science and the Arts on Achievement in Primary Schools (4) have argued that teacher initial and in-service training should take more account of the need to help teachers communicate with other adults, especially parents, but improvement is slow.

The DES must know well that some of parents' new rights to information, access to school curriculum documents and syllabuses and governors' papers, are empty while so few parents have a place of their own in schools: a parents' room, drop-in centre, or family centre. One cannot read such documents in a busy office or from a notice board in a corridor without seeming a suspicious busybody. If these rights are to be real and routinely exercised, all schools should have a parents' place. Yet not only does no government department encourage and facilitate these developments, but the DES actually issue lots of advice about mothballing surplus classrooms to save light and heat and cleaning costs. All measures to make parents feel at home in schools, listed in more detail below, should be centrally promoted, researched, encouraged and funded, if the government is serious.

LOCAL EDUCATION AUTHORITIES

Some LEAs do care very much about school links with home and community, but only a minority - all honour to these - have positive polices to ensure that these links are strengthened throughout the area. Very few have an adviser for home-school relationships. Few fund parents' rooms or drop-in centres, home-link teachers, or encourage the development of true community schools, which are not just places where the lights are on all evening. Even fewer maintain or assist any

independent parents' advice centre. Hardly any do the simplest and cheapest thing of all which is to organise the
spread of the best practice among their own schools. This is
a shame, since everywhere I go I find heads and teachers
intensely interested and desperate for ideas on how to do it
better. There is very little research on communication with
homes to discover what works best. When one does find LEAs
setting shining examples there is great sense of purpose in
their schools. I cannot understand how the rest can read one
report after another over a period of twenty years or more,
all saying that home support is the greatest single contribution to effective learning, and yet not accept the proper
harnessing of that support as part of their responsibility for
an effective total service. After all it is there that the main
legal responsibility rests, and to know that a factor is vital
and to take no steps to act on the knowledge seems as bad as
not to supply any textbooks. Even the systematic encouragement and advertisement of schools which through impro-
visation, imagination and commitment have done something
good on their own would be a start. Many LEAs will blame
lack of money for failure to take initiatives, but my
impression is that if they got a windfall most of them would
not spend it that way, and I also believe that with the right
priorities much could be done without expense.

As far as governors are concerned, there is a good deal
to be done at LEA level. Training is such a big subject that I
have dealt with it separately, but there is much besides that
LEAs could do to improve their contribution. The work they
give governors, the substance of the discussion material, the
habit of consulting on major local policies, the notice they
take of what governors say, all contribute to giving the role
respect. Election arrangements must be good not just technically but in their encouragement to wide participation. Good
general leaflets, publicity in local press and radio, preparation for elections well before they are imminent, all help
to encourage interest. Schools should be encouraged in all the
good habits dealt with in the section on schools' policies
below. Some attention should be given to improving head
teachers' reports, if only by circulating some good models.
Heads often tell me they never see any but those of their
predecessor, and if these have been scrappy or perfunctory,
interest will have waned and the standard is only likely to go
down further. Much depends on the tone the LEA establishes.
It soon gets through to schools that better involvement of
governors in the life of schools is something to which the LEA
attaches importance at high policy levels. The messages will
be conveyed by the way governors are consulted, responded
to and serviced, by the publicity given to the schools which
display good practice, and by the firm treatment of any kind
of default. One very good practice is to circulate governors'

resolutions to the Education Committee.

Attention needs to be given to arrangements to give effect to the right to open access to governors' non-confidential papers in schools. I have already referred to the need for a proper place to read them, but publicity is important and so is timing. Parents should know that they can see the agenda before the meeting: it makes no sense unless they have a chance to comment. As for minutes, if they are not available until governors have ratified them at their next meeting, it could be as long as five months before parents see them. This seems to me to be very unsatisfactory, and the new regulations under the 1986 Act (5) seem to recognise this by referring to 'draft' minutes. It is very unsatisfactory - and very common - for governors to see the minutes only just before the next meeting. It is difficult to check accuracy or to discover whether action has been taken on decisions, and if the minutes are useless and dull to those who were at the meeting, how much more so they will be to those who were not! In any committee, minutes should be circulated as soon as possible after the meeting, with a week for any member to question points of accuracy through the Chair. After that they could be available in the school 'subject to formal ratification'.

LEAs need to be specially careful to ensure that all governors share equally in the work of the governing bodies. They themselves are sometimes guilty of putting unnecessary restrictions on parent and teacher governors particularly, but even when their practice is impeccable, they need to watch that within the school and/or the governing body itself no bad habits are developing, such as excluding teachers and parents from confidential items and excluding them from serving on selection panels. (It is clear from the regulations that teachers are intended to play whatever part their colleagues as a whole wish, save only in cases where they stand to gain directly and personally from the outcome.) An officious chairperson will often try to monopolise the representation on selection panels and choose colleagues as necessary. This if not right - governors should make their own choice of people to represent them.

A frequent complaint of parent governors is that they are discouraged from communicating with other parents; most want to seek views on issues, and report back after meetings. They regularly report that LEAs or schools imply that they have no more obligation to communicate than other governors, and, rather sententiously, that they are 'not parent representatives, merely representative parents'. There is a sound point, of course, that any governor is a governor first and a representative of an interest group second, and that governors are not mandated delegates. To use this good point to discourage communication, however, seems quite wrong. Parents do not have the routine opportunities for communication which councillors and teachers have, and it would seem quite undemocratic for them to take no further interest in the views of their constituency once elected: at least they should be listening and reporting as best they can. This the Taylor Committee described as making sure they could 'act with maximum awareness' of the views of those they represent.

In consulting governors about general matters, it is surely right that LEAs should interpret widely the nature of governors' interest as a vital middle tier of decision-making. They should not only consult governors of schools directly affected by change or governors in sectors of the service involved. They should assume - because this is the way to make it happen - that governors feel a concern for, and loyalty to, the local system as a whole. Apart from anything else, such a practice will help LEAs by liberating decisions from narrow and parochial, and often predictable patterns. For the same reason it is wise to arrange for governors sometimes, to have conferences, or joint meetings, as well as training events, genuinely taking them into the authority's confidence and asking them questions which are not cut and dried.

SCHOOLS AND GOVERNORS

This to a large extent, of course, means head teachers and governors. Since governors will in future be making vital choices for schools it is essential that they be equipped to make wise ones. Headteachers play a crucial part.

Attitudes and Expectations

Since the publication of the Taylor Report in 1977 I calculate that I have had contact with some ten thousand head teachers on in-service courses. That is at least one occasion a week during term time, each involving between twenty and fifty participants. I always talk to them about their perceptions of governors.

Only very rarely do heads see themselves in a dynamic relationship with their governors. If I ask if it is true that they accept them as though they fell from heaven and then whinge to each other about them, they laugh with guilty good nature. The generally poor performance of governors is not seen to be anything to do with them.

Heads' views of governors fall into three broad categories. The poorest experience is of governors who scarcely get involved at all, but who would be expected on the whole to be harmful if they did, the harm ranging from ill-informed comment to dangerously ill-judged intervention. The objective is therefore to tell them as little as possible and to accept that if their impact on school life is marginal, it is just as well.

Next comes what one might call the Victorian wife view: 'My governors don't trouble me much'. This view is of governors again not very deeply involved but at worst harmless and at best vaguely well-disposed. Heads with this experience are clearly on the whole pleasant with their governors and glad to see them in school now and then, but perhaps relieved that not much more is expected.

The highest praise accorded to governors - and this comes from a majority of heads - is that 'My governors are very supportive'. If I'm in a mischievous mood I refer to the drunk and the lamp-post, grateful for the support but not keen on the illumination. They don't mind, because it isn't seen as a very important issue, and anyway they have, as I said, this curious detachment from it all. Governors in this category come into school as often as they can, write strong letters in advocacy of any concessions to the school or in protest against anything which threatens it, act as energetic and positive ambassadors in the community.

Almost all the comment fits into one of these categories. Occasionally there is real damage to report, governors who meddle destructively, play party games with schools, are disloyal, or seriously neglectful. At the other extreme one does very rarely meet a head who rejoices in having governors who support, but not blindly, who promote the school's good, but not always uncritically, who share problems, with trust on both sides, and who bring a fresh and valued viewpoint to the management of the school. Perhaps one does not yet often encounter governors who deserve to be viewed in this way either.

The only question to ask, is whether the relationship needs to be so static? In all other aspects of their work, head teachers would accept the importance of high expectations in getting the best from people. They would expect to create a climate for development. They would actually try to inculcate more positive attitudes. They would see it as primarily their responsibility to set standards, to initiate, to make the best use of resources, including people, and to plan for steady progress. Put like that, it may seem clear what has to be done. The only reason for not doing it is that on the whole governors have not been considered necessary or relevant to the work of schools, and have typically been viewed as an intrusion whose nuisance value can with care be kept within bounds.

It is obvious that this view will have to be modified. Even then head teachers have the choice of accepting the responsibility because the alternatives are terrifying or accepting it because they see an opportunity for a new dynamic in school management.

Either way, expectations are of major importance. One would not have to argue this in relation to teaching staff, children, or dinner ladies. I find it embarrassing to have to say it about governors. The head teacher has all the best lines in this particular script. The process of induction will in future be much more controllable, since with governors each having a statutory term of office of four years they will not all arrive new on the same day - thus putting the school at the mercy of <u>their</u> expectations - but will join a body whose ethos is already recognisable, and which ought already to be reflecting the school's expectations to an increasing extent. I am not, I hasten to say, encouraging head teachers to manipulate or to influence opinions, but merely to create a climate of high expectations in respect of commitment, loyalty, frankness, trust, and generosity with time. Governors who don't feel comfortable with the high standards set will be squeezed out, and that's no bad thing either. I don't need to tell head teachers how to convey and establish their expectations - that would be rightly considered impertinent. They have these skills in abundance, and my role is merely to suggest governors as a deserving cause for them.

Before moving on to the consideration of structures, I would like to make a plea for head teachers to share some of the insoluble or near-insoluble problems. As a governor with some experience, I know that increasingly head teachers bring plans to us for approval, take great trouble to explain their policies and rules, seek our understanding when they have to do unpopular or difficult things, and are increasingly rewarded by our positive identification with the school's aims and programmes. Sometimes governors are even presented with options requiring a choice. It is very unusual for governors to be invited to think about something when the school has not yet found an answer or even range of alternative answers. It is very natural for educators not to feel comfortable appearing at a disadvantage. Traditionally their role was to have the advantage, and if in teaching the young that tradition has changed, the process has been very slow. They still feel a little naked without the answer book. Increasingly today government policies by forcing schools into competition are encouraging any natural tendencies to hide wounds and make light of problems. But infallibility makes new friends, and apart from the fact that in present conditions schools do have appalling problems which sharing would soften if not solve, there is nothing quite as effective in bringing out the best in governors as the honest plea for help.

Structures for involving Governors

The last ten years have brought me into contact with even more governors than head teachers. Thousands of them have told me that they don't know how to move from ceremonial involvement in the school - carol service, harvest festival, school play - to something more real, more casual, more conducive to the kind of insights which will produce better decisions.

Obviously governors find it hard to make these opportunities for themselves. I suppose it is the bureaucrat in me, but I always think structures make things easier for people, especially shy people. To say to someone who is more than an acquaintance but less than a friend, 'Drop in some evening' is very unlikely to lead to a visit. S/he won't know what time you get home from work, what time you eat, what time you go to bed, what television programmes you watch, and won't know what to say when you open the door. It is the same with visiting schools. An open invitation to drop in isn't as helpful as a specific or regular arrangement. Best of all is a clear responsibility. I know two good ways - both on the initiative of head teachers - which schools have devised to involve all their governors routinely. One is the 'duty governor of the month' idea. Of course all governors are expected to attend meetings and to support sports, harvest festivals, concerts and the like, but instead of the chairperson attending to all the little duties which come up between meetings, every governor is for one month of the school year the first point of contact on anything needing governors' attention.

The most obvious occasion is an interview for staff appointments. The duty governor would be the first contact, and if not free would be responsible for finding a colleague who is. S/he would be there when the pupils returned from the sponsored walk, or when the school had an important visitor; would help with any disciplinary issue in its early stages; would nag the LEA about any building matter not attended to; would lend an ear to any cherished plan or project; would plant a tree, present the badges for swimming; might, if invited, attend an internal meeting; might take an assembly. The month would certainly include a day spent routinely in school getting to know people and - remembering the importance of structure - looking at some manageable aspect of the school's work on which to report to fellow governors.

The benefits are obvious. The chairperson is relieved of a heavy load, and the governing body works in a more participatory way. Governors feel responsible for the school, not just on meeting days but always. Pupils and staff are encouraged. Governors learn, and make better decisions. The sum of governor contact is greatly increased. Governors become demystified, more 'visible' in the school, and this in turn helps participation. Involvement becomes ordinary, unthreatening.

A variant is giving governors each a special area of

interest. One will give particular attention to maths, another
to sport, another to the arts, another to welfare and pastoral
care, another to site and building matters. Invitations to visit
and do what has to be done will be built into school routine.
Having a governor take a special interest in the arts will
enormously encourage those concerned. Having a governor go
round with a notebook and progress building matters will
keep a lot of junk off the agenda, and will help to avoid a
very nasty phenomenon, which is that because of governors
every job is guaranteed to take three months. I said this to
one head, who replied as from a dark pit of experience, that
at least the existence of governors ensured that no job took
more than three months.

Some schools have tried setting up a special relationship
between a governor and a staff member, or a governor and a
class or tutor group. Some have a regular lunch attended by
governors. Some arrange an occasional social evening for
governors and teachers.

However it is done, it is essential that governors get to
know staff other than the teacher governors. It is good
practice for a different staff member to attend every
governors' meeting to talk to them about his or her subject or
special responsibility. Above all, because of their very
specific responsibility under the Education Act 1981 for using
their best endeavours to ensure that children with special
needs are identified and helped, governors should have
regular reports from the staff member in charge of special
needs.

If the election of parent governors in particular and the
relations between governors and parents more generally are to
be lively, it is important that governors should be 'visible' in
the school and this means identifying the best supported
parent events which should have priority in governors' attention. Generally these are those centred on children's work, or
open occasions in which parents can ask questions about the
school. In the secondary school where I am a governor, there
is always a meeting for new parents before the first half
term. This attracts almost 100% - some member of a family
comes even if a parent can't - because of the concern associated with travelling a longer distance, perhaps using buses
and crossing town centres, new teachers, new subjects, new
friendships. Governors always try to attend this, and the
parent governors are given an opportunity to introduce
themselves, saying something about their work in an informal
way. Thus new parents are introduced immediately to parent
governors and know what it's all about when elections come.

Schools should really be preparing for elections all the
time, not just when they are imminent. This is the secret of
widespread participation: people will take an interest if they
can see that governors are not remote and forbidding but
play a real part in school life. Efforts need to be made to

inform parents generally about what is involved well in advance of seeking nominations: many are deterred only by not knowing exactly what governors do.

Governors' annual meetings with parents were not very well attended on the whole in the early days of the 1986 Act, and initially some head teachers were either nervous about the occasions - losing control of the agenda is always disconcerting - or ambivalent about whether they wanted them to succeed. I think that if heads set their minds to success they could help governors a great deal behind the scenes. There were a number of factors working against good attendances. The requirement was rushed through, and the summer term was probably the worst time. No financial provision had been made, so many reports were perfunctory or dull in format. The teachers' unions did not help to give parents the right messages when they advised members to boycott them. Some of the invitations read like rate demands. Above all, the tone of the communications was negative at best, at worst legalistic and intimidating: the object was not just to avoid saying unpleasant things about teachers after all. In future perhaps a suggestion of celebrating the work done with and for children at the school might not come amiss. Honesty about problems, and a welcome to parents to assist, would also win more hearts, and some suggestion of joint effort to improve the effectiveness of learning - that mutual accountability never far from our thoughts.

When all this has been said, however, I do not think we should make too much of head-counting at these statutory meetings. They are not inquorate if 20% don't attend: that is merely the requirement for formal resolutions. There were good and useful meetings with fewer parents than that. The important thing is the opportunity to come and meet governors - who long remained mysterious and unaccountable - and discuss the school. The right to have a report is in itself valuable, and if parents are satisfied with the report, and don't want to ask any more questions, then perhaps it is a good school and perhaps it was a good report. I would fight to keep the right to a meeting on the statute book even if a good attendance were a rarity. By the same token I would certainly not regard a poor attendance as a necessarily black mark for the school or the legislation, but even sometimes the reverse.

Head teachers' reports are the raw material of governors' discussions, and deserve more attention. They can be bare records of numbers and events, or they can be windows on a living school. I have already spoken of the need for LEAs to help improve the standard, but most heads will be able to think of ways in which reports can be used to enrich governors' perceptions, prompt good questions, solicit positive advice and support, as soon as they have made the breakthrough into a sense of their responsibility for creating a favourable climate. A good starting point is to think of how closed and impenetrable a school's affairs, particularly its curriculum, appear to governors, and to visualise the report as a series of entry points. Again I would emphasise the helpfulness of sharing problems and asking difficult questions.

Helping parent governors to communicate can be an important task for a head who really wants to improve governors' work. Many parent governors feel frustrated because they have a sense of obligation to those who elected them, and know that it is right to keep in touch, but they are wholly dependent on head teachers for the means to communicate efficiently. They can listen in the launderette, question in the queue, and gossip at the gate, but all forms of communication not based on the school and addressed to all parents are selective and potentially undemocratic. In the end it is in the interests of the school that there should be widespread understanding among parents of what the governors are doing, and support for the whole process, but it is again hard for educators to let go of the communications system, and overcome fear of the consequences. I think it is worth risking the occasional indiscretion to allow parent governors to communicate with parents through the school's pupil post to get views and report back; to give them facilities at meetings to talk to other parents: to encourage parents to go to them with their concerns.

This leads naturally to the difficult issue of individual complaints to parent governors. The latter need to be wary of being turned into a complaints box, and equally wary of becoming a PRO for the head. I always tell parent governors that it is not their job to filter questions or complaints of a purely individual nature, and that if the school has good arrangements for enabling parents to raise matters concerning their children as they arise, if the point really does only affect the individual, and if the parent is confident enough to use the normal channels, they must be firm about encouraging them to do so. A parent with no confidence may need support to approach a teacher: this is a reasonable thing to expect of a parent governor. An issue may come up so often that it may have general implications and need to be on the agenda. A very large number of unconnected individual complaints suggest that parents do not think they have access to the school, even if the school sees itself as very open, and this needs attention. A wise head will not adopt defensive attitudes to a parent governor who is trying to say this: it is parents' own perceptions of access which are important. Even the most well-intentioned arrangements don't always work, and may simply need to be better publicised. Complaints to a parent governor are a valuable safety valve, and parent governors may be a useful source of information. My postbag suggests that this is a very sensitive issue, again because it makes head teachers feel threatened by outside intervention in communications networks. In this and all delicate matters involving heads' self-esteem, very minor acts of clumsiness by inexperienced parent governors and very minor displays of defensiveness cause a disproportionate amount of pain all round. It would be such a step forward if they could be laughed off a little more often.

Teacher governors are another common source of sensitive behaviour. At least they are usually aware of the risks they run, and in general this seriously limits the contribution they make. They may find the process of discussing school affairs in the presence of the head and assorted outsiders very disturbing. A mixture of loyalty, embarrassment and concern for their careers may sometimes reduce them to total silence. This is a pity, since teaching staff, like parents, bring a valuable fresh perspective, and if the governing body is to discuss the school curriculum effectively, professional input is crucial, and should be frank and confident. Thoughtful heads can do a great deal to encourage and reassure, and impress upon staff governors how much their contribution is wanted and how free they should feel to make it.

Schools, Governors and Parents

If participation in school affairs becomes yet another privilege, hogged by those who have all the other privileges, we shall have failed. Heads fear this, and rightly, and I am always telling new governors that if they sometimes find professionals defensive, it may be for the most laudable reason, namely that the best heads and teachers are much concerned for the children who do not have the support of confident, well-informed adults, and are afraid lest intervention on behalf of the already privileged should rob the most needy in schools.

Many schools would say that their policies are dominated by two equally troublesome minorities, the parents who care almost too much and would like to run the school, and those who may appear not to care at all, as long as the children are missing between 9 and 4. In between we often have the majority, well-disposed, bewildered about the part they can play, a little frightened of schools, and fairly busy doing other things. It is absolutely vital to involve these more actively, if governors are to represent properly the interests of the whole school community; if decisions are not increasingly to be made in education by or on behalf of extremists; and if the governing body is to become, as the Taylor Committee's vision would have it, a focus of good relationships and good communication.

Much that has been said about preparing for parent governor elections all the time, not just when they are imminent, making governors visible in the school and striving always to make their job real and to present it as real to the generality of parents, has an obvious bearing. But I know from the contact I am privileged to have with head teachers that one of their most pressing anxieties is that involvement in schools is largely confined to those whose children already enjoy home support. Sometimes the obstacles to broadening the base of participation to include those whose children desperately need such support, seem almost insurmountable. It is the problem most frequently mentioned, and the great majority of heads would do anything to solve it.

Chapter Four suggested that when progress in the second decade after Plowden was reviewed, we might find that home-school relationships had advanced less spectacularly than in the first. There are a number of obvious reasons for this. Firstly schools in the Seventies were still stretching their limbs in the now-fading glow of expansion, while in the Eighties cuts damaged morale and used up a lot of energy. Secondly the Eighties were characterised by growing teacher dissatisfaction. But I think there has been another, more obvious reason. We have now got to the hard bit. It was easy to open school doors to those who were only waiting for an invitation, harder to bring in those who saw barriers even where there were none. It was easy to show the eager and confident how they could help their children and their children's schools, very hard to motivate those who had such low self-esteem, such keen awareness of their own educational deprivation, so little self-confidence as parents, that they could not believe their contribution could be significant. Many headteachers, seeing the dangers of minority participation, and despairing of extending its boundaries to embrace the majority, even decided that it had all been a mistake, and that it was better to discourage PTAs and other forms of home involvement, better oneself to pursue relationships with individual parents, and be sure it was done even-handedly.

This seems a wrong prescription following a correct diagnosis. Though the next stage is hard, it is surely the only way to health. It is especially important to say that at this time, when teachers are frightened that parents are being propelled into a threatening role by government policies, and may find the prospect of retreat from the good habits of the last twenty years all too tempting. Such a retreat would be dangerous, because a failure to win the understanding of the ordinary well-intentioned majority would expose schools cruelly to those few who are interested in power.

Involving the less confident is hard work. If there were a bit of magic, I'm sure every head would go to the ends of the earth to find it. I think I may have stumbled on something, a habit of thought rather than a programme or formula, like most magic, and I only presume to judge it helpful by the way faces have lit up when I have mentioned it. It is this. Most schools nowadays make parents feel welcome: very few make them feel necessary. Anyone who can swim even a little will plunge into an icy river to save a child. But try telling a weak and inelegant swimmer, when there is no drowning child, that the water is really lovely once you're in, and you'll get nowhere. To the parents we have in mind, the water is icy and forbidding, and surely only the belief that their bravery can decisively affect their children's chances is strong enough motivation. There is abundant evidence in the researches of the early Eighties that even the least educated, even illiterate parents, can advance their children's learning, but teachers have to accept and assimilate this humbling, yet exciting message before they can convincingly communicate it to parents. I return to the theme of parent help with learning later on.

Teachers' expectations of children and their parents are vitally important. Many working class parents believe that teachers do not expect much of their children. I hear this all the time. Most teachers would hotly deny that this is so. They certainly devote infinite patience and skill to those who don't bring very much to the process, but whether they expect enough at the end I am less sure. One often hears remarks like 'We can't expect to compete with St. Cuthberts' or 'We do very well considering our catchment area'. It is legitimate to say that schools are not given the resources to make good the shortcomings of experience. But that is not the same as believing the task to be impossible.

Even excessive kindness can be unkind. With the best possible motives, it's not uncommon for schools to make so many allowances for children with lots of problems that they might unwittingly convey the message that they are undeserving of high hopes or disappointed anger.

Communicating well with parents and making them feel welcome are the pride of any good school. It will be working all the time to make its style more vivid and direct, and will be considering the design of head teachers' rooms, the welcome conveyed at school entrances and the simplicity of the route to where parents might need to be. In many of the schools built during the boom following the Second World War, beautiful as they are, it is often hard to find the main entrance. Nothing is more destructive of confidence than walking three times around a building and then entering the kitchen or the broom cupboard. If main entrances are not a strong design feature, can anything be done to make them so? I return to the question of parents' rooms, mother and toddler clubs, drop-in centres. I know that many schools have space problems, and little encouragement to use surplus space even when they have it rather than close it down. Yet it is so important that I would urge all concerned to keep on campaigning for such facilities and meanwhile consider whether even a bend in a corridor could be made suitable for parents to sit and wait for their children, talk, pin up their own notices and read the things they have new rights to read.

Parents' organisations would repay a little attention to the nuts and bolts. New groups establishing such organisations might well welcome advice. I do not accept that, because parents' organisations sometimes become a bit 'clubby', one should resist setting them up and rely wholly on head teachers to organise relationships with parents. I think it is important for parents to have a place of their own in schools, visibly and invisibly. I also think this should include some ownership of the agenda in debating their own concerns. There are many open and totally unauthoritarian heads who are convinced that they do not in any way inhibit the activity or the discussions of parents, indeed would not wish to. Yet even in such schools as these parents often feel that their role is in some way circumscribed. It is all part of the common phenomenon of the barriers which exist only in the mind of the beholder.

Apart from parents' feelings, there are advantages to a school in having a structure for parents' activity. It is always easier to deal with misunderstanding or conflict within a structure. One problem which has been brought to me a hundred times by governors or heads is that of a school - often one changing its style - where a minority of parents are trying to force a more formal and traditional curriculum, sometimes because they have aspirations to have their children prepared for private schools or entry to the next academic stage as they visualise it. The problem is always how to mobilise the support of the majority for what the school is doing, and in nearly all these cases it has been because the school has no structure within which that aim can be pursued.

So what is the answer to a parents' association which has been allowed to develop an undesirable cosiness? Dispose of it, like the money-changers in the temple? We all know that people can exclude people, not always intentionally. There is no simple answer, except hard work to involve more people, and vigilance, and finally frankness with those concerned about the dangerous consequences of what they are innocently doing, the desirability of creating a more open structure. If any structural changes are possible, it is a very good idea to break down the concentration of activity in one central committee, and have a lot of work done in open class or year groups, which will have much in common anyway. On the vexed question of the involvement of teachers, I would resist the too ready assumption that teachers ought to be involved in the social or fund-raising activities of PTAs. I would myself hotly defend teachers' rights not to be so involved unless they happen to like it, and as long as they are generous with their help when parents want meetings about educational matters. I think the ideal is an association in which all staff and parents are automatically members, and in which either group can supply committee members in any proportion (I would judge a teacher takeover unlikely). Then if at any time there are teachers who like that sort of activity they have a role, but there should be no moral pressures.

Most voluntary organisations these days find it hard to recruit enough people with time to take on major responsibilities. It is not merely that for economic reasons a high proportion of mothers in poorer homes have long since had to work but also that at the other end of the social scale it is far more common now for mothers to return to a profession or study for one when children are old enough, and - sometimes forgotten - this also makes demands on good fathers' time, since they will do their share not only of household chores but also of ferrying children around, helping with homework, shopping and hobbies. For this reason and obvious others it's well worth thinking about how responsibilities can be broken down into even smaller individual assignments, so that nobody is given an impossible or daunting load. The job of secretary does not have to involve the same person in minutes, correspondence, social events, membership records and newsletters. In my own organisation, the Campaign for the Advancement of State Education, what is frequently done by a secretary involves five people, and every committee member has a job. Some of the most successful campaigns I have been involved in have had street representatives, and I can testify that to break jobs up into such small bits not only makes it easier to get help but also extends commitment. It may take a bit more communication time, but this can be turned into a bonus.

Training and Supporting Governors

A minority of LEAs involved themselves in training programmes for governors before the 1986 Act, and a handful had very good arrangements. A variety of other institutions had some involvement in governor training in different areas: the National Association of Governors and Managers has organised training courses, produced training materials and encouraged others to do so for many years. Some university extra-mural departments - outstandingly Sheffield and Southampton - have programmes run in partnership with LEAs, and a few university Schools of Education - I recall Nottingham and Exeter with particular pleasure - have laid on good training days either open to anyone or for a group of LEAs. The Workers' Education Association, the Co-operative Movement, the PTA movement, the Campaign for the Advancement of State Education, and an assortment of local adult, community and FE (Further Education) colleges have all had some worthwhile enterprises in particular localities. The courses run at the City Literary Institute for the Inner London Education Authority over the years deserve particular mention, and more recently there has been excellent more structured co-operation between the ILEA and the National Association of Governors and Managers in London to train governors, the written material being of a particularly high standard. Finally one must pay tribute to the excellent Open University course which combined written, audio and video materials, and which is still available as a pack although it is in need of up-dating now.

Sometimes governor training has been good, varied, participatory but in general it has been patchy and ludicrously inadequate to meet the needs. There has never been any serious attempt to fund it, and during a period when education has been under financial strain, LEAs have been understandably reluctant to spend on an important but invisible resource when the supply of teachers and books and the maintenance of school buildings were all under-funded.

The Taylor Committee recommended that all LEAs should be required to ensure the provision of training (the words were deliberately chosen to make the point that simple provision by the LEA was not necessarily desirable) and all governors required to undertake it as soon as practicable. The 1980 Act did nothing about this, but the 1986 Act provided that LEAs should provide such training as they considered requisite: there was no absolute requirement and no obligation on governors to take up the opportunity. Since 1986, despite the qualified nature of the obligation, there has been a great increase in LEA activity in this field, and the majority are at least thinking and talking about it, and a large number making some provision. As a minimum it will be an introductory lecture and a handbook, as a maximum an ambitious rolling programme with lectures, workshops, seminars and other activities. In the middle many LEAs will be organising a programme of evening lectures, either alone or in association with a college of some kind, or providing a single Saturday training conference with some group work.

The Government have been unwilling to accept that the training of governors requires substantial new funding. In 1986 they did make available a sum by way of Educational Support Grants of £100,000, and this gesture has since been used to justify many refusals of financial help for governor training. This grant was distributed in the most efficient way by inviting bids based on good ideas for pilot schemes, and given to only ten LEAs. The process of thinking about projects to put forward would clearly be very constructive for those LEAs who put in bids, and if my own LEA is anything to go by, many of the ideas which emerged could be pursued without any money by some of the unsuccessful applicants. This is quite apart from the long term advantages of funding a limited number of pilot schemes and ensuring that the results are later well publicised.

The ESG exercise does spotlight the need for some mechanism to exchange information and materials among LEAs and others concerned to improve both the quantity and quality of training available to governors. An awareness of this need led in 1986-7 to a remarkable initiative in which something like fifteen organisations were involved, all of them with practical experience of or a direct interest in governor training. AGIT, Action for Governors' Information and Training, began its work early in 1986, hosted and serviced at first by the National Consumer Council, which had itself organised three very successful pilot training days for school governors a year or two earlier. A steering group of voluntary, academic and official agencies met regularly during 1986, and reached agreement on the need for a service aimed at all those engaged in governor training and support. Within a year the steering group had established itself as a consortium and begun to seek funding. The nature of the service to be established was readily agreed: no one wanted to take over or control the work of any other group, but to encourage cooperation, to exchange information, to find out what was happening in governor training and publicise it, to make existing training resources available more widely, and to spread good practice.

The organisations concerned included the two local authority associations, the Open University, Southampton University, the National Consumer Council, the Community Education Development Centre, the Advisory Centre for Education, the National Association of Governors and Managers, the National Confederation of PTAs, the Campaign for the Advancement of State Education, the National Council for Voluntary Organisations, and the Health Education Authority. It was agreed that the service should operate from outside London, and economic considerations dictated that it would have to be hosted by an existing agency which could provide not just a roof but some expert services such as graphics. Without much argument it was agreed that the Community Education Development Centre in Coventry would be appropriate, with possibly at a later stage a second centre for training materials at the Open University. The DES refused financial support, but AGIT secured a grant from Gulbenkian to start its operations, and immediately obtained a dozen or so LEA affiliations, the idea being that it would soon offer member services which would make it attractive to LEAs, diocesan boards, academic institutions and other agencies. Its constitution provides that LEAs, academic institutions and voluntary organisations should each provide a third of its management committee, to safeguard the balance of the original initiative and particularly the vital, if financially insignificant, involvement of grass roots organisations.

A group of volunteers worked all through the summer holiday of 1986 on a constitution, articles of association and terms of membership, in order to proceed with registration as a company and later a charity. By the beginning of the academic year 1987-8 the group had also held two conferences for LEA officers engaged with governors and planned a third, begun to assemble and catalogue training resources, compile a compendium of training materials contributed by members, and issue a newsletter; this in addition to all the formalities and financial planning and a small survey of LEA activity. This had all been done largely by voluntary effort, aided by modest use of consultancy and the services of a clerk/information assistant in CEDC. By the end of 1987, AGIT was able to proceed with the appointment of a Development Officer to put its activities on a sound professional footing. It was a remarkable example of cooperation by groups with immensely varied character and aims, united only by a conviction that governors were important and their effective training and support vital.

Clearly the Government will, if it is serious, have to accept that the 1986 Act commitment to governor training will need to be backed with appropriate resources. Money alone, however, is no guarantee that governor training will be good, and the subject deserves the most intensive and imaginative investigation. I believe the Taylor Committee was right to suggest that the best training would emerge from partnership between LEAs and other agencies, and that LEA efforts alone might result in training which was dull and which concentrated too much on conformity rather than independent thought, though already many honourable exceptions are emerging.

When I approached the task of serving as a parent on the Taylor Committee, I was aware that if I had been taken straight from the school gate, my ignorance would soon have become obvious and what I said would have been discredited - ever so kindly - because I was an ordinary typical mum knowing little of the subject. If on the other hand I worked hard to inform myself, I was quite likely to be described as an untypical mum, a professional parent, or even - worst abuse of all - an articulate parent! In this case what I said would be discredited, not because I was too ordinary, but because I was not ordinary enough. I believe this confusion runs right through the education service. It has a bearing on governor training. I feel quite sure from my reading of history that the role of a school governor has always been about ordinariness. The effort to find ways in which the community interest in education could be given expression has been based on the belief that it is healthy and necessary that the precious light of ordinariness should shine upon expert affairs, bringing to them an innocent common sense and experience gained in the outside world. This has implications for governor training. The object is not to produce shadow teachers, pretend inspectors, trainee managers, imitation accountants, but to give governors the information and the confidence they need to be effective in their ordinariness. I don't think we should lose sight of this.

One of the reasons so many LEA officers find the whole subject daunting, is that the range of tasks governors will have to perform and their complexity, the number to be trained and the turnover rate, and the number of Saturdays and evenings in a year, produce an impossible assignment.

The only way to look at this is to accept that no governor can be taken through all the tasks s/he might ever have to perform, and even if it were possible the indigestion would be acute. If governors are indeed to be effective in their ordinariness, they need a basic knowledge of the education system and of how schools work, especially what decisions are made at school level and how. They need some helpful approaches and attitudes to enable them to build good relationships. Above all they need insights into the education process, windows on the school. Whichever window you look through, it is the same school, so any process in which governors can be involved will help them to tackle a quite different process with insight. The insight, and the knowledge that it is their ordinariness which is wanted, will help their confidence. So will contact with others, and the respect with which their work is regarded.

Evening lectures alone can be terribly dead. People come and go, listen, perhaps learn, but remain unchanged. It is best if the training starts with a Saturday of not too ambitious a kind, to introduce governors to their role, put it in its setting, give them a little practice in problem solving, and contact with each other. The written material to go with the day should be simple, self-contained, and encouraging. I think it is important to build in plenty of time for casual contact and to have lunch, however simple, on the premises. This day can be followed up with instructional evening lectures on specific subjects, because then people will know someone to sit by, talk to over coffee, and to go the pub with afterwards, and, less tangibly, will feel part of a group.

The next stage offers scope for governors to meet in smaller more local groups with perhaps some good distance-learning material; but with all training exercises the quality of the group leader is crucial. Videos are helpful, and one LEA used part of its ESG grant for making six videos. These are best if they don't tie up every issue but leave scope for stopping and debating, but again a good guide is needed, and one who lets people find their own answers. Groups of governors in a neighbourhood ought to meet sometimes anyway, though wider contact is also important. Then one comes to school level, and in many ways with a wise and skilled head the school can be the best training ground of all. One can gain more of those precious insights from sitting in on an internal school meeting or taking part in a staff selection process than in a year of lectures, as long as it is combined with other experiences.

It goes without saying that governors' training needs to be participatory and not prescriptive. Alas it is also true that the supply of people with the skills to direct that sort of training, and with the ability to write in a simple and lively fashion about the education system and the functioning of schools, is grossly insufficient, and it is urgent to identify these skills up and down the country and enlist them. This is something AGIT may be able to help with. When you have some good case studies to work from, the role-playing possibilities need careful thought. The first Saturday ought to be fun, and cases must be brought to life. To make everybody role-play seems to me harsh: we are not dealing with big executives on management courses. A few will hate it so much that the entire learning experience will be destroyed. A proper public presentation is very difficult to hear unless you have a drama studio and/or very small numbers, and realistically most will have a not very cosy big hall and a hundred or more governors. The solution may be to identify a few key roles and find some extrovert volunteers to play them, and get the leader or chairperson to interview them each in turn about how they viewed the events in the story, and this way they speak audibly direct to the audience. It serves to bring the case to life and make people think, but it is quite quick. It needs very little preparation if the participants understand the issues and are confident, and they don't need acting skills of a high order.

Before ending this section, I should like to make one or two comments which are related more to giving governors support and status than training in the narrow sense. It is a good idea to provide them with a very local resource centre, where they can consult Education Acts and circulars and borrow books and audio-visual material. Audio cassettes are very useful for busy people who spend a lot of time in cars, or ironing, or listening in bed. This provision need not be expensive, since much of the material exists and needs only assembling, and suitable places would include a room in the branch library, a teachers' centre, or a school.

Secondly I would favour a loose leaf system rather than an LEA handbook, or best of all a very short handbook about the governors' place in the system, simple and timeless, accompanied by a loose leaf system. I think many handbooks spend a lot of time in some busy officer's in-tray waiting to be up-dated, and anyway if they are any good, given the complex and changing nature of the material, they get longer and longer. A loose leaf system gives more hope that each item will be updated promptly when occasion arises. Schools could be encouraged to put their own basic documents in the same form. Governors <u>must</u> be convinced that this is reference material to look at when the subject comes up, not to pass an exam on before you go to your first meeting. It is important that the information is not daunting, and anyway an effective governor will be one who knows how to get up-to-date information when s/he needs it, rather than one with a rapidly digested and half remembered encyclopaedia.

Finally a governors' newspaper at LEA level is a very good way of keeping governors informed on national and local developments relevant to their work, courses or lectures which might interest them, exhibitions at a school or teachers' centre, changes in personnel in the local system, achievements of schools and children, new books, and so on. This information can be given in other ways, but a newspaper dropping on everybody's mat on the same day has status value too. Some day perhaps a local governor might be found to edit it.

The task is certainly vast, but may have benefits far beyond its immediate objectives. A little-publicised implication, of which the Taylor members were conscious, is that it will involve hundreds of thousands in the most ambitious programme of adult education ever undertaken, and the awareness engendered by such a programme could surely spread beyond education into the wider field of public and community affairs, with great benefits to the democratic process.

Common Problems Raised by Head Teachers

In my contact with head teachers, certain questions crop up over and over again, and the same is true of governors. Sometimes the two sets of questions are halves of one problem and answer each other. Governors say head teachers are defensive. Head teachers say governors don't show any interest - or in the very rare case show too much. Head teachers say governors come to school on special occasions but don't seem disposed to become involved more routinely in school affairs. Governors say they don't know how to advance beyond the ceremonial involvement to something more real. Heads say governors are obsessed with lockers and lavatories and show no interest in the curriculum. Governors say they are afraid of a rebuff if they venture too near territorial waters. They stay with the paving stones and the plumbing because they understand them, and because they don't constitute a challenge to anybody, except the poor LEA whose broad back is far away. Governors say it's hard to get information. Heads say governors don't respond to being given information. They really should get married.

This is indeed the institutionalised abuse of couples too long engaged. There are more serious issues, and I shall list those most often mentioned.

'It's always the same few'. Heads get understandably anxious about governors developing a narrow base, and far from helping parents to feel closer involvement with the school, actually discouraging it. This is a serious danger, and heads and governors alike should take it upon themselves to tackle the causes. It remains true that only the engagement of the majority can keep the process healthy, but this is hard work for schools, and I can only reiterate that heads cannot expect it to happen without constant efforts to make the governors' job not just a real one, but seen in the school to be real; to try diligently to improve the election arrangements, and to prepare for elections all the time, not just when they are imminent; to keep at the mammoth task of making parents feel wanted, overcoming their diffidence, and increasing their self-esteem.

'Will enough parent governors come forward?' Swopping tales about seven parents turning up to elect two parent governors from two candidates, these only as a result of arm-twisting, is a favourite occupation wherever two or three heads are gathered together. The 1986 Act provision that there should be a chance to return votes by post or by child should help – there is no less satisfactory method of election than at a school meeting. I actually think it's likely to be easier to elect three, four or five parents than one or two, because it takes away some of the fear. Having said all this, one still comes back to the dull but inescapable formula: make the job real. make governors visible, prepare the ground well, keep on improving the arrangements.

'How can I be sure the right parents will get elected?' In a democracy there is surely only one right person, the one elected. Degrees of effectiveness certainly exist, and more effective governors come from wider support both for the elections and for the representative process thereafter. Hard work again.

'Won't governors always care only about the sunny side of school life, the achievement, the successes?' We do like to be proud of our schools. You wouldn't like if if we were not. But governors need telling often that the success of a school is made up of many different things, and they will win more lasting friendships among professionals if they can demonstrate their care for all the school's pupils, especially those who don't have it easy. Heads can help by encouraging governors to come closer, and resisting the temptation – fostered by government policies – to hide their wounds.

'Won't the well-provided schools in the affluent areas benefit even more, and the deprived schools suffer more, because the strength of their governors will reflect the area they come from?' There is no real evidence that people in deprived areas are any less effective in the support of their schools than others. It is undoubtedly serious if governors keep pushing for luxuries for already well-endowed schools against the common good. Heads can do much to raise awareness, if they really want to, and it is very helpful if governors can meet governors from contrasting situations and visit other schools. I can well remember the moment when, with heavy hearts, we decided not to push for some mouthwatering flexible drama studio staging which the manufacturers came to demonstrate to us at the school. It was just the thought of all those primary schools built in the last century which held us back, though drama was very dear to our hearts.

'Isn't there a danger that governors will be old-fashioned in their educational thinking, adding to the pressure for a narrow curriculum, elaborate uniform, heavy discipline?' If influential people outside schools have these ideas, it's about time schools started promoting themselves a bit more effectively. There is expert evidence that heavy concentration on the basics does not even work to advance basic skills. Let's publicise that, and win public support for what schools are doing. If such support cannot be won, something is wrong. It seems vital to debate schools' aims and methods if governors are to assume such major responsibilities. Perhaps it will be encouraging to record that our experience in Richmond does not support this particular apprehension about governors. When our elected members gave up their control in 1974, they were almost certainly assuming that the kind of people who came forward could be relied upon to keep traditional flags flying and educational costs down. For most governors, close contact with schools has produced a determination to fight for maximum resourcing for education, concern for justice to children and protective attitudes to the less fortunate pupils. It has also produced an attachment to the broad curriculum and child-centred learning among the great majority: we have had no complaint at all from professionals that governors are a reactionary force in curriculum matters or any school policies. This must be reassuring in an area of high educational aspirations.

'Isn't there a danger that, as governors become more important, parent governor elections will become politicised?' In theory this is possible. If such tendencies develop, we must take them very seriously, and there are enough who would deplore such a trend to deal with it. Again I can only report that it has never happened in my own authority. Unbelievably, I was in the middle of this page when I heard of an angry scene about a candidate in a parent governor election who had kept some political allegiance dark. So great was the public reaction against the political character of LEA nominations that there is even an excessive suspicion of a candidate with a party affiliation. My impression from visiting many schools is that the majority of school parents are frightened of politics in school affairs and very suspicious of anyone who introduces party issues. There may be exceptions, and one especially needs to watch racial issues.

'Should I exercise my option to be a governor?' Heads seem to want to be confirmed in their instinctive wariness of full governor status. This wariness is a very understandable reaction to the bad experiences of some heads in heavily political systems, and I would agree with them that there was little to be gained from full involvement in such a governing body. Now that we are to have a balance of the various interests, however, I would expect heads to realise gradually that their interests lie in full involvement. The Taylor Committee believed that it would seem absurd that they should not have such involvement when all other groups are represented. Remember the distinction I made about partnership with the governing body, which makes it merely a consumer council, and partnership within the governing body, a concept which could surely not exclude the head. More practically, remember the occasions when a head teacher's vote could, with the new balance, become more important - in co-opting community governors, choosing parent governors in the exceptional case where a vacancy could not be filled by election, deciding on the budget, and making vital choices perhaps about the school's future.

Heads regularly make two points. One is that they think they have more influence as detached professional advisers than as governors with a vote. I do not think these roles are a matter of either/or: I think they will always be seen as detached professional advisers as well, and the commitment and influence as governors are an extra dimension. Secondly they seem fearful of losing the argument in a matter where they have a strong professional opinion. I suggest that this is a serious matter whether or not they are governors. It is always in theory possible, though I would think it will be very rare, for a governing body to come to a conclusion which does not accord with the head's professional judgement. It is no worse if the head has been involved in a formal vote, and as a voting governor s/he can perhaps argue with less inhibition for the preferred course.

Common Problems Raised by Governors

'We never discuss anything important.' This is going to be a less common complaint in the years to come! Meanwhile governors need reminding that they can ask for items to be on the agenda, that any three can request a special meeting, and that any meeting at which the business is not concluded must now be continued another day. This last point is a new rule under the 1987 School Governing Bodies Regulations. Above all they can help by making the content of their reports more conducive to discussion of real issues.

'Professionals are very defensive.' When I talk to governors, I always emphasise that many professionals are defensive for good reasons – they have had poor experiences of the old system, they worry lest governors promote only the interests of the already privileged, they want to be free to adopt fair and caring policies towards the disadvantaged. It is up to us, I say, to prove that we are different, and that will take time, patience and tact. I also stress always how vital it is for governors to build on positive things in their initial contacts with schools. So often with the best motives, they will begin with a demonstration of the watchdog role. They have waited a long time for a say, and thoughtlessly may be tempted to start at 9am the first Monday morning trying to tackle some minor issue, thinking their general support and friendliness can be taken for granted. They must learn that the best way to build enduring good relationships is to find out what a school does best, is proudest of, go and see it, get talking to the people responsible, encourage and praise. Shared enthusiasms, I say, are the best possible start. No, we are not a supporters' club, we will be critical now and then, but as in a marriage, the odd disagreement or nag can be accepted because there are shared values, trust, and the memory of a lot of good days.

Head teachers must be tolerant of the inexperienced governor, realising that nervousness, and waiting for a turn, often makes an innocent question come out all wrong and aggressive. They can gently offer opportunities for the shared-enthusiasm event. They can be reassuring, generous with information, expect the best of governors. Our only enemies within schools are clumsiness and misunderstanding. Outside there are more serious dangers.

'I don't know how to get beyond the carol service level of involvement.' Indeed many head teachers don't know how to get you beyond this level of involvement. Governors must be assured that such routine involvement is wanted, and heads encouraged to suggest positive means to achieve it. Governors in turn must understand that a lot of their predecessors were not very interested, and perhaps the head would be delighted and surprised that they wanted to come in. On the other hand, if there is real defensiveness, governors must realise that there may be fear, and proceed by easy stages, perhaps offering to help in areas where parents help, like outings or old people's parties, asking if they can come on the day the school prepares for harvest festival, dress children for the nativity play. All that is said about structured involvement in the section on heads' problems will come in useful in time.

'Everybody seems frightened governors will gossip and consequently, confidentiality is taken to extremes.' It is surely
offensive to suggest that parent governors are more likely to
engage in careless talk than others. Provided they know the
rules, they must be trusted, as it is the only way. All concerned must accept that governors' proceedings are not
confidential unless they have voted for them to be so treated
on a particular item. For the rest, all governors should be
pleasantly reminded of the undesirability of discussing the
affairs of an individual pupil or staff member outside school,
and of the unwisdom of revealing the detail of governors'
debate, as distinct from the majority conclusions.

'I want to report back to my fellow parents, and seek their
opinions on matters which come before governors. This is
discouraged.' This point has already been covered in the
section on the LEA's responsibilities and that on the role of
head teachers. Parent governors should in my view be allowed
and indeed encouraged to communicate, within the rules. I
know many head teachers find it hardest of all to let control
of communication slip through their fingers, but I also know
that tensions vanish and relationships improve if they can
only bring themselves to relax about this and help parent
governors to do what they know is right.

'We have this one really weak teacher. The parents know, the
children know, yet there's no evidence that it is known in
the school.' Governors rightly feel that if they can't do
anything about bad teaching there isn't much point. The first
thing to say, of course, is that they must have an explanation, in general terms, of how careful one has to be to
approach such matters within the rules, if one is not to
expose one's LEA to the risk of defeat on technicalities should
the matter ever come to a wrongful dismissal appeal, and in
particular why professionals are so wary of discussing teacher
weaknesses behind their backs.
    This is so important that it must be discussed in general
terms with governors before an individual case ever comes
up. Governors' induction must include a clear statement that
it would be very unlikely that any head would be unaware of
any weakness in a teacher, and an explanation of the legal
difficulties, which does not mean that a governor should not
report in confidence any vital information which might not be
known. Governors must know they are not exempt, corpor-
ately or individually, from libel and slander laws. Above all,
they must be familiar with what the school and the LEA do to
support teachers, to help any in difficulties, to counsel and,
in the last resort, discipline. They need to know what in-
service opportunities exist, and what appraisal arrangements.

MAKING PARTNERSHIP WORK

It is better to have such an exchange of information in the abstract and, routinely, not wait until there is a case. What is most frustrating to governors is the feeling that the problem is not being recognised and dealt with in the school. Just to know there are recognised procedures is greatly reassuring.

PARENTS AND CHILDREN

The last word in this chapter, indeed in this book, must take us back to the intractable problems of reconciling parental choice with equal chances for children; building partnerships with all parents, including the least confident; enlisting the support of the strong and articulate in the cause of 'whole schools, whole neighbourhoods, even whole nations'. I quote only from myself, for I want to take you back to the questions I formulated when I visited Australia, set out on page 5 and trying to get to the fundamental issues of providing good public education anywhere in the world.

I know that all teachers wrestle with the problem of responding to the aspirations of those who have any, without damaging their chances of responding to the needs of those whose parents have none. Teachers know that parents' rights and children's needs are not always synonymous, not in this far from ideal world anyway. By now I must have made it clear how much I too fear a state of affairs in which children's chances depend even more cruelly than now on their parents' ability to support them, help them and choose for them. The danger is that schools will be so afraid of the influence of the confident and well-organised, and so tender in their concern for the children whose parents find it hard even to provide at home the minimum framework of care, security, order and play, that they will too lightly dismiss the possibility of better relationships with either group. I do not think the problem can be solved by keeping the most demanding at arm's length and trying to be social worker, nurse, priest, mother and father to the others. Only the strong and articulate can in the short run fight for a better-resourced and respected public education service, so schools must go on trying, by letting them come closer, to tap their compassion, and by at least putting over the message that the world the achievers will grow up in will be made up of others people's children. I have seen governors act as a focus of this awareness, and they can be strong allies.

But in the end people must be helped to solve their own problems. It is not enough that others champion their cause or that teachers care for their children. The process of educating has to be shared between teachers and parents. All the researches agree that teachers alone cannot prevail against all the problems children have without a degree of cooperation from home. More recent researches have produced the message that even the most disadvantaged parents can advance their children's learning if the school can manage to convince them that it matters. The lessons of Haringey and Belfield (5) (6) and many other pioneering LEAs and schools were clear. It doesn't matter if people are poor, uneducated, non-English speaking, illiterate. The only thing which had made them in the educational sense inadequate parents was the belief that they were inadequate. The message that anything they did could make a measurable difference to their children's progress was enough to work the magic. The lesson comes over with startling clarity from the Haringey research, in particular, since in the catchment area of the chosen schools it was not just that parents were <u>told</u> they did not have to comment or correct, merely be there: many <u>could not</u> have commented or corrected. It is clearly not about helping children to read. If their chimneys had been photographed on alternate evenings instead, and they had believed that it would advance their children's reading, it probably would have done. The vital thing was that they had a new perception of their own worth, and that their children had regular practice, the encouragement of their parents, and a bit of guaranteed adult time to themselves.

Many teachers will say that the standard of parenting leaves much to be desired across the social spectrum. Children, they say, are victims not just of poverty but of parents' ambition, materialism, or plain dislike of being with their offspring. I accept the evidence, and I understand how frustrating it is for teachers to know that, apart from the many children who come to school too late, too early, unsuitably dressed, unslept, unbreakfasted, there are also quite a few from homes where there is no excuse, who have no nursery rhymes, no bedtime stories, no walks or talks with parents. But I am less sure about the reasons. I think we have all of us devalued parenting, for quite a long time, and that many parents of all classes think it's not a very important job. It was not helpful that a generation of teachers used to tell us we might confuse our children if we helped them, might teach them to write in capital letters or wrongly describe the process of borrowing in subtraction sums. Teaching was overmystified, and yet the best teachers now seem to be the ones who can persuade parents that there's not so much to it! That's an exaggeration, but certainly the most successful are those who are beginning to invest the process of learning at home with some dignity and worth. The most fascinating part of nearly all the researches I have read is that apart from the gains directly to the children, there have been changes in the parents' attitudes to the school and the school's expectation of parents.

You will guess that I believe home help with learning schemes, chances for parents themselves to learn in schools, an early start with parental involvement through mother and toddler clubs or family centres, and greater respect for parents and their role, are the most hopeful directions. I should like to enter one word of concern about the home learning schemes. I hope they won't become too structured. I am glad to hear that in some form they are now beginning to spring up everywhere in the form of Parents and Children and Teachers (PACT), paired reading, and other variants, but less pleased to hear of the odd school making such a meal of briefing and instructing parents in the precise techniques, and definitely disturbed to note that publishers are having a field day with books designed to inaugurate parents into teaching their children at home. Such elaboration may drive away those for whom the simple early schemes were such a success, and we could have yet another middle class takeover of measures designed for the needy.

Involving parents successfully as partners in the process is the key to so many of the other problems. We have the beginnings of mutual accountability, or at least the climate for it, in that parents have naturally accepted that something is expected of them. As they become identified with school purposes, they will be motivated to support the cause of education more generally, and we have the beginnings of that public pressure which was the subject of another of the basic questions I took to Australia. We perhaps begin to see light also on the perennial question of choice, and how we can break its deadly association with inequality: if parents feel that schools are open to their influence and that they have an active role in their children's learning, it matters much less where that process takes place, and choice loses some of its obsessive significance. What's more, if the school in a poor neighbourhood is really achieving very good results with parent help, it will be noticed. I believe a great deal more could be done by teachers and LEAs to sell the positive advantages, in social and curricular terms, of a neighbourhood system with strong links between schools as children move on, and successful parent involvement. This would be particularly helped if LEAs were willing to inspect schools parents were not choosing, publish the results, and where necessary openly discuss remedies. We must try absolutely everything to arrest the vicious way in which choice, parent helplessness, professional defensiveness, LEA hand-wringing, combine to make the gloom of 'unto him that hath shall be given' a way of life.

Schools still have great power to change people. We may have been disappointed that they could not alone achieve social mobility, but perhaps we were looking for the wrong things. Laws can confer new choices and new rights. Structures can promise us more effective partnership. Action groups can tell us what to fight for. Books can tell us how to do it. But what can be done for those who have not the confidence to accept their rights or make good choices, do not feel that anyone wants partnership with them, don't join anything, don't read anything, never rise far enough above despair to hope for anything? Schools, and only schools, can reach everybody. They might even offer the confidence, the partnership and the hope. I spoke of a race between rival ideologies, one based on responding to wants, the other based on meeting needs. John Stuart Mill was fascinated by a now obscure writer called Henry Taylor, who in a book called 'The Statesman' written in 1836 and reviewed by Mill in the 'London and Westminster Review' the following year, wrote simply that education was 'the greatest want of the people, though the least felt'. Mill kept echoing these words as though they had the key to something important. I think that the task is to help people themselves to be aware of this least-felt want, and thus motivated, to insist on the right to have it satisfied. Until they do, their children will never sit with the children of 'the good and the wise', better described, perhaps, as the lucky.

NOTES

1. DES, Parental Influence at School, (HMSO, May 1984).

2. DES, Better Schools, (Cmnd. 9469, DES, March 1985).

3. Joan Sallis, School Managers and Governors: Taylor and After, (Ward Lock Educational, 1977 not now in print).

4. House of Commons, Third Report from the Education, Science and Arts Committee. Achievement in Primary Schools, (HMSO, September 1986).

5. J. Tizard, W.N. Schofield and J. Hewison, Collaboration between teachers and parents in assisting children's reading, (British Journal of Educational Psychology, Vol. 52, 1-15, 1982). See also J. Hewison, Home is where the help is, (Times Educational Supplement, 16 January 1981).

6. Peter Hannon and Angela Jackson, The Belfield Reading Project: Final Report, (Belfield Community Council with National Children's Bureau, 1987).

APPENDIX ONE

A SUMMARY OF THE TAYLOR REPORT

In April 1975 a Committee of Enquiry was appointed under the chairmanship of Mr. Tom Taylor, CBE, (later Lord Taylor of Blackburn) by the Secretary of State for Education, Mr. Reg. Prentice, and the Secretary of State for Wales, Mr. John Morris. It had the following terms of reference:

> To review the arrangements for the management and government of maintained primary and secondary schools in England and Wales, including the composition and functions of bodies of managers and governors, and their relationship with head teachers and staffs of schools, with parents of pupils and with the local community at large; and to make recommendations.

The Committee's Report, 'A New Partnership for our Schools', was submitted to the Secretaries of State (Mrs. Shirley Williams was by then Secretary of State for Education) on July 6th 1977, and published on September 20th that year. A list of the Committee members is given at the end of this summary (Annex A).

The Committee was not concerned with the management of nursery schools or special schools (the education of children with special needs was still at the time under consideration by the Warnock Committee).In a letter to the Chairman on May 5th 1975, Mr. Prentice suggested that the Committee should also exclude from its terms of reference those aspects of the management and government of voluntary schools which arose from the dual system. The same letter suggested that the Committee should consider whether the arrangements for the management and government of schools should include an obligation upon head teachers to consult their staffs about internal policies. In response to a specific enquiry from the Chairman following the speech by the Prime Minister (Mr. James Callaghan) at Ruskin College in October 1976, expressing concern about standards in schools and the relevance of the school curriculum, the Secretary of State replied that there were no plans for national control of the curriculum, and that the Committee should work on the assumption that the division of responsibility between central and local government would remain unchanged. So much for the scope of the enquiry.

As to its method of working, the Committee held 21 meetings, often of two days' duration, and two residential weekend conferences. It received over 400 items of written evidence, but instead of hearing oral evidence in London, Committee members, in groups of around a dozen for each visit, went to nineteen selected LEAs for full discussion of local arrangements and experience, the visits generally lasting two or three days. The LEAs were chosen after discussion based on members' knowledge, so had some interesting practices to demonstrate. On each visit members spoke to elected councillors, LEA officers, head teachers and teachers, parents, sometimes pupils, and of course managers and governors. In most areas visited they attended governors' meetings. The Committee was also represented at a few governors' courses and conferences, and met some overseas visitors concerned with the subject of its enquiry. A list of the LEAs visited is given at the end of this summary (Annex B).

All but one of the Committee's 23 members signed the Report: this member's minority report is discussed later. In addition eight members dissociated themselves from the recommendation on the frequency of meetings; one dissociated himself from recommendations on pupil governors under 18, governors' say in finance, and governors' involvement in teacher appointments; and seven (different) members agreed fully with the Report but felt that in the matter of parents' rights and responsibilities it did not go far enough, and entered a Note of Extension on this subject, discussed later.

GENERAL PRINCIPLES UNDERLYING THE REPORT

In the Preface, the Committee attempted to set out 'a recognisable guiding philosophy'. It described its task as to identify those areas of decision-making which ought to be school-based, given that most people were concerned about standards but also about independence and variety; to identify the interests with a legitimate contribution to make to school decisions; and to devise a way in which those interests could work together to produce 'a school with enough independence to ensure its responsive and distinctive character, taking its place in an efficient local administration of an effective national service.'

The three principles of fundamental importance in the Committee's thinking were those of equal partnership in the constitution of governing bodies; the responsibility of those

181

APPENDIX ONE

bodies for the success of the school in all aspects of its life and work; and their duty to promote good relationships and effective communication, both within the school and between the school and its parents and community.

THE SYSTEM AS THE COMMITTEE FOUND IT

In Chapter 2, supplemented by Appendix B, the Committee looked at the history of school government, the legal framework, and the working of the system in practice. They found that between 1944 and 1969 the system was almost universally ineffective and full of abuses, in particular large-scale grouping of schools, with some individuals holding many governorships, excessive party political influence, and failure to assume any of the more important responsibilities assigned to governors in law. After 1969 there had been reforms in some areas, though in the main these were confined to the composition of governing bodies, giving some seats to parents and teachers, and were not associated with a widespread revival of governors' responsibilities. Nevertheless, by the time the Committee started its work, at least two thirds of LEAs had begun to give representation to parents and teachers, and just a few were attempting to give governors a better image and a more significant role.

THE COMMITTEE'S RECOMMENDATIONS

1. Governors' Place in the Local System
All powers relevant to school government should be formally vested in the LEA, from whom governors derive delegated authority (3.15). There should be as much delegation to governors by the LEA as is compatible with the LEA's duty to run an efficient local service, and as much delegation by governors to head and staff as is compatible with the governors' responsibility for the success of the school as a whole (3.17).

2. Use of Terms
The terms 'governor' and 'governing body' should be used for both primary and secondary schools. The terms 'manager', 'managing body', 'instrument of management' and 'rules of management' should become obsolete (3.26).

3. Separate Bodies for Every School
Every school should have its own governing body. Section 20 of the Education Act 1944, which permitted grouping, should be repealed (3.24).

4. Composition of Governing Bodies

Governing bodies should be established on the principle of four equal shares. One quarter of the members should represent the LEA (minor authorities no longer being represented as of right, thus Section 18 of the 1944 Act should be repealed - 4.10), one quarter the staff (including the head teacher ex officio, and in larger schools non-teaching staff), one quarter the parents, shared with older pupils in secondary schools, and one quarter the community served by the school (4.6).

> Parent governors should be parents of children currently attending the school, and should be elected by a secret ballot of all parents, with efforts to secure maximum participation, the arrangements to be made by the LEA (4.20, 4.22, 4.23).
>
> Pupil governors should be permitted the full degree of participation allowed by the law: in view of the doubt about whether their involvement is legal below the age of 18, the Committee wished the DES to seek clarification, since all but one member would wish pupils over 16 to be eligible. Pending clarification, pupils not able to be full governors could be allowed observer status (4.26).
>
> Community governors should be chosen by the other three groups from lists of individuals willing to serve or organisations desiring to nominate, drawn up by the LEA. The Committee did not wish to be prescriptive about, eg ethnic minorities or the business community, though it hoped that both would be well represented (4.30).

5. Size of Governing Bodies

There should not be less that two or more than six representatives of each interest group. Governing bodies should vary in size, depending on the size of the school, from 8 to 24 (4.7).

6. Rules About Being a Governor

No governor should serve on more than one school catering for the same age-group (4.42). Governors' term of office should normally be within the four-year framework of local elections (4.39), but where teacher turnover is high, LEAs might have discretion to require teacher governors to submit to re-election after two years. There should be no compulsory retirement age (4.43). LEAs should be required to provide training, and governors required to undertake it as soon as practicable (10.8).

7. Communication

This the Committee placed first in its consideration of governors' functions, making it clear that the satisfactory discharge of other responsibilities depended upon a firm supporting structure of good relationships.

Staff. The Committee hoped that through the head teacher and the teacher governors there would be free exchange of views between the governors and the staff as a whole, with teachers presenting papers and making oral submissions to governors. It did not consider that consultation between head and staff needed to be mandatory. It recommended that governors' agenda and minutes be made available in the staffroom (5.11) and that the governors should invite the head to submit for their approval details of his/her arrangements for consulting staff day-by-day (5.12). These should include the non-teaching staff, who should also be kept informed of governors' discussions and encouraged to contribute ideas (5.16).

Pupils. Pupils should certainly be encouraged to sit in on governors' meetings, quite apart from the possibility of becoming governors. Governors should have the power to authorise the formation of a pupils' council in secondary schools, should make sure that such councils operate effectively, with pupils deciding their own agenda, and that they were given access to the governing body to express views (5.18).

Parents. 'The special role of the parent governors is to foster relationships between the school and its governing body and the general body of parents' (5.20). Parents' organisations should be encouraged and facilities for their work made available in the school (5.20). Parents should have the opportunity to set up an organisation based on the school (5.22), and the governors should ensure that as a minimum such an organisation was given access to the school for an evening meeting once a term, and the means to publicise their activities (5.23). Governors should also protect the interests of the individual parent, who has a right to expect the school to provide the means by which s/he can communicate about the child's progress and offer effective support. The Committee lists in 5.28 the ways in which a school should inform and involve parents, and recommends that the governing body should satisfy itself that adequate arrangements were made to inform parents, to involve them in their children's progress and welfare, to enlist their support, and to ensure their access to a teacher by reasonable arrangement (5.28). Furthermore in order to emphasise the mutual responsibilities of school and home, governors should send a letter to all parents at the time of enrolment, setting out what the school would undertake to do to involve parents and what parents in turn could do to support their child at school (5.29). A possible form of letter (but not intended as a model) was set out in the Report and is reproduced as an annex to this summary (Annex C).

The community. Governing bodies should survey the range and nature of the community interest in the school (5.32), and make known their desire to be accessible to community representations (5.33) as well as encouraging local people to attend school functions and use the school. They should do all they can to smooth children's transition between different stages of education (5.35). They should endeavour to improve the links between schools and the wealth-producing sector of the economy (5.36). They should build co-operation between schools and the other agencies responsible for children's welfare (5.37). LEAs should draw on the knowledge and experience of governing bodies in framing their general policies (5.38). Governing bodies for different schools in an area should consult each other about shared concerns (5.39).

8. The Curriculum

Starting from the belief that a school is not an end in itself, but part of society, the fact that schools today have much broader aims, and aims closer to home and community than formerly, and the impracticability of dividing responsibility (either in terms of functions or levels of generality) for today's much more complex and integrated process of learning, the Committee recommended that the life and work of a school be conceived as an indivisible whole, and that there should be no aspect from which governors should be excluded and no aspect for which head and staff should be solely accountable to themselves or the LEA (6.19 and 6.22). Thus the governors should have delegated responsibility from the LEA for setting the aims of the school, for considering the means by which they were pursued, for keeping under review the school's progress towards them, and for deciding on action to facilitate such progress (6.23). In making these recommendations, the Committee accepted that teachers have expertise in finding the most appropriate methods of implementing curriculum policies, and that governors can bring to the task no more than 'can reasonably be expected of informed, interested and responsible lay people'. At the same time it emphasised, firstly that consistency and continuity in teaching methods throughout the school were a reasonable concern of governors; secondly, that the public had views on teaching methods which governors should seek to communicate to the school; thirdly, that even such a technical process as timetabling could express fundamental educational philosophy; and finally, that debate and the search for consensus were themselves healthy processes, and that all concerned, including professionals, would benefit from having to 'discuss, debate and justify the matters which any one of them may seek to implement'.

Significantly, school <u>discipline</u> is dealt with in the chapter on curriculum, and so, in so far as they are dealt with at all, are <u>pastoral care</u> and <u>school organisation</u>. The Committee said that 'to be effective the learning experience must be supported first by an organisation which directs resources in accordance with the needs of each child, second by sensitive pastoral care, and third by the encouragement, through precept and example, of the consideration for others which alone in the long run can ensure pleasant and orderly behaviour' (6.32). Conversely, 'a curriculum devised to give every child experience of success' is the best guarantee that the majority will behave well. Thus the Committee recommended that, in harmony with the principle of indivisible responsibility, the governors should <u>formulate guidelines to ensure high standards of behaviour, with such minimum rules and sanctions as were necessary to maintain them</u> (6.33).

Governors should see classes at work, not as inspectors but to enable them to do their work with greater insight. The Committee saw the role of LEA inspectors as crucial to its recommendations, since they would be the bridge between governors' view of the school and plans for it, and the translation of that view and those plans into professional terms and strategies. Their number should be greatly increased - a yardstick of one for every 20,000 population was suggested - and every school should have a general adviser to be available for consultation with governors. Such general advisers should receive in-service training provided co-operatively by LEAs on an area basis (6.24).

Governors should build up a system of information on every aspect of the school's life and work, including factors outside the school having relevance, to aid them in their regular reviews. This should be maintained in co-operation with the head teacher (6.44). Reviews should take place at intervals determined by local agreement, but the Committee thought it would be reasonable for the first to be after the governors had been in post for about four years, and subsequent reviews after two or three years (6.46). A short report should be sent on each occasion to the LEA (6.55).

9. Finance

The Committee accepted that general responsibility for the distribution of resources in the area as a whole was for the LEA, but considered that governors should have as much involvement in finance as was compatible with this responsibility. They should receive estimates of expenditure on the school and have an opportunity to suggest changes (7.13). On school spending, the Committee wished schools to have maximum flexibility in the use of such allowances as were made to them (7.14 to 7.21) with as many heads of expenditure within school control as practicable. The clear implication is that governors would be involved in decisions about school spending priorities, and the DES were asked to investigate the whole question of how money was allocated to schools (7.18). It was also considered important for governors to have early and significant involvement in determining priorities for the school in the LEA's building programme (7.26).

10. Appointments and Dismissals

The Committee considered that the selection of head teachers should be the responsibility of a joint panel of governors and LEA, the governors to elect their representatives, the LEA providing a chairperson who would if necessary have a casting vote (8.10 and 8.11). Responsibility for other staff appointments should be vested in the governors with professional advice, but the governors should be free to make (and at any time to vary) arrangements to delegate it (8.12).

The Committee considered that governors should be better informed about the LEA's procedures concerning teachers' contractual arrangements and in particular the arrangements relating to teachers whose professional competence became a cause for concern. While recognising that teachers' contractual arrangements were outside its terms of reference, the Committee believed that governors would find it difficult to carry out their new functions without becoming involved in such problems. It therefore recommended that the DES initiate discussions with employers and teachers' organisations on the whole issue (8.17).

11. Other Functions of Governors

Admissions. The Committee saw no reason to change the general practice, namely that LEAs had ultimate responsibility for admissions to county schools, but consulted governors about general policies. The Committee considered, however, that the criteria for allocating places should be made public (9.5).

School premises. Governors should continue to be responsible for inspecting school premises and reporting to the LEA on their state of repair (9.21). It was also recommended that governors should have discretion to have urgent repairs, up to a specified amount, carried out without reference to the LEA (9.22).

Lettings. The LEA, in consultation with all governors, should draw up a general policy on lettings, which should be implemented in individual schools by governors. In practice they would exercise this responsibility by laying down guidelines for the head to apply to individual applications (9.31). Any dispute should be determined by the LEA (9.32). The Committee was concerned about the rising level of charges and its effect on community use of schools. While recognising the financial problems of LEAs, it would wish consideration to be given when possible to extending community access (9.34).

Holidays. The Committee considered that the LEA should standardise half term holidays, in consideration of the problems of employers, working mothers, and the providers of school services, and that governors should have a limited power to grant occasional holidays at other times, subject to LEA agreement, for events individual to the school. The Committee was inclined to frown on the tradition of the use of holidays as rewards (9.42, 9.43, 9.44).

Suspension of pupils. The Committee was very concerned about many aspects of current practice. There was widespread confusion about the use of terms (exclusion, debarment, suspension, expulsion); about the objects of suspension; about the question of who had responsibility, and in consultation with whom, for the initial decision and subsequent action to resolve the problem; and especially about the role of governors. Above all the Committee was disturbed by evidence of excessive resort to suspension for indeterminate long periods in many areas, with no clear procedures for arriving at agreed solutions. In the Committee's view LEAs should make and publish arrangements which clearly defined terms and allocated responsibilities. There should be a limit on the time a head teacher could suspend a pupil without reference to governors; parents should be kept fully informed (and told before matters became so serious if a pupil's behaviour had been causing concern); and the governors' role was to authorise suspension for a further limited period if necessary, to bring together all parties and agencies in a search for a resolution, and to make sure all concerned had a fair hearing. Only the LEA should have power to make a suspension permanent, and parents should have a right of appeal (9.18).

12. Training

The Committee considered that governors should receive training, that LEAs should be responsible for its availability, and that ideally its provision should be a partnership between the LEA and some other appropriate agency. The Committee therefore recommended that LEAs should be required to ensure the availability of both initial and in-service training for governors, designating a person for co-ordinating such training, and that all governors should have a short period of initial training and regular in-service training (10.8).

13. Governors' procedures

Three governors, or one-third, whichever is greater, should constitute a quorum (11.2).

One-third should be the proportion of governors necessary to call a special meeting (11.3).

At least two governors' meetings should be held each term (11.6). Eight members dissented, on the ground that this should be a matter for local rules.

The time of governors' meetings should be determined by governing bodies themselves, to suit the convenience of the majority (11.8).

Governors' proceedings should not be confidential except in so far as they themselves rule them to be so (11.9).

Copies of all governors' working papers should be sent to the LEA and every governor (11.10).

Information about the membership of governing bodies should be widely available to parents and others (11.11).

The chairman should be elected, and the office should be open to any governor other than a paid employee of the school (11.13).

The LEA should decide in the light of local circumstances the most effective and economic method of clerking governing bodies (11.18).

No attendance allowances should be paid to governors, but governors should receive loss of earnings allowances, and LEAs should have power to pay travel and incidental expenses to ensure that no-one would be debarred from serving by the cost (11.21).

14. Voluntary Schools

The Committee accepted that its recommendations could not be applied to voluntary schools without changing both the statutory balance of representation on their governing bodies and the greater independence of the LEA which their governors in many respects enjoyed. It considered neverthe-less that the implementation of its recommendations in county schools with no change at all in voluntary schools would cause problems. It accordingly recommended that the arrangements for voluntary schools should be brought into harmony with those for county schools to the extent that this was possible without undermining the essential character of the dual system, and that the Secretary of State for Education and the Secretary of State for Wales should to this end put in hand consultations with the providing bodies and the LEAs as soon as possible (12.9).

15. Implementation

Legislation should be introduced to require LEAs to make arrangements for the government of county schools on the lines recommended, and to publicise the arrangements (13.6).

The aim should be to have the new arrangements working within five years.

Three recommendations were picked out for earlier implementation. The Committee recommended that the grouping of governing bodies should be made illegal as soon as possible; that the requirement to have representation of minor authorities, the only legal obstacle to the equal partnership formula, should similarly be removed promptly; and that LEAs should be required to implement without delay the recommendations on suspension of pupils (13.14).

Within five years of the implementation of the main recommendations of the Committee, the Secretaries of State should review the operation of the new system and introduce any necessary modifications. Arrangements should also be made for the government of schools to be kept under continuous review by an independent body such as a university research group, working in close collaboration with the DES and the LEAs (13.8).

16. Minority Reports

(a) One member, who at the time of his appointment was Chairman of an Education Committee, was unable to sign the Report. He fully accepted the need for schools to be more accountable, and for parents to be better informed, but he was unconvinced that these objectives would be attained by its recommendations. He feared that scarce resources would be committed for little real gain. Confidence in schools could best be restored by firmer LEA control of their affairs, and concentration on basic skills and preparation for adult life. Only the elected council had real accountability. Parents wanted more information and assurances about their own children's progress and more attention paid to incompetent teachers, not a policy role.

(b) Another LEA Chairman recorded reservations on three issues. Firstly, he thought it undesirable and unrealistic to involve governors in finance: the LEA had to bear responsibility for determining priorities, and it would only be frustrating for governors to give them the false hope that they could influence spending much beyond the school's capitation budget. Secondly, he was opposed to vesting responsibility for staff appointments below the level of head in the governing body: he believed that LEAs should be free to decide on appointments procedures for themselves. Finally, he opposed the recommendation that student governors' minimum age should be reduced to sixteen.

(c) Seven members of the Committee, Jocelyn Barrow, Eleri Edwards, Fred Flower, John Hale, Geoff Hett, Joan Sallis, and Judith Stone, accepted the Report in its entirety, but wanted it to go one step further in its recommendations on parents' rights and responsibilities. They put their views to the Secretaries of State in a Note of Extension.

The seven members applauded the Committee's recognition of parents' corporate rights – to be represented on governing bodies and to form associations – and its endorsement of a list of measures which a good school would take to involve individual parents. They considered, however, that it was not enough to say that it would be reasonable for parents to expect schools to observe such a code of good practice: every parent should have a right to a good school in this sense and to the information, the access, the involvement necessary to enable him or her to carry out responsibly the duty imposed on parents in law to see that their children were appropriately educated. The individual right would include information about the school, regular reports and consultations on progress, access to teachers by reasonable arrangement, and access to all information relevant to the individual child, including permanent school records.

The group made it clear that they were not asking for unstructured access to school buildings, school staff or school records. It would be the responsibility of the governors to ensure that the arrangements made by the school were adequate to give effect to the right of each parent, and that those arrangements were not abused by any parent.

ANNEX A: LIST OF COMMITTEE MEMBERS

Chairman
Councillor T. Taylor, CBE, JP
Leader of Blackburn Council

Members
Professor G. Baron,
Professor of Educational
   Administration,
University of London

Miss J. Barrow, OBE,
Senior Lecturer,
Furzedown College

Mrs. M.B. Broadley,
Headmistress,
Dick Sheppard School

Mr. D.P.J. Browning,
Chief Education Officer,
Bedfordshire

Councillor E. Currie-Jones,
   CBE,
Chairman,
South Glamorgan County
   Council

Mrs. A.E. Edwards,
Parent

Mr. F.D. Flower, MBE,
Principal,
Kingsway Princeton College

Councillor P.O. Fulton, JP,
Chairman of Education Committee,
Cleveland County Council

Mr. J.E. Hale, MBE, JP,
Headmaster,
Shears Green County
   Primary School

Mr. G.M.A. Harrison,
Chief Education Officer,
Sheffield

Mr. R.N. Heaton, CB,
formerly Deputy Secretary,
Ministry of Education

Councillor E.G. Hett,
Member,
Clwyd County Council

Councillor J.R. Horrell,
   TD, DL,
Chairman,
Cambridgeshire County Council

Mr. J.A.R. Kay,
formerly director of various
industrial concerns
(Resigned 24th Sept. 1975)

Miss B. Lynn,
Teacher,
Beech Hill Primary School,
Calderdale

Mr. J. Macgougan,
General Secretary,
National Union of Tailors and
   Garment Workers

Miss A.C. Millett,
Deputy Head,
Tile Hill Wood School

Mr. M.J. Moore, OBE, JP,
Deputy Chairman,
Electricity Consultative Council,
Merseyside and North Wales

The Rev. J.P. Reilly,
Secretary,
Birmingham Diocesan Schools
   Commission

Mrs. J. Sallis,
Parent

Mrs. J. Stone,
Parent

Mr. K.J. Turner,
Headmaster,
Foxhayes County Primary School

Canon R. Waddington,
Bishop's Adviser for Education,
Diocese of Carlisle

Assessors
Mr. M.W. Hodges,
DES

Mr. C.A. Norman,
HMI
(from Nov. 1976)

Mr. S.K. Bateman,
Welsh Office
(until Sept. 1975)

Mr. J.B. Davies,
Welsh Office
(from Jan. 1976)

Secretary
Mr. J.K. Sawtell

Asistant Secretaries
Mr. C.R. Appleby
(until 31st Dec. 1975)

Mr. D.,A. Wilkinson
(from 9th Feb. 1976)

APPENDIX ONE

ANNEX B: LIST OF VISITS MADE BY THE COMMITTEE

The following LEAs were visited:-

Bedfordshire,
Birmingham,
Calderdale,
Clwyd,
Devon,
Ealing,
Gwent,
Gwynedd,
Harrow,
Humberside,
ILEA,
Isle of Wight,
Lancashire,
Northumberland,
Nottinghamshire,
Richmond,
Sheffield,
Solihull,
Staffordshire.

In addition, the Committee attended the following events:-

a seminar for managers and governors in Warrington, Cheshire,

the 1975 Annual Conference of the British Educational Administration Society,

a conference on the government of secondary schools at Cumberland Lodge, Windsor,

a conference for school managers and governors at Nottingham University School of Education,

an induction course for managers, governors and clerks in the London Borough of Ealing.

ANNEX C: SAMPLE LETTER WHICH GOVERNORS MIGHT SEND TO PARENTS ON ACCEPTANCE OF A PLACE AT THE SCHOOL

We understand that your child will be coming to this school, and as governors we welcome him and hope that he will be happy and successful here. He will be in the care of teachers who will do their best to see that he enjoys school and learns well, and we hope that the school will in every way earn your confidence.

We also welcome YOU, his parents. Your support for your child and your interest in the school are vital to his education. Because the part played by parents is so important, the school will always try to involve you in its life and work. You will be invited regularly to meet your child's teachers to hear how he is getting on and perhaps how you can help him. But we hope you will feel that the school is a friendly place where you are welcome at any time, and that you will not wait to be asked if you have any worries or questions. A member of staff will always see you by reasonable arrangement. We promise in turn that the school will contact you promptly if any problem arises with your child. You will be fully informed about its aims and methods, its rules and the reasons for them. You will see among our names and addresses given below those of governors representing parents. It is your right as parents to be represented, and you may be asked at some time while your child is here to take part in elections for the governing body. The school also recognises parents' rights to form their own organisations and we welcome you to our PTA/Parents' Association/Friends of the School Association, which we encourage and support.

You will know that while your child is a pupil of the school it is your legal duty to see that he attends regularly and punctually; we hope that you will seek the help of the school if you have any difficulties in meeting this obligation. But this letter is not about legal matters: it is about the many ways in which schools and parents can work in willing partnership for the child's good. We have told you about the arrangements which the school makes to keep in close touch with you. You can best help your child if you take full advantage of these arrangements, joining as often as possible in the consultations with teachers, meetings and activities for parents, and coming to discuss any problem which your advice and support may help the school to solve. You can help us by trying to make sure that any work set by the school is done, and by supporting us in our efforts to encourage pleasant and considerate behaviour at school.

This is in a very important sense YOUR school, and your child's education is a responsibility we share with you. Please accept this letter of welcome as a promise that we will do our best to win your trust. No school is perfect, teachers are human and have a very difficult job. With parents' help and support they can do it a lot better. You will see that we enclose two copies of this letter. We thought you might like to keep one as a reminder of a big occasion in your child's life. Perhaps you will kindly return the other after filling in the slip confirming that you have accepted the place at the school. We shall then know that an important message has reached you, and we too shall have a reminder of what we hope to achieve, with your help, for your child.

A SUMMARY OF THE EDUCATION (NO 2) Act 1986

THE LEGAL FRAMEWORK BEFORE 1986

A condition of the grant aid given to voluntary bodies from 1830 was that they appointed local boards of managers to oversee the conduct of the schools thus aided. This was at times a source of grievance, and thought to be unwarranted interference. When the Forster Act of 1870 established locally elected school boards to fill the gaps in voluntary provision and thus secure elementary education for all, it also required some of the functions of the boards to be delegated to school managers. The 1902 Education Act, which established local education authorities with responsibility for primary and secondary education, stipulated that primary schools should have managers and secondary schools governors. For many years this led to conflict between the Board of Education and a few, mainly large city, LEAs, who resisted any delegation of their powers: this was never really resolved.

The Education Act of 1944 repeated the requirements about managers and governors, but it allowed schools to be grouped for the purpose, a provision much abused in the Fifties and Sixties and in a significant number of LEAs until 1985 when the 1980 Act took full effect. At extremes it gave those few LEAs who opposed any kind of delegation a loophole which enabled them to circumvent the law by making a sub-committee of the council the governing body for all its schools. The Act gave no guidance about the interests which local authorities should seek to represent when making appointments to county school managing and governing boards. In voluntary schools it laid down exact proportions of foundation and LEA members, two thirds foundation and one third LEA in aided schools and the reverse in controlled schools. No functions were prescribed in detail in the Act, but Model Articles were issued in 1945, and these provided in broad terms the basis for local arrangements. They gave governors care of school premises, a share in budgeting for the school and appointing its head teacher and other staff, and 'the general direction of the conduct and curriculum' of the school. Though not prescriptive, the Model strongly influenced local practice, and the fact that the Minister's approval was required for Articles of Government for county secondary schools, and that he made the Articles for voluntary secondary schools himself, prevented too much drift from the departmental guidelines.

There was no requirement to provide representation of parents and teachers until 1980: the Education Act of that year laid down that all county schools should have two parent governors elected by secret ballot, and one elected teacher governor in schools with under 300 pupils, two in schools above that size. The head teacher could be a governor if s/he wished. Voluntary schools had the same representation of parents and teachers, with optional membership of the head, the only difference being that only one of the two parent governors had to be elected, the other being a member of the foundation group. But whereas in county schools the LEA remained free to constitute the rest of the governing body as it wished, in voluntary schools there was prescribed representation of the voluntary interest - one fifth of the total had to be foundation governors in controlled schools, and in county schools the foundation governors were to have a majority of two over all others in boards of up to 18 members and three in larger boards. Grouping of schools was normally only allowed for two related primary schools.

Regulations made under the Act (SI 809 of 1981) established important rules about governors' proceedings. They were to elect their chairman and vice-chairman annually, and only employees of the school were ineligible. No governor could be on more than five boards. Any three governors could request a special meeting. Only the governors themselves could rule an item confidential, and apart from such items their agenda and minutes had to be available to the staff, parents and pupils of the school. A governor could be required to abstain from voting on an issue only if s/he or a close relative stood to gain from the outcome.

The Act said nothing about governors' functions, so these remained subject to local Articles based on the 1945 Model. It removed the difference in nomenclature between primary and secondary schools: all were to have 'governors' and the terms 'manager', 'Instrument of Management' and 'Rules of Management' became obsolete.

OVERVIEW OF THE 1986 ACT

Against this background the 1986 Act represents a very radical change. It prescribes precisely the constitution of governing bodies for different types and sizes of schools, with little scope for local variation. By providing for exactly equal numbers of LEA and parent representatives, it brings to an end the possibility of the LEA holding a majority of seats on county school boards, a widespread practice from the earliest days. It provides for all schools to have some co-opted governors from the wider community. It prescribes not only the composition of governing bodies, but also their functions in relation to the curriculum, financing, staffing and discipline of schools, so precisely that it became unnecessary for the Secretary of State to be concerned any longer with making and approving Articles and Instruments of Government, save in disputed cases involving voluntary schools.

The Act makes schools more accountable to parents by providing for parents to have the right to see all curriculum documents and syllabuses, and by requiring governors to report annually to all parents and to arrange an annual parents' meeting to discuss the report and any matters concerning the school. It provides new safeguards for schools, pupils and parents in disputed suspension cases, and makes corporal punishment illegal. It gives LEAs the power to pay governors' travel and subsistence expenses, and imposes on them a duty to provide such training as they think necessary.

The new Act empowers the Secretary of State to require teachers to be regularly appraised. Finally, it provides for the Secretary of State directly to finance approved schemes of in-service training for teachers.

THE ACT IN DETAIL

Constitution of Governing Bodies

LEAs must make for each school an Instrument of Government and Articles of Government in every respect consistent with the requirements of the Act and other operative legislation and any trust deed applying to the school (Section 1).

Before making these orders, LEAs must consult the head and the governors (Section 2 (1)). In voluntary schools they must secure the agreement of the governors, and the agreement of the foundation governors specifically on any matter which concerns them (Section 2 (2) and Section 2 (4)). They must consider any requests for alteration made by governors of any school (Section 2 (3)), but in the case of a voluntary school any disagreement must be determined by the Secretary of State on the request of either party (Sections 2 (5) and 2 (6)). The Secretary of State may vary the trust deed where it seems to him necessary and expedient.

County, Controlled and Maintained Special Schools.
Schools of less than 100 pupils (Section 3(2)):

2 parent governors
2 LEA governors
1 teacher governor
The head teacher if s/he chooses
EITHER
2 foundation + 1 co-opted governor (controlled schools)
OR
3 co-opted governors (county and maintained special schools)

Schools of 100 to 299 pupils (Section 3(3)):
3 parent governors
3 LEA governors
1 teacher governor
The head teacher if s/he chooses
EITHER
3 foundation + 1 co-opted governor (controlled schools)
OR
4 co-opted governors (county and maintained special schools)

Schools of 300 to 599 pupils (Section 3(4)):
4 parent governors
4 LEA governors
2 teacher governors
The head teacher if s/he chooses
EITHER
4 foundation + 1 co-opted governor (controlled schools)
OR
5 co-opted governors (county and maintained special schools)

Schools of 600 pupils and above (Section 3(5)):
5 parent governors
5 LEA governors
2 teacher governors
The head teacher if s/he chooses
EITHER
4 foundation + 2 co-opted governors (controlled schools)
OR
6 co-opted governors (county and maintained special schools)

LEAs have the option of treating schools in this largest category (600+ pupils) as though they were in the second largest category (300 to 599 pupils), i.e. settling for a maximum size board of sixteen governors (Section 3(6)).

Aided and Special Agreement Schools. Each school, regardless of size, shall have among its governors (Section 4 (2)):
at least 1 governor appointed by the LEA

at least 2 teacher governors in schools of 300 pupils
in primary schools, at least 1 governor appointed by the
   minor authority, if any
foundation governors
at least 1 parent governor
at least 1 teacher governor in schools under 300 pupils
   and over
the head teacher if s/he chooses

The foundation governors must have a majority of 2 over
other interests combined in schools having a governing body
of up to 18 governors, and 3 in larger governing bodies
(Section 4(3)(a)). One of the foundation governors must be a
parent of a registered pupil at the time of his/her appointment (Section 4(3)(b)). Where the head teacher elects not to
be a governor, s/he shall be treated as such for the purpose
of determining the majority of foundation governors (Section
4(4)). The number of representatives of various interests on
aided and special agreement school boards are minimal, but
any increases must be balanced by sufficient additional
foundation governors to secure the required majority (Section
4(5)).

General Rules about Governors

Minimum Age. Governors must be over 18 (Section 15(14) and
Section 61). Student governors of FE Colleges, but not
schools, are excepted from this rule.

Term of Office. Governors' normal term of office will be four
years (Section 8 (2)). There is no provision, as there was in
the 1980 Act, for parent governors to cease to hold office
when their connection with the school comes to an end.

Elections. The election of parent and teacher governors shall
be by secret ballot (Section 15(4)). Election arrangements are
made by the LEA in county and controlled schools and the
governors in aided schools (Section 15(2)(b)). They must
allow for the return of voting forms by post or via pupil as
well as in person at the school (Section 15(5)). All concerned
must take care to communicate effectively with parents about
the arrangements (Section 15(6)). It is for the LEA or
governors, as the case may be, to determine what constitutes
a parent or a teacher for election purposes (Section
15(2)(a)). In boarding schools (Section 5(1)) and hospital
schools (Section 5 (3)), where the LEA consider it impracticable to hold elections for parent governors, or in other
schools where insufficient parents come forward (Section
5(2)), parent representatives may be appointed by their
fellow governors. Such appointed governors may not be
members or employees of the LEA (Section 5(4)(b)), and they

must if possible be parents of registered pupils (Section
5(4)(a)(i)) or failing that, parents of school-age children
(Section 5(4)(a)(ii)). The rules made by the LEA on elections
may not specify that a minimum number of votes are needed
for the election of a parent governor (Section 15(3)).

Co-options. In making co-options, governors have a duty to
strengthen links with the local business community where
these do not already exist among their number (Section 6).
Otherwise, no restrictions must be placed on governors'
freedom to choose (Section 15(12)). In a county or controlled
primary school where there is a minor authority, a representative of that authority must be substituted for one co-opted
governor (Section 7(1)). In a hospital school, a representative of the district health authority shall be thus substituted (Section 7(2)), and in a special school the LEA may
appoint one or two representatives (depending on the size of
the school) of an appropriate voluntary organisation, or two
such organisations acting jointly, in place of a co-opted
governor or two co-opted governors (Section 7(3) to (6)).
These variations are clearly designed to provide appropriate
expertise in schools for children who are ill or have particular difficulties.

Training and Information for Governors. All governors must
be given copies of the Instruments and Articles of Government for their schools, such other information about their
functions as the LEA consider appropriate, and such training
as the LEA consider requisite, free of charge (Section 57).

Governors' Expenses. LEAs are empowered to defray
governors' travel and subsistence expenses (Section 58(1)).
All classes of governors within a particular institution must
be treated alike (Section 58(2)) in respect of any allowances
so paid. No other forms of payment may be made to governors
(Section 58(7)). (Note: In the past some LEAs had paid
elected members attendance allowances for governors'
meetings.)

Governors' Papers. The Education (School Government) Regulations 1987 made under the Act (SI 1359 of 1987) provide
that the governors' agenda, draft minutes (approved by the
chairman), signed minutes, and any other documents,
reports, etc. considered by the governors, must be made
available in the school to any person wishing to see them.
They may exclude any items relating to a named person, or
such other items as the governors rule confidential (Regulation 25). This is an extension of the provision in the regulations made under the 1980 Act (SI 809 of 1981) which gave
parents, staff and pupils of a school access to the agenda
and signed minutes, and the 1987 regulation also adds that

access must be afforded 'as soon as may be'. Under Section 56 of the Act itself, governors may be required to make reports to the Secretary of State.

Governors' meetings and procedures. Section 8 of the Act gives the Secretary of State power to make regulations about governors' meetings and procedures, and these are contained in the Education (School Government) Regulations 1987. Regulation 5 provides that no person may be a governor of more than four schools, (one less than previously). Regulations 6 and 7 list the circumstances which lead to the disqualification of governors (bankruptcy, criminal convictions, etc.) and Regulation 8 disqualifies a governor who fails to attend meetings for twelve months. Regulations 9 and 10 require governors to elect their chairman and vice chairman annually (in the case of a temporary governing body of a new school for its duration) and provide that any governor who is not an employee of the school shall be eligible. Regulation 11 allows the head teacher to attend meetings whether or not s/he is a governor. Governors must meet at least once a term (Regulation 12), those of temporary boards for new schools as often as necessary, and any three governors may requisition a special meeting. Teacher governors are disqualified when they cease to be employed at the school (Regulation 15). Seven days notice of a meeting is required unless the chairman decrees otherwise on grounds of urgency (Regulation 19) and any uncompleted business must be considered at an additional special meeting. Governors themselves decide whether to allow outsiders into their meetings (Regulation 22). A quorum shall be three governors or one third, whichever is the greater, except that if local Instruments prescribe a higher quorum this may be substituted up to a maximum of two-fifths (Regulation 13). For certain purposes, namely choosing co-opted governors, appointing parent governors in special circumstances where election is impracticable, and co-opting teacher governors to temporary boards, the quorum is increased to three quarters. Schedule 2 sets out the circumstances in which individual governors must refrain from participating in a particular discussion or vote, and these all hinge on the possible pecuniary or career interest of the governor or a near relative in the issue, or his/her involvement in a disciplinary incident. It is particularly stressed that these restrictions are intended to be maxima: local rules may not be more restrictive. In cases where the involvement of a governor is a pecuniary or career interest (but not in disciplinary matters), the governors may allow him or her to remain at the meeting, though not to take part.

New Schools

Newly established schools, which include technically 'new' schools formed by reorganisations requiring statutory notices, had to comply with the requirements of the Act from September 1st 1987, in advance of existing schools. For the first time the law establishes firm and detailed arrangements for 'caretaker' boards for schools in the planning stage, so that decisions about staffing, curriculum, organisation and, where appropriate, admissions are taken by bodies following as closely as possible the rules laid down in the Act.

As soon as a new school has been through the period of public notices (and received Secretary of State approval where necessary) a temporary governing body must be set up by the LEA, after consultation with the promoters in the case of a voluntary school (Section 12 and Schedule 2). This temporary governing body must be constituted on the same basis as the Act prescribes for an existing school and must exercise the same functions. The temporary parent governors, who must if possible be parents of pupils likely to attend the proposed school, or, failing that, parents of school-age children, are appointed by the LEA in county and controlled schools and the promoters in aided schools, and where appropriate the governors of schools to be discontinued may be asked to nominate parent or teacher governors. Teacher governors may also be co-opted by the appointed governors, and they must be teachers in maintained schools. No person may serve on the temporary governing body of a school in more than one capacity, and no temporary parent governor may be a member or employee of the LEA. Temporary governors must be suitably experienced, through service as a governor or better still a governor of a contributory school whose pupils will attend the new one.

Temporary governing bodies must be replaced by permanent ones, constituted in accordance with the Act, as soon as possible after the opening of the school, at the latest by the end of the first term in which the school admits pupils.

Grouping of Schools

In general schools must have individual governing bodies, and grouping requires the consent of the Secretary of State. The only exception is that two primary schools serving the same area, neither of them a special school, and if in Wales having the same language policy, may share a governing body if the LEA wish (Section 10(1)). They must first consult the governors and the head teacher, and if voluntary schools are involved they must obtain the consent of the governors. If any school sharing a governing body (with Secretary of State consent where necessary) is a voluntary school or a special school, the arrangements for the government of the grouped schools must follow the rules for voluntary schools of the appropriate category and special schools respectively (Section 9(1)(3)). The constitution shall be the same as that for a single school of the type concerned, except that the head teachers of all the grouped schools may serve as governors (Section 15(1)). Arrangements must be made to ensure that parents of each school have the opportunity to participate in the election of at least one parent and at least one teacher governor.

Responsibilities of Governors

General. The conduct of a school is under the direction of the governing body, except to the extent that the Act assigns functions to anyone else (Section 16(1)).

The Curriculum. The LEA must determine, keep under review and publish its policy for the curriculum of all its maintained schools (Section 17(1)), and must have regard to balance and breadth (Section 17(2)). The governors of county, controlled and special schools shall study this statement of policy, consider whether it needs modification in relation to their school, and decide what the curricular aims of the school shall be. Their conclusions must be the subject of a written statement which is kept up to date (Section 18(1)). In addition they must decide whether sex education should be provided in the school, and if so what form it should take (Section 18(2)). If they decide that it shall not be given, they must give reasons. If sex education is given, governors and head teachers must do their best to ensure that it is given in the context of moral values and family life (Section 46). They must publish their policy statement. Governors and head teachers also have a duty to try to ensure that where political education is given, the issues are presented in a balanced way (Section 45). The LEA, the governors and the head teacher shall forbid the participation of any junior pupils in any partisan political activities and the teaching of partisan political views in any school (Section 44). In exercising any of their functions in relation to the curriculum, both governors and head teachers must take account of any views expressed by persons in the community, including the chief of police (Sections 18(3)(a) and 18(6)(b)). Head teachers of county, controlled, and special schools must consider the curriculum policy statements of the LEA and the governors, and in the light of these statements determine the curriculum to be followed in the school (Section 18(5) and (6)). This curriculum must be compatible either with the LEA's statement or the governors' statement (Section 18(6)(c)(ii)) and with the governors' policy on sex education (Section 18(6)(c)(i)). It must also be compatible with any enactments on education including those on special needs (Section 18(6)(c)(iii)). In aided schools the governors have the control of the secular curriculum (Section 19(1)(a)), but they must have regard to the LEA's statement of curriculum policy (Section 19(1)(b)) and to representations made by the community and the chief of police (Section 19(2)). They must ensure that the head teacher has the necessary delegated authority 'to determine and organise the curriculum and see that it is followed within the school' (Section 19(1)(c)).

Finance. The LEA must furnish the governors with an annual statement setting out expenditure on the school, suitably itemised, and including at their discretion capital as well as revenue expenditure, so that governors may judge whether resources are effectively used (Section 29(1)(a)). They must also make available to governors an annual sum for books, equipment, stationery, etc. to be spent at their discretion (Section 29(1)(b)) - explanatory material published by the DES indicates that it is intended that a significant proportion, sufficient to give governors a real share in the financial management of the school, or even the whole, of the school allowance, should be at the disposal of governors. They may delegate the spending of this allowance to the head teacher (Section 29(1)(d)) and in any case they must not incur any expenditure which is inappropriate, in the head teacher's view, to the curriculum of the school (Section 29(1)(e)).

Discipline. It is the duty of the head teacher to regulate the conduct of pupils, encourage pleasant behaviour and self-discipline, and 'respect for authority' (Section 22(a)), but s/he must have regard to any general principles or guidance laid down by governors (Section 22(b)). Corporal punishment became illegal from 15th August 1987 (Section 47 and 48). Complex procedures are established concerning the exclusion of pupils in Sections 23 to 27 and Schedule 3. Only the head teacher may exclude a pupil, but the whole process is subject to rigorous safeguards to ensure that parents are kept fully informed, that pupils are not out of school for long without consultation with governors and LEA to achieve a solution, and that in particular such consultation takes place quickly if through suspension a pupil will miss more than five days' school in any one term, or any public examination. In county and controlled schools the LEA, and in aided schools the governors, may endorse the permanent exclusion or direct the reinstatement of a pupil, but both parents and the governors of the school have the right of appeal to an independent appeals board (set up by the LEA in county and controlled schools and the governors in aided schools), similar to the choice of school appeals boards under the 1980 Act, against permanent exclusion or reinstatement, as the case may be. (Schedule 3 sets out procedures in detail.)

Section 28 of the Act gives the LEA a reserve power to take such action as they think necessary (after informing the governors) when they consider that discipline at a county, controlled or special school has broken down.

Appointments. The LEA appoint and dismiss staff in all schools other than aided schools (Section 35(1)), while in aided schools appointments and dismissals are the responsibility of the governors. LEAs may, however, only appoint as a head teacher a person recommended by a selection panel consisting of at least as many governors as LEA representatives and no less than three of each (Section 36). This panel also short-lists (Section 37(1)(d)), and in the event of failure to agree, either the governor members or the LEA members may add up to two names (Section 37(1)(e)). If the panel cannot agree on a recommendation to appoint, they must repeat various steps until they do. Other teaching staff are appointed on the recommendation of the governors, but governors themselves decide how to discharge their responsibility, which they may delegate to one or more of their number, the head teacher, or both acting jointly (Section 38(6)). If the LEA wish to appoint a redeployed teacher to a school, the governors may draw up a job description and the LEA must take heed of it (Section 38(4)). If nevertheless the LEA appoint someone the governors do not approve, the matter must be reported to the next meeting of the Education Committee (Section 38(4)(c)(ii)). The appointment of deputies may, depending on the size and type of school and other circumstances, be conducted in accordance with the head teacher model or the other staff model at the LEA's discretion, but the head teacher has a right to be present and to advise, and must be consulted even if he or she is not present (Section 39(1) and (2)(a) and (b)).

The governors may recommend to the LEA the dismissal of any teacher or the premature retirement of any teacher, and the LEA must consult governors (and the head teacher unless it is s/he) before making any such proposal themselves (Section 41(1)(a) and (c)). They must also consult governors before confirming successful completion of probation or extending that probation (Section 41(1)(b)). Headteacher or governors may suspend any staff member, but must inform the LEA and must end the suspension if directed by the LEA to do so (Section 41(1)(d) and (e)).

Admissions

The Act does not change the situation whereby the LEA control admissions to county schools and the governors admission to aided schools, but Section 33 of the Act provides that where the LEA are responsible they shall consult governors annually about the arrangements, and at any time when it is proposed to change the arrangements, and that governors, where they are responsible, shall so consult the LEA.

Premises
Section 42 gives to governors the responsibility for deciding the use of premises outside school hours, subject, however, to any general directions given by the LEA and having regard to the desirability of encouraging community use.

Communication with Parents
Governors must issue an Annual Report to be sent to all parents, and must arrange an Annual Meeting of parents to discuss the Report and other matters concerning the running of the school (Sections 30 and 31). The Report must contain governors' names, with the details of the interests they represent and their period of office, and the address of their chairman and clerk. It must give examination results where appropriate, give details as provided by the LEA of the expenditure on the school, a statement of how the allowances made by the LEA to the governors were spent, and of any gifts to the school. It should give information on the steps taken to improve links with the community and the police, and on the action taken in response to resolutions passed at the last Annual Meeting. In addition to this specific information, governors must report on the discharge of their responsibilities during the year. Parents may pass resolutions at the meeting provided a number equal to at least 20% of the school roll are present. Parents have a right to see all curriculum statements by the LEA, governors and head teacher, and under Section 20 of the Act the Secretary of State has made regulations giving them access to all syllabuses followed by their children.

Miscellaneous Matters

Clerk to the Governors. If the Articles of Government do not lay down procedures, the LEA must agree with governors the arrangements for appointing a clerk. A clerk may not be dismissed except in accordance with such procedures or agreed arrangements. If the clerk fails to attend a meeting, the governors may elect one of their number to act as clerk (Section 40).

School Terms, etc. The LEA shall determine school terms and session times in county and controlled schools, the governors in aided schools (Section 21).

Freedom of Speech. Governors of universities, polytechnics and other defined colleges must use their best endeavours to facilitate free speech on the campus (Section 43).

Teacher Appraisal and Training. The Secretary of State has power (Section 49) to require LEAs, governors and others to arrange for the regular appraisal of teachers, and to fund (Section 50) approved schemes of in-service training for teachers and other education service employees.

Recoupment. The provision of the 1980 Act whereby pupils attending schools outside their home LEA must automatically have their education paid for by the home LEA is now extended to students in colleges of FE (Sections 51 and 52).

Transport. In deciding whether they are required to provide school transport, LEAs must take into account the age of the pupil and the nature of the route (Section 53 - supplementary to Section 55 of the 1944 Act).

Change from Controlled to Aided Status. A controlled school may now apply to the Secretary of State for aided status. Public notices are required, and any objections must be considered. The Secretary of State must also be satisfied that the governors can meet the financial obligations of aided status, including the payment of any compensation to the LEA in respect of the building (Sections 54 and 55).

Secretary of State's Annual Report. Section 60 removes the obligation on the Secretary of State to publish an Annual Report.

Central Advisory Councils. These are abolished by Section 59.

Timing

Governors' duties in respect of political education and moral values in sex education, and their obligation to issue Annual Reports and hold Annual Meetings, came into force on January 7th 1987. The option for controlled schools to become aided operated from April 1st 1987. Corporal punishment became illegal on August 15th 1987. Most LEAs' responsibilities - financial reports and delegation to governors of spending powers, training of governors, power to make arrangements for paying governors' expenses, duty to make curriculum statements - operate from September 1st 1987. On that date also, the new constitutional arrangements and responsibilities of governing bodies take effect for new schools. County and special schools comply fully with the Act from September 1st 1988, and voluntary schools from September 1st 1989, on which date the Act is in all respects functioning.

SOME HELPFUL READING

GENERAL

Stewart Ranson and John Tomlinson, The Changing Government of Education (Allen and Unwin for INLOGOV, 1986)

John Lello (ed), Accountability in Education (Ward Lock Education, 1979)

A.H. Halsey, A.F. Heath and J.M. Ridge, Origins and Destinations: Family, Class and Education in Modern Britain (Clarendon Press, 1980)

William Bacon, Public Accountability and the Schooling System (Harper and Row, 1978)

Maurice Kogan, Daphne Johnson, Tim Packwood, Tim Whitaker, School Governing Bodies (Heinemann, 1984)

NFER, Report on Parental Involvement in Primary Schools (NFER, 1980)

Andy Stillman and Karen Maychell, Choosing Schools: Parents, LEAs and the 1980 Act (NFER Nelson, 1986)

Alistair Macbeth, The Child Between (Commission for European Communities, 1984)

Nicolas Beattie, Professional Parents (Falmer Press, 1985)

PARENT HELP WITH LEARNING

Centre for the Teaching of Reading, Parents in Partnership, ideas for involving parents in school reading programmes (Reading University, 1983)

210

J. Tizard, W.N. Schofield, J.P. Hewison, <u>Collaboration between teachers and parents in assisting children's reading</u> (British Journal of Educational Psychology, Vol. 52, 1-15 1982)

Barbara Tizard and Martin Hughes, <u>Young Children Learning: Talking and Thinking at Home and at School</u> (Fontana, 1984)

K. Topping and S. Wolfendale, <u>Parental Involvement in Children's Reading</u> (Croom Helm, 1985)

Peter Hannon and Angela Jackson, <u>The Belfield Reading Project: Final Report</u> (Belfield Community Council and National Children's Bureau, 1987

TRAINING GUIDES FOR GOVERNORS

Barbara Bullivant, <u>School Governors Guide</u> (Home and School Council)

Elizabeth Wallis, <u>Education A to Z</u> (Advisory Centre for Education)

Joan Sallis, <u>The School in its Setting</u> (Advisory Centre for Education)

Joan Sallis, <u>More Questions Governors Ask</u> (Advisory Centre for Education, 1987 edition)

Joan Sallis, <u>Summary of the Education Act, 1986</u> (Advisory Centre for Education)

Peter Newell, <u>Special Education Handbook</u> (Advisory Centre for Education)

Tyrell Burgess and Anne Sofer, <u>School Governors' Handbook and Training Guide</u> (Kogan Page)

E. Wragg and J. Partington, <u>A Handbook for School Governors</u> (Methuen)

K. Brooksbank and K. Anderson, <u>School Governors</u> (Society of Education Officers and Longman)

Peter Harding, <u>A Guide to Governing Schools</u> (Harper and Row, 1987)

(1971) 15; South
Glamorgan school choice
16; Tameside, House of
Lords ruling 15
Lettera a Una Professora
(Italy) 89
Liverpool Association of
School Parents (LASPA) 83
Local Authorities (Access to
Information) Act 1985 28
local education authorities
(LEAs)
accountability 29-30;
Articles of Government
109-10, 133; curriculum
responsibilities under 1986
Act 141, 142; extreme
decisions, consequences of
64-5; failing schools,
Plowden recommendation
49-50; governing bodies,
consultation with 153;
governor training 151-2,
164, 165-7, 168-70; home
school relations policies
52-3, 150-1; 'national
service locally admin-
istered' 108-9; parents'
choice of schools policies
63; partnership with
central government 109-10;
Rules of Management
109-10; school closure or
reorganisation 29-30;
unpopular schools, how to
remedy 178; 'unreasonable
behaviour', right of appeal
against 14-15
local education authority
governor appointees
domination ended by 1986
Act 140-1, 142; Green
Paper proposals for
minority influence 135;
nominees in minority prior
to 1986 Act 120; Taylor
Report, opposition to equal
partnership 132; Taylor
Report, recommendations
129, 133, 134, 135
Local Government Act 1980 28

local government
Maud Commission 28, 112,
113; reforms 129

Macclesfield grammar school
trustees 100
managing bodies
church schools 104; city
authorities refusing to
create 106; Cross
Commission report, chapter
on 104-5; elementary
schools 106, 108; name
change under 1980 Act
106; primary education
109-11; see also governing
bodies
Manchester LEA
governors' training day
99-100; Poundswick
teachers' strike over
graffiti 99-100
Manpower Services Commission
involvement in education 2,
29
market place approach to
education see consumer
view of education
mathematics, new maths 12
Maud Commission 28, 112, 113
Mercers' Company 100
Mill, John Stuart, quoted 179
Ministry of Education 103
money raising see fund
raising
Morant, Sir Robert 106
mother and toddler clubs 52,
162

National Association for
Primary Education (NAPE)
80
National Association of
Governors and Managers
(NAGM) 78, 80-1, 112,
113, 135, 164, 165, 166
National Confederation of
Parent Teacher
Associations (NCPTA)
address 84; co-operation
with other parents'

against cuts 122-3;
examination results
publication 31; governing
bodies reform 9, 113-14,
115, 118-25, 141; governor
training 125; out-borough
pupils in schools 16;
Richmond Parents
Associations 81; teachers'
pay dispute, parents'
support 81-2
Roman Catholic education
grant aids conditions
103-4; relationship of
church and state education
86, 89, 90, 91, 92
Rowntree Trust 80, 83
Ruskin Speech of James
Callaghan 2, 138

Save Our Schools group 17-18
schools
aims, Taylor Report view
132; appraisal 37; Better
Schools: Evaluation and
Appraisal, DES conference
37; Better Schools, White
Paper 136, 146; blamed for
problems of society 42-3;
closure or reorganisation
29, 30; failing, Plowden
recommendation 49-50;
home input low, problem 5;
parental choice affect on
17, 20, 22; parent
perception of 39, 40-1, 43;
responsiveness, Taylor
Report 129; spare
accommodation for parental
use 52, 162-3; unpopular
schools, how LEAs can
remedy 178
Schools Council, NCPTA place
on 71
Scotland, school councils 91
Scottish Consumer Council
address 84; parents,
support for 91; school
brochures study 33
Scottish Parent Teacher
Council 71, 91

secondary education
Bryce Commission 105;
Education Act (1902)
developments 105-6;
governing bodies 105-6,
108, 109-11, 133; parental
involvement 51-2
Select Committee on
Education, Science and the
Arts
Achievement in Primary
Schools 29, 150
sex education 139, 140
Sexton, Stuart, adviser to Sir
Keith Joseph 17-18
Sheffield
governor training 164;
school government reform
112, 113, 114-15, 116-18,
141
small schools 12
Southampton University
extra-mural department
governor training 164, 166
South Glamorgan legal case on
school choice 16
special needs, governors'
responsibilities 157
standards in education
compatibility with choice
and variety 5; consumerist
attitudes 12; Great Debate
2, 138; see also schools
state education
centralisation see
centralisation; church
system in other countries
86, 92; community purpose
concept 128; extremist
influence 64-6, 139, 146;
financial expenditure see
financial expenditure; good
practice 52; Great Debate
2, 138; moderate majority
passivity 65-6; parent
pressure for higher
priority 62, 81-3, 176;
post 1944 changes 106-7;
power not participation
viewpoint 139, 141;
privatisation 13, 69, 146;

public pressure 6, 8-9;
school level democracy 141;
significance beyond
individual 128; two-tier
system developments 7, 132
State of Schools in England
and Wales published by
NCPTA 13, 68-9
Stierer, B.M. survey of
voluntary help with
reading in schools 27
Sussex University
parents' thirst for
information evidence 33
Sweden, parent participation
88

Tameside LEA, House of
Lords ruling 15
Taunton Commission 1864 on
grammar and other schools
101
Taylor, Henry, quoted 179
Taylor, Lord of Blackburn
chair of Committee on
School Government 3, 127
Taylor Report on School
Government
background to setting up
3, 127-9; better
communication with parents
call 48; commenced work 1,
3, 138; dominant themes 3,
129-32; 1980 Education Act
response 133; governor
training recommendations
165, 167; implications of
recommendations 137,
141-2; initial reactions
hostile to 6, 132-3, 142;
LEAs visited 113-14;
members of committee's
affiliations 138; opposition
to recommendations 132-3;
proposals 3, Appendix 1;
terms of reference 127
teacher accountability
client/professional model
25-8; consumerist view of
24, 42; definition 25;
education service

responsibility 24, 25; home
support essential for
child's success factor 5,
41-2; individualistic based
62; mutual with parents
28, 30, 32-7, 150;
parents' views 25-7;
pressure for 4, 9-10
teachers
appraisal 37-40; bad,
parents' views 25-6, 175-6;
communication with parents
150; confidential reports
on 39; consumerist view of
11-12; curricular freedom
effect 98; democracy in
schools, viewpoint 130,
142; governing bodies
relationship with staff 157;
governors' role 129, 130,
133, 134, 152, 160; home
liaison teachers 50, 52, 56,
150; independence 1, 2,
24; morale 4, 161; parent
movements co-operation 70,
82-3; parent movements
co-operation in other
countries 85; parent
participation, views on 8,
9-10, 27; pay dispute
37-8, 69-70, 77, 81-2, 130,
138, 145; pay dispute,
withdrawal of contact with
parents 145; parent
pressures, fears of 62,
148, 161; payment by
results 104; power to
influence 42-3; professional
status 24, 27-8, 137, 174;
PTA involvement 163-4;
redeployment, 1986 Act
provisions 143; respect for
3, 24; skills required 3-4;
Taylor Report, hostile
reactions to 6, 132-3, 142;
Taylor Report recom-
mendations not implemented
130, 147
teacher training
importance of 148; LEA
responsibility, Education